GRACE UPON GRACE

Thomas A. Langford

GRACE
UPON
GRACE

Essays in Honor of
Thomas A. Langford

EDITORS

Robert K. Johnston

L. Gregory Jones

Jonathan R. Wilson

Abingdon Press
Nashville

Copyright © 1999 by Abingdon Press

This book is printed on acid-free, recycled, elemental chlorine–free paper.

Library of Congress Cataloging-in-Publication Data

Grace upon grace : essays in honor of Thomas A. Langford / Robert
  K. Johnston, L. Gregory Jones, Jonathan R. Wilson, editors.
     p.   cm.
  Includes bibliographical references.
  ISBN 0-687-08609-4 (alk. paper)
     1. Grace (Theology) 2. Methodist Church—Doctrines.
  I. Langford, Thomas A. II. Johnston, Robert K., 1945–
  III. Jones, L. Gregory. IV. Wilson, Jonathan R.
  BT761.G67 1999   99-28178
  234—dc21   CIP

Scripture quotations, except for short paraphrases or unless otherwise noted, are from the New Revised Standard Version Bible, copyright © 1989, by the Division of Christian Education of the National Council of the Churches of Christ in the United States of America. Used by permission.

Those noted RSV are from the Revised Standard Version of the Bible, copyright 1946, 1952, 1971 by the Division of Christian Education of the National Council of the Churches of Christ in the USA. Used by permission.

Those noted NIV are taken from the *Holy Bible: New International Version.* Copyright © 1973, 1978, 1984 by the International Bible Society. Used by permission of Zondervan Bible Publishers.

Those noted NKJV are from The New King James Version. Copyright © 1979, 1980, 1982, Thomas Nelson Inc., Publishers.

Those noted NAB are from the New American Bible, © 1986 Confraternity of Christian Doctrine.

Those noted KJV are from the Authorized or King James Version of the Bible.

99 00 01 02 03 04 05 06 07 08—10 9 8 7 6 5 4 3 2 1

MANUFACTURED IN THE UNITED STATES OF AMERICA

CONTENTS

CONTENTS

PART II: HISTORICAL ESSAYS

PART III: THEOLOGICAL ESSAYS

CONTENTS

PART IV: CULTURAL ESSAYS

PREFACE

Thomas A. Langford, theologian and lifelong Methodist, observed:

> The centering theme of Wesley's thought was grace, expressed in Jesus Christ and conveyed to individuals by the Holy Spirit: Christian life is rooted and fulfilled in grace. Wesley explicated this theme—from prevenience to justification, to assurance, to sanctification, to final glorification—and this theology possessed the power to inaugurate and nourish a tradition. . . . In every tradition . . . there are commitments that stand at the center of corporate awareness . . . the theology of the Wesleyan movement has been an extended consideration of the grace of God as expressed in Jesus Christ. This theme has constituted the pivot point of this theological tradition and, over time, has functioned as a creative center. The tradition has been formed, not by continuous conformity, but by acknowledgment of grace as the criterion for judging theological value.[1]

Here is the center of the gospel, "the grace of the Lord Jesus" (1 Cor 16:23). Here also is the theme of this volume of collected essays, *Grace Upon Grace*, which honors the life of Thomas A. Langford, on his seventieth birthday. Langford has worked out of the Wesleyan tradition, even while extending its influence and understanding outward to the broader church. Serving his entire career as a faculty member at Duke University, he has been a theologian teaching and writing from a church and for the Church. Not all the contributors in this book are Methodists: for example,

9

Roland Murphy is Roman Catholic, Mary McClintock Fulkerson is Presbyterian, and Jonathan Wilson and Robert Johnston are members of the Evangelical Covenant Church. But all share with Tom, their colleague, mentor, and friend, a commitment to the grace of our Lord Jesus Christ.

The title, *Grace Upon Grace,* is taken from John 1:16 and was used by John Wesley in his sermon "Salvation by Faith." He wrote, "If then sinful man [and woman] find favour with God, it is 'grace upon grace.'" [2] It is indeed!

As editors we invite you to read this volume not just as a collection of theological essays, but as an extended meditation on the heart of the Christian faith that might lead you further into the fullness of God's grace. In his sermon "The Scripture Way of Salvation," John Wesley counseled, "And as we are more and more dead to sin, we are more and more alive to God. We go on from grace to grace."[3] May "the grace of the Lord Jesus Christ, the love of God, and the communion of the Holy Spirit" (2 Cor 13:13) be with you on your continuing journey into grace.

> Robert K. Johnston
> L. Gregory Jones
> Jonathan R. Wilson
> *editors*

Notes

1. Thomas A. Langford, *Practical Divinity: Theology in the Wesleyan Tradition* (Nashville: Abingdon Press, 1998), 248, 250.
2. John Wesley, Sermon 1, "Salvation by Faith," 3, *The Works of John Wesley* (Nashville: Abingdon Press, 1984–), 1:118.
3. Wesley, Sermon 43, "The Scripture Way of Salvation," 1.8, *Works,* 2:160.

A GRACEFUL LIFE:
An Appreciation of Thomas A. Langford

Both the church and society need Christian intellectuals. . . . An intellectual, as I am using the word, is not only a smart person but a person of learning, a person who has mastered a discipline and who, in addition, possesses both wider knowledge and wisdom. . . . The intellectual I want to commend is a person who, while thoroughly rational, has integrated reason with feeling, will with work, understanding of the world with changing the world. . . . The Christian intellectual, as I use the term, is a person who brings resources of Christian faith to bear upon contemporary issues and who brings these issues to bear upon Christian faith.

Thomas Langford spoke these words at a banquet celebrating forty-four years of Dempster Scholars. One of the first persons to receive a Dempster Scholarship, Langford exemplifies the program's aim to support the importance of biblical and theological scholarship for the Methodist church. Indeed, Langford embodies powerfully the Dempster's vision of Christian intellectual leadership, so it was fitting that he would deliver the address at the banquet.

Thomas Langford has been a Christian intellectual through his service to the academy, the church, and the world. He has sought to mine the riches of the Christian tradition for the sake of contemporary understanding, even as he has sought to understand the challenges that contemporary scholarship have posed to Christian faith and life. As Langford puts it later in his address, "Christians do not engage the world simply to convey the truth in final form, rather it is

11

a Christian responsibility to attempt to live the truth, and to point to the truth, and thereby engage in the discovery of new truth with others." Such has been a hallmark of Tom Langford's life and work as a Christian intellectual.

Langford rightly emphasizes in his address the link between theory and practice, understanding and embodiment. This is true of any Christian inquiry, but it comes to particular focus in the work of Langford's own scholarly discipline, Christian theology. When rightly done, Christian theological reflection and lived life mutually reinforce and enrich each other. We hope that our theological reflection bears fruit in our actual living, even as we recognize that our reflection might also challenge us to repent of aspects of our lives and allow God to reshape us for the sake of more faithful, holy living. Similarly, we hope that our lived life will provide a significant context for our theological reflection, even as we recognize that our lives might also challenge us to admit inadequacies and distortions in our reflection and allow God to reshape the questions we ask and the modes by which we understand God.

Obviously, there are asymmetries between theological reflection and lived life that compel ongoing reflection, engagement, and critique. Yet we also hope to discover, over the course of Christian life, a sense of increasing symmetry between the faith that is believed and the people who believe it. This is true of our own lives as well as those we encounter. To be sure, we recognize, with Paul, that at times "I do not do the good I want, but the evil I do not want is what I do" (Rom 7:19). Even so, we hope that we will eventually be found to be faithful hearers, speakers, and doers of the Word.

While this is a theme common in diverse understandings of Christian theology and life, it receives emphasis in those traditions identified with holiness. In such traditions, including especially those that point to John and Charles Wesley as exemplars, God's grace embraces us in ways that fundamentally reshape our lives as holy people. Wesleyans emphasize that theological reflection, rooted and fulfilled in God's grace, aims at faithful understanding and holy living.

Langford stresses this theme in *Practical Divinity: Theology in the Wesleyan Tradition*. He notes, "Theology, for John Wesley, was intended to transform life. Always in the service of presenting the gospel, theology was to underwrite the proclamation of the grace of

God given in Jesus Christ for the redemption of all people."[1] In this sense, theology—for Wesley and for Wesleyans—is eminently practical, focused on the gift and the task of transformed living. Practical divinity, however, requires rigorous intellectual engagement with a variety of texts, traditions, and sources—supreme among them Scripture and the doctrinal traditions of Christian faith—precisely because of their importance in cultivating holy people.

Theology so understood requires us to be able to find congruence between the faith that is believed by Christians and the lives of those Christians who believe it. Where there are asymmetries, we look for ways to correct misunderstandings and to deepen understanding on the one hand, and to repent of sin and grow in grace on the other.

We are honoring Thomas A. Langford with this volume of essays because of the remarkable ways in which he has embodied the life of a Christian intellectual and enriched our understanding of the connections between Christian theology and lived life. He has done so through his scholarly activity, his teaching and churchmanship, and his ministries of administration. Though each of these areas of his life can be identified separately, they ought not to be separated. For, indeed, Tom Langford's distinguished career has been marked by the convergence of his scholarship and his life: a man whose scholarly work on grace is both rooted and fulfilled in a grace-filled life.

Tom's life and work reflect the graceful character of a person whose skill seems effortless. But Tom has understood, and has helped others to understand, that it is only because we have been graced by God that we can live gracefully. Tom's extraordinary character has been cultivated by hard work and patience, displaying a quiet confidence that as we do what we can to serve God and the needs of communities, we will also receive the grace we need from God and others. As the grace of a ballet dancer, pianist, or basketball player displays a person at the top of her form, reflecting years of hard work and habits of attention, so also Tom Langford's graceful life and work reflect the character of a Christian intellectual at the top of his form.

Before turning to an exploration of his impact as a Christian intellectual in the areas of scholarship, teaching and churchmanship, and administration, a brief biographical sketch is in order.

Biographical Sketch

Thomas A. Langford was born on February 22, 1929, in Charlotte, North Carolina. He attended Davidson College, and then studied for the Methodist ministry at Duke Divinity School. He was ordained as a Methodist minister, and retained throughout his career membership in the Western North Carolina Annual Conference.

After completing seminary, Langford stayed at Duke to work on a Ph.D. in Christian Theology under the tutelage of Robert E. Cushman. His dissertation was entitled "Paul Tillich's Method of Correlation."

Langford remained at Duke throughout his professional career, first in the Department of Religion and then in the Divinity School. He received several awards for outstanding teaching, including a Distinguished Teaching award from the Danforth Foundation in 1965–66. He chaired the Department of Religion from 1965 to 1971, and then became Dean of Duke Divinity School in 1971. He served as Dean until 1981, when he returned to the faculty of the Divinity School.

In 1986, Langford was appointed as the inaugural William Kellon Quick Professor of Theology and Methodist Studies. From 1984 to 1988, he served as Vice-Provost of Duke University. He served as Provost of Duke from 1990 to 1994, when he returned again to full-time teaching. He retired from Duke University in 1997. He is the author or editor of fourteen books, including most notably *In Search of Foundations: English Theology 1900–1920,* and *Practical Divinity: Theology in the Wesleyan Tradition.*

Throughout his career, Langford has been active in leadership positions in The United Methodist Church. He has served the church at a variety of local, regional, national, and international levels. He was a delegate to five General Conferences, and in 1988 he chaired the important Legislative Committee on Faith and Mission that shepherded through the General Conference a revised understanding of "Our Theological Task" within The United Methodist Church.

Langford has served on a wide variety of boards in higher education, the church, and society. He became a trustee of the Duke Endowment in 1992, and currently serves as Chair of the Rural Church Division. Throughout his service, Langford has been noted for his careful attention to the ways in which diverse organizations can best serve their own mission.

Even so, Langford's extensive and impressive accomplishments fail to do justice to the impact he has had on students and colleagues. For as influential as he has been on institutions, it has always been people who mattered to Langford. His service to institutions has embodied the conviction that we need strong institutions in order to enable people and communities to flourish.

Scholarly Activity

Thomas Langford began his career as a scholar, and he has continued to nurture that activity. His early work focused on philosophical theology, and he edited or co-edited several works designed to introduce students to classical philosophical work. His first major book, *In Search of Foundations*, displayed Langford's greatest intellectual strength: an ability to probe deeply into others' thought, interpreting traditions as well as particular thinkers in a sympathetic yet critical vein.

Once Langford became Dean of Duke Divinity School, his scholarship became more focused on interpreting the Wesleyan theological tradition as well as the directions of United Methodist theology. He continued to be a thoughtful interpreter of others' work, genuinely moving the tradition forward through irenic yet engaging analyses of diverse streams of the tradition. In the 1980s Langford published several works that have had a strong impact on theology in the Wesleyan tradition: *Practical Divinity*, which went through several printings and has been reissued in a second, revised edition, as has the accompanying *Practical Divinity: Readings in Wesleyan Theology*, which he edited; and *Doctrine and Theology in The United Methodist Church*, which he edited and to which he contributed four essays.

In reflecting on the 1988 statement on United Methodism's theological task, Langford offers us a guide to his own scholarly activity:

Practical divinity is intentionally transformative, it underwrites proclamation and the nurturing of Christian life; on the contrary, practical theology is neither a distanced reflection upon life nor an intellectual interpretation of life. Practical divinity is pragmatic in the sense that it operates on the conviction that knowledge is only gained through engagement; contrariwise, knowledge is not found through spectatorship as an abstract observer. Practical divinity holds text (biblical) and context (social and cultural) in tight tension; each requires the other for insight and interpretation. Conversely, practical theology never allows an ahistorical text or an independent social order to function as a matrix of interpretation. Practical divinity, as I see Wesley practicing it, is a mode of life-thought which is engaged in revival and reform, in confrontation and challenge, in service and sanctification. It could be no other.[2]

True to his own insights, Langford wrote not only for other scholars and clergy, but also for laypeople seeking to cultivate their own theological reflection. Throughout his time as an administrator and a teacher, Langford practiced the art of practical divinity even as he reflected upon it. In such books as *Christian Wholeness, The Harvest of the Spirit, Prayer and the Common Life,* and *God Made Known,* Langford forged a theology meant to shape the practices of the church.

Langford's scholarship, particularly as it interprets and extends the Wesleyan tradition, has been shaped by his conviction about how traditions ought to be understood. He has reflected on the nature of traditions in several places, including notably "A Wesleyan/Methodist Theological Tradition." There he describes traditions in the following terms:

A tradition is a fluid, changing, malleable reality which is not static or set; tradition is a process, a shaping, forming ongoing strain of experience. A tradition is defined by communal themes, and the corporate character of a tradition is primary and persistent. This means that a tradition is a rich and complex set of relationships which can never be fully explicated but which conveys formative power through a corporate sphere. . . . Tradition should be recognized as an ongoing process which is always interrelating with its particular environment in such a manner that new configurations are formed.[3]

Langford's engagement with the Wesleyan tradition reflects this ongoing process. He offers a reading of the persistence of central communal themes, and in his gracious, generous way he puts diverse figures in conversation that makes the whole greater than its parts. At the same time, he provides room for those who read the tradition in significantly different ways—including those who would give a more prominent place to doctrine in the Wesleyan tradition—to see themselves in argumentative continuity with him. Though to my knowledge Langford does not anywhere quote Jaroslav Pelikan's pithy characterization, I think Langford would find it quite congenial: "Traditionalism is the dead faith of the living. Tradition is the living faith of the dead."[4]

Langford has contributed significantly to understanding and extending the Wesleyan theological tradition. Even so, partly because he has spent his career as a significant participant at Duke University, a leading research institution, and partly because of his own commitment as a Christian intellectual, Langford has continued to develop his scholarship in conversation with other disciplines. This has appeared less often in print than in his own habits of intellectual engagement. He has sought out colleagues in other disciplines—philosophy, literature, economics, as well as more far-reaching areas such as neurobiology—in an ongoing attempt to deepen his understanding of intellectual inquiry in general, and specific intellectual achievements in particular. Tom Langford has, with justice, been characterized as a scholar with a renaissance spirit of inquiry.

Teaching and Churchmanship

This vigorously engaged yet generous inquiry has borne great fruit in his teaching and churchmanship. It might seem odd to group these two together, for they are often seen as contrasting vocations—or, at the very least, as having different audiences and purposes. Yet Langford's intellectual inquiry is manifested most richly in his collaborative approach to teaching and learning—an approach he has richly articulated in teaching and churchmanship through his service in a university-related divinity school.

Langford has long been recognized as a master teacher. He has received formal recognition as well as the informal accolades that have come from generations of grateful students. It is difficult to capture Langford's teaching style, for it is less a technique than a manifestation of his own character. He has the remarkable ability to teach in a way that conveys knowledge while, at a deeper level, inviting the student into a process of discovery of what it means to engage in the inquiry oneself. He rarely lectures from a text, or even notes. Typically, Langford would come to class to engage in theological reflection, often—in trademark fashion—leaning on the podium, closing his eyes, and running through his mind an extraordinarily rich canvas of texts and ideas that could be brought to bear on the subject at hand. Yet his lectures would also typically conclude with a rhetorical flourish that drew together the wide-ranging discussion into a compelling vision.

A typical theology course would include standard readings, but the class discussions would likely also include references to such topics as Plato, Dante, Eugene O'Neill, and recent research into biological diversity. Moreover, he liked to teach courses for undergraduate and divinity students focused on such broad yet central questions as "What does it mean to be human?" Regardless of the course he was teaching, Langford's intellectual style opened up new avenues of exploration— even as, indeed especially as, he understood his inquiry to be part of a rich theological tradition. It is no wonder that many graduates of Duke University, going back to his early teaching days in the 1960s, remember Langford as the teacher who most inspired them to be lifelong learners.

Similarly, Langford's churchmanship has been characterized by the same approach. He has given generously of his time helping to deal with difficult issues in the church, typically opening up new avenues of exploration even as he sought to be faithful to the church's tradition. Langford has done this in countless local church settings, as well as on church-related college campuses, and in settings of the national and international church. Langford is as comfortable teaching and learning in a rural church as he is at the National Humanities Center.

Throughout, Langford has lived as a teacher who continually learns, and as a learner who continually teaches. In the university as well as the church, Langford's life reflects a process of joint inquiry in which Christ is the only true Teacher. Indeed, Langford has made a signal contribution by insisting that the university and the church continue to need each other. His career spans a period of American culture when higher education and the church have found themselves in significant tension or, worse, in an increasingly distant relation where each has tried to ignore the other. Langford's insistence to the church of the importance of intellectual inquiry, and to the university of the importance of theological engagement, has provided a compelling personal and institutional witness within Duke University and beyond.

A Ministry of Administration

It is ironic that a person who has continually sought to serve as a preacher, teacher, and scholar was repeatedly drawn into administrative service as a department chair, dean, vice-provost, and provost. In part, this has been because he displayed the gifts necessary for effective administrative leadership. But, more profoundly, people have continually turned to Langford because his intellectual and personal character draws people together in ways that enable institutions and communities to flourish. He understands that administrative leadership is an important exercise of Christian ministry.

Langford's leadership has been marked by attentiveness to the needs of others, to the broad intellectual and theological issues facing the university and the church, and to the importance of discerning and sustaining a center that holds. Langford spent much of his life in administration, but he never became an administrator. He consistently pursued an active intellectual life even amidst the demands of full-time administration. He continued to read and write, even as he recognized the prior claim of setting aside his own research in order to devote extra time to a junior faculty member on her research, a student seeking to understand a text, or a particularly knotty budgetary problem.

Even more, Langford recognized that effective administrative leadership requires theological and intellectual creativity. It is no accident that he reflected on the central communal themes of the Wesleyan tradition during his service as Dean, for those themes also contributed to his vision for Duke Divinity School. Nor is it accidental that he continued to think about broad issues of what it means to be human while serving as Vice-Provost and Provost, for those are central questions across the disciplines and schools of a research university.

Langford continues to develop such creativity as a trustee of The Duke Endowment. He has been instrumental in developing new ways in which that foundation's resources can be used to further the work of churches, universities, health-care institutions, children's homes, and communities throughout North and South Carolina.

Langford's irenic spirit and effective administrative leadership have brought healing during difficult times in Duke Divinity School's history, and have brought divided university factions together to find a future not bound by the divisions of the past. He has been an able

19

and effective mediator, because all sides of a conflict cannot help recognizing him as a person of intellectual integrity, a diplomat as well as a leader.

Grace Upon Grace: A Remarkable Legacy

Thomas Langford could have achieved many more personal accolades during his career, if that was what he wanted. He could have devoted himself more selfishly to his scholarship; he could have more carefully guarded his time so as to produce monographs and lectures that would have brought him personal acclaim; he could have avoided getting involved in disputes that required enormous amounts of energy; he could have refused the administrative assignments that meant that he supervised fewer Ph.D. students. But then he would not have been the Thomas Langford who has touched and enriched so many lives, who has helped to shape and sustain institutions and communities of higher education and the church, and to whom so many of us are indebted.

Yet Langford has left some extraordinary, important legacies, even beyond the impact he has had on those privileged to know him. Theologically, Langford has helped recover a christological shape to Methodism; his work through the church, in his writing, and in his leadership of Duke Divinity School have all shown how a recovery of Wesley's practical divinity represents not a retreat into the past or a narrowing of perspective, but rather a dynamic way forward that requires openness to the world. Administratively, Langford embodied a commitment to both the church and the university in a time when each was tempted to abandon the other. Even when it has not been clear how to maintain those ties, Langford's graceful leadership has offered a powerful example of how to go on even when we are not sure of where we are going. Duke University is a different and better place because of his leadership.

Langford has achieved a beautiful symmetry between his theological perspective and his own life. He has shown what it means to work within a tradition in a way that opens up an opportunity for others to engage that tradition as well as other traditions, to extend or to revise them, and even to disagree fundamentally with his own proposals.

Tom Langford's work focuses on grace, and specifically the claim that grace is embodied in the person of Jesus Christ. His life has reflected that commitment to grace. He will no doubt be embarrassed by the appearance of a collection of essays in his honor, for he has consistently focused his attention on the needs and contributions of others. Yet precisely because of his generosity to others, and his exemplary commitment as a Christian intellectual, it is difficult to imagine a person more deserving of such a collection.

We hope these essays, in their variety of focus yet unity of appreciation, will bear witness to the life and work of a wonderful teacher, scholar, and colleague. They are written by colleagues, friends, and former students, people who have been influenced by Tom Langford even as they have worked in their own distinctive ways. Many others would no doubt like to have offered contributions.

One of the people who would have wanted to contribute to this collection was Tom's longtime friend and colleague at Duke, Stuart Henry. Unfortunately, Stuart died on June 28, 1997. At Stuart's memorial service in Duke Chapel on July 1, 1997, Tom Langford delivered the remembrance. His concluding words, eloquent and truthful about Stuart Henry, also aptly summarize what many of us think is true of Tom:

> It is rare to have a friend who has been befriended by truth:
> It is rare to have a teacher who has been taught by Beatrice:
> It is rare to see light refracted by one who has stood in pure light:
>   and
> It is rare to catch rays from one whose virtue was love.

Dean L. Gregory Jones
Duke University Divinity School
February 1999

Notes

1. Thomas A. Langford, *Practical Divinity: Theology in the Wesleyan Tradition* (Nashville: Abingdon Press, 1998), 20.
2. Thomas A. Langford, "A Wesleyan/Methodist Theological Tradition," in Thomas A. Langford, ed., *Doctrine and Theology in The United Methodist Church* (Nashville: Kingswood Books, 1991), 10.
3. Ibid., 11.
4. Jaroslav Pelikan, *The Vindication of Tradition* (New Haven: Yale University Press, 1984), 65.

PART I:
BIBLICAL ESSAYS

GRACE UPON GRACE
IN THE GOSPEL OF JOHN

D. MOODY SMITH

The title of this volume dedicated to Tom Langford and to his central theological interest, is *Grace Upon Grace*. That is, of course, a direct quotation of John 1:16, at least according to the NRSV and other modern English versions (RSV, NEB, REB). The term *grace* appears four times in the prologue of John (1:14, 16-17) and nowhere else in the Gospel. Its occurrence probably does not seem surprising to most careful readers of the New Testament, although *grace* does not appear with this clear theological sense in the Synoptic Gospels. As we shall see, it is principally a Pauline theological term and concept, occurring mostly in Paul's letters and those written under his influence.[1]

Yet there is a problem of translation in John. The older, KJV translation, "grace for grace," is also possible, and arguably better than "grace upon grace," because the Greek preposition *anti* is ordinarily translated "instead of " and thus "for." If this translation is adopted, then verse 16 may seem to be explained by verse 17: the grace of the Mosaic law would be succeeded by the grace and truth of Jesus Christ. Such a translation seems apposite against the background of a biblical theology in which God acts in history, with one act of grace displacing another. But is such a biblical theology Johannine? (At the same time, the implication of the phrase "grace for grace" could also be supersessionist, for the grace of Moses and the law can easily be perceived as displaced, superseded by the grace and truth of Jesus Christ.) There is a difficulty, for in verse 16 Mosaic law seems to be specifically contrasted with the grace and truth of Jesus. Thus most modern commentators prefer the translation "grace upon grace," on the assumption that Christ only is full of grace and truth.[2] Without doubt John is a skilled writer, as well as a theologian, one who is fond of deliberate ambiguity and double meaning. Could he possibly have both meanings in view?[3]

Another, related problem is whether John knows or has in view other early Christian writings. The problem of John and the Synoptics has recently received another thorough and vigorous airing.[4] John 1:14, 16-17, however, raises the question of John and Paul. In fact, John 1:17 sounds like a summation of an important aspect of Pauline theology, which John would seem to embrace. Paul writes that Christ is the end of the law (Rom 10:4). Does John mean that? Perhaps he does. Similarly, John 8:30-36 on freedom from sin seems to echo Pauline theology, as does John's apparent limitation of the love commandment to the community of Jesus' disciples (cf. 13:34 and Gal 5:13-15; Rom 13:8).[5] It is possible that John plays on Pauline sayings and themes. If so, these passages, like James 2:14-26, bespeak the dissemination of Pauline theology, if not Paul's letters, at an early date.

John 1:16-17 may then represent such a play on a Pauline theme. Jesus Christ is full of grace and truth (v. 14), which he himself has brought (v. 16), or God has sent through him. He supersedes Moses, through whom the law was given: "The law was given by Moses; grace and truth by Jesus Christ." Yet like Paul, John does not dismiss the law as of no account. Its origin is God, and if the law (or as John prefers to say, Moses) is understood correctly, it testifies to Jesus (5:39, 45-47; cf. 1:45). Even though Jesus refers to the law as "your law" (8:17) in the same breath he assumes its validity (cf. 10:35: "Scripture cannot be annulled"). So perhaps one could understand "grace instead of grace" as also "grace upon grace," for John loves *double entendres,* words and expressions with double meanings. Surely the most famous such case is 3:1-10, in which Nicodemus misunderstands *anothen* as "again" (born again), when the more fundamental meaning is "from above." Yet those who are born from above are also necessarily born again. There is a fundamental meaning, but given that, a secondary meaning is also not untrue. So in the case of "grace for grace" or "grace upon grace" the fundamental idea may be the latter: grace abounding through Jesus Christ. Yet "grace for grace" in the sense of "grace instead of grace" is not an invalid idea insofar as Moses, like Jesus, was sent from God, although his meaning is now given by Jesus, who follows him. Jesus has displaced Moses, who was likewise sent from God, or, better, Jesus now redefines Moses' role.

So even as the term *grace (charis)* appears in John it has clearly Pauline overtones. *Grace* is, of course, a characteristically Pauline theological term. It appears more than sixty times in the uncontested letters, and frequently in the deutero-Pauline letters as well. It also occurs ten times in 1 Peter and eight times in Hebrews, perhaps under Pauline influence. (The verb *charizomai* is also fairly frequent in Paul.) "Grace" in the benediction of 2 John 3 sounds Pauline, as it does in Revelation 1:4. *Grace (charis)* in the Pauline theological sense, appears in Acts (e.g., 20:24), but not in Luke or the other Synoptic Gospels. One might also ask whether the theological idea of grace, with its Pauline overtones, is otherwise present in John, even where the term is absent. It is often said in Johannine exegesis that the prologue is a kind of overture to the Gospel, in which basic theological terms or themes are first introduced. Some, like *light* and *life*, recur throughout the Gospel. Others like Word (*logos* used of Jesus) never appear again, but nevertheless convey an important aspect of the Gospel's message. Arguably this is true also of *grace.*

Moreover, one might pursue the linguistic side of the investigation and ask whether grace, *charis,* is significantly related to other Johannine language. Here one thinks first of all of the eschatological joy *(chara),* which Jesus promises and brings. There is an obvious linguistic relationship. Is there not also within this linguistic relation a theological one? We shall return to this question.

We look first at the general theological concept. *Webster's Third New International Dictionary* includes in its definition of grace "a free gift of God to man for his regeneration or sanctification." Certainly a definition strongly influenced by Paul, as well as the historical Christian theological tradition. Similarly, Van Harvey defines grace as "perhaps the most crucial concept in Christian theology because it refers to the free and unmerited act through which God restores his estranged creatures to himself."[6] Again a definition strongly influenced by Paul's usage. As Conzelmann has aptly put it, "In Paul *charis* is a central concept that most clearly expresses his understanding of the salvation event."[7]

Does John share Paul's theological concept, if not his extensive use of the term, in a fundamental way? Bultmann evidently thinks so: "*[charis]* . . . denotes the character of revelation as a pure gift; the formulation is appropriate in this context because . . . the recipients of the gift are here speaking, and v. 16 is their confession of thanks."[8] Perhaps not surprisingly, Bultmann interprets the relationship between law, on the one hand, and grace and truth, on the other (v. 17) as sheer contrast, not continuity, and asserts that it "is otherwise foreign to John and comes from the Pauline school."[9] (He means the terms, not the concept represented by "grace," are otherwise foreign to John.)

That John understands the gospel in this fundamental, seemingly Pauline, sense is rather clear. As in Paul's theology grace is closely related to the idea of God's initiative and election. This becomes clear in John's classic statement about God's giving of the Son in 3:16 (echoed in 1 John 4:9), in which Christian readers have often seen a statement of the essence of the New Testament's message, the gospel. (With it one may compare Galatians 4:4-5; Romans 5:6-8; 2 Corinthians 5:18-19, on the Pauline side.) As Bultmann observed, the giving of the Son is a clear allusion to his death, for only in 3:16 is "gave" rather than "sent" used by John of God's action in dispatching his Son.[10] In any event, the priority and initiative of the Father, God, are obviously important in John as in Paul, so that they have become a fundamental aspect of the Johannine gospel message.

God's initiative and intention are, of course, closely and integrally related to God's election, in John as well as Paul. Perhaps the classic statement of this relationship in Paul is Romans 8:28-39, where God's election is grounds for Christians' assurance. Even though the Johannine Jesus' statement (15:16), "You did not choose me, but I chose you," is found in the context of exhortation, its burden is the same. Moreover, Jesus repeatedly states that he will not lose those whom the Father has given him (6:37, 39; 18:9). This is the ground of their assurance. Everything comes from God: the Son, but those who believe in, and belong to, the Son as well. God's intention, initiative, election, and grace are closely bound together in John as in Paul. Bultmann observed that although there is a difficulty in establishing a historical connection, that is, a connection of dependency, between Paul and John, their theologies are nevertheless closely allied. He speaks of *"the deep relatedness in substance that exists between John and Paul in spite of all their differences in mode of thought and terminology."*[11]

Of course, it goes without saying that both Paul and John are indebted to Israel's scriptures for this concept of grace, Paul perhaps more immediately or directly than John. The frequently occurring Hebrew terms *hēn,* verb *hanan* (grace, favor), and *hesed* (favor, grace, mercy) testify to faith in the God who in his mercy elects a people and is gracious and faithful to them, even in their waywardness. Thus the famous blessing of the Israelites (Num 6:24-26), which Tom Langford knew in his youth as the MYF benedictions, runs: "The Lord bless you and keep you; The Lord make his face to shine upon you, and *be gracious to you;* the Lord lift up his countenance upon you and give you peace." Presumably God's graciousness may be invoked because it is promised to Israel by virtue of her election. Thus the Lord says to Moses, "I will be gracious to whom I will be gracious, and will show mercy on whom I will show mercy" (Exod 33:19, quoted in Rom 9:15).

Within the Johannine corpus the concept of grace may be developed in an unusual and unique way, if the etymological connection between grace *(charis)* and joy *(chara)* is of any theological significance. It may be a sheer coincidence, although an intriguing one, that the term *chara* appears toward the end of the First Epistle's prologue (1:4), even as *charis* occurs toward the end of the Gospel's prologue. That in itself proves nothing, but it is suggestive, inasmuch as the prologue of 1 John seems to presuppose and reflect that of the Gospel.[12]

Moreover, the believers' existence after the death and departure of Jesus will according to the Gospel, be characterized by joy *(chara)*. Immediately after Jesus has spoken of the Father's love for him and his love for the disciples, admonishing them to abide in his love (15:9), he goes on to tell them that keeping his commandments is tantamount to abiding in his love, even as his own keeping of the Father's commandments is his abiding in the Father's love (15:10). Then, before reiterating the love commandment (15:12), Jesus speaks of joy: "I have said these things to you so that my joy may be in you, and that your joy may be complete" (15:11). Obviously joy is the fruition of the proper relationship between Jesus and the Father and between the disciples and Jesus.

In using the analogy of a woman in childbirth, Jesus compares her labor and pain with that of the disciples' anguish at his departure. In the one case the birth of a human being begets joy (16:21). In the disciples' case Jesus' seeing them again will end their pain and cause rejoicing (*chairō;* 16:22). At that time their asking in prayer in Jesus' name and receiving will complete their joy *(chara).* One might suggest that what they receive is a free gift *(charisma)* and a mark of grace *(charis),* although those terms are not used here. In his final prayer Jesus says that his very speaking in the world is "so that they may have my joy made complete in themselves" (17:13).

Bultmann points out that *chara* (joy) "is a word used to describe the eschatological, otherworldly salvation" and notes its occurrence in Jewish and Hellenistic sources.[13] "Joy" is, so to speak, the eschatological *Heilsgut,* the very stuff of salvation.[14]

Commentators generally do not, however, observe or make much of the similarity of *chara, charis,* and *chairō* (although they appear in the same word group in *Theological Dictionary of the New Testament).* Obviously, etymology can lead exegesis astray, whether in antiquity or modern times.[15] So I do not want to make too much of the relationship of *charis* to *chara.* Words acquire meaning through use rather than merely through morphological and phonetic relationships. Grace is one thing and joy is another. But the phonemes are close in Greek as they are not in English, and one should not assume that their similarity was something of which John was oblivious, especially in view of the fact that in ancient Greek *charis* was apparently not always clearly differentiated in meaning from *chara.*[16]

If Brown is correct in his reading of 1 John 1:1-4 over against John 1:1-18, then "beginning" and "word" at the beginning of both prologues may be matched by *charis* (grace) and *chara* (joy) at the end. (One may note also that *plērōmatos* in John 1:16 is matched by *peplērōmenē* in 1 John 1:4, even as the name Jesus Christ is first mentioned in John 1:17 and at the end of 1 John 1:3.) John the author of the Epistle (whether or not the author and the evangelist are the same individual) would have matched and replaced *charis* with *chara* and this would have been theologically appropriate. For the *charis* of God given in Jesus Christ finds its fruition or realization in the believer as *chara,* joy as the eschatological substance of salvation. Moreover, that grace does not relieve believers of responsibility for their actions, but rather puts them for once in control of their actions is a point made or assumed by Paul and John, as well as many theologians since. In John the first promise of eschatological joy is set in the context of exhortations or commands to love one another (15:11). Otherwise, grace is negated and joy cannot be realized. This reflects a common New Testament ethical paradigm that has managed to maintain itself, and for good reason, down through the centuries.

Once upon a time Tom Langford drove around Durham in a pickup truck—I think he still has it—with a personalized tag that read "Joy-in-it." I always wondered what that might mean, but never had the nerve to ask him. At first I assumed it meant joy in the truck, but that seemed inappropriate for a theologian, divinity dean, and university provost. Then it occurred to me that "it" might be the Holy Spirit, which, after all, is neuter in Greek, as Tom would know. But now, having run down the relationship of *chara* (joy) to *charis* (grace), particularly in John, I am quite certain of what the tag means and how it epitomizes his central theological interest. Obviously, the antecedent of "it" must be *grace,* and thus "joy-in-grace" brings into focus Tom's theological interest and the etymological, as well as theological, relationship between *chara* and *charis.* Too bad the tag doesn't read *chara en chariti,* but even if that were not too long for the space provided it could not be appreciated by most other drivers, whose knowledge of Greek ranges downward from minimal to nonexistent. But was such a meaning intended? In a day when the question of authorial intention does not necessarily govern exegetical results, and reader-response criticism is taken seriously, such a consideration is by itself no longer decisive. It is enough to maintain that like so much of Tom Langford's work the license tag is highly suggestive theologically!

Notes

1. The principal English-language work on grace in the New Testament is still James Moffatt, *Grace in the New Testament* (New York: Ray Long and Richard R. Smith, 1932). Among the entries under *grace* in the standard biblical and theological dictionaries one should note particularly the articles on *charis* (grace) and related terms such as *chara* (joy) in G. Kittel et al. (eds.), *Theological Dictionary of the New Testament,* trans. G. W. Bromiley et al. (Grand Rapids, Mich.: Wm. B. Eerdmans, 1964–76), vol. 9, 372-415, in which H. Conzelmann wrote the New Testament sections. As far as I can see, monographic or similar treatments of grace per se in the New Testament are relatively few, although of course the subject is dealt with in theologies of the New Testament and of Paul. See, e.g., Rudolf Bultmann, *Theology of the New Testament,* trans. Kendrick Grobel (New York: Scribner's, 1951), vol. 1, 288-314.
2. Philo, *De Posteritate Caini,* 145, is frequently cited by commentators in favor of this translation. See, e.g., the commentary of C. K. Barrett, *The Gospel According to St. John,* 2nd ed.

(Philadelphia: Westminster, 1978), 168; also Raymond E. Brown, *The Gospel According to John (i-xii)*, Anchor Bible 29 (Garden City, N.Y.: Doubleday, 1966), 16.

3. Double meanings in John are usually involved in the evangelist's characteristic technique of misunderstanding, whereby Jesus' interlocutors fail to understand him because they are talking on a different level, so to speak. See R. Alan Culpepper, *Anatomy of the Fourth Gospel: A Study in Literary Design* (Philadelphia: Fortress Press, 1983), 152-65. Such misunderstanding is replete with irony (*Anatomy* 165-80). Yet the prologue is not a conversation, and the readers themselves become potential victims of misunderstanding. But, as we shall see, there may be here not so much an alternative of understanding or misunderstanding as of two possible understandings, one more profound or appropriate than the other.

4. For an assessment of this extensive, and intensive, discussion, see my *John Among the Gospels: The Relationship in Twentieth-Century Research* (Minneapolis: Fortress Press, 1992).

5. Commentators generally note the possible relationship of John to Paul, but it has not been the topic of very intensive discussion in the latter half of the century. I have recently engaged the question in "The Love Command: John and Paul?" in *Theology and Ethics in Paul and His Interpreters: Essays in Honor of Victor Paul Furnish*, ed. Eugene H. Lovering and Jerry L. Sumney (Nashville: Abingdon Press, 1996), 207-17.

6. *A Handbook of Theological Terms* (New York: Macmillan, 1964), 108.

7. *Theological Dictionary of the New Testament*, vol. 9, 393.

8. Rudolf Bultmann, *The Gospel of John: A Commentary*, trans. G. R. Beasley-Murray, R. W. N. Hoare, and J. K. Riches (Philadelphia: Westminster, 1971), 78.

9. Ibid., 79.

10. Ibid., 153-54 n. 3.

11. *Theology of the New Testament*, vol. 2, p. 9.

12. See Raymond E. Brown, *The Epistles of John*, Anchor Bible 30 (Garden City, N.Y.: Doubleday, 1982), esp. 176-80.

13. *Commentary*, 505.

14. Cf. Rudolf Schnackenburg, *The Gospel According to St. John, Volume Three: Commentary on Chapters 13–21* (New York: Crossroad, 1982), 104: "The joy of Christ that is mediated to the disciples can become a full measure approaching that of the fullness of eschatological salvation. It is also a joy that cannot be taken away (16:22)."

15. As James Barr, *The Semantics of Biblical Language* (Oxford: Oxford University Press, 1961), pointed out many years ago (see esp. 107-60, "Etymologies and Related Arguments"). A couple of Barr's comments are to the point of our interest (p. 107): "It [etymology] studies the past of a word, but understands that the past of a word is no infallible guide to its present meaning. Etymology is not, and does not profess to be, a guide to the semantic value of words in their current usage, and such value has to be determined from the current usage and not from the derivation." As we shall note, however, there seems to be a connection in usage of *charis* and *chara* in the Jóhannine literature.

16. See Walter Bauer, William F. Arndt, and F. Wilbur Gingrich, *A Greek-English Lexicon of the New Testament and Other Early Christian Literature*, 2nd rev. ed. (Chicago: University of Chicago Press, 1979), 877.

AVE MARIA, GRATIA PLENA:
An Exemplar of Grace in the New Testament

C. CLIFTON BLACK

Ave Maria, gratia plena;
Dominus tecum;
benedicta tu in mulieribus,
et benedictus fructus ventris tui Jesus.
Sancta Maria, Mater Dei,
ora pro nobis peccatoribus nunc,
et in hora mortis nostrae.
  Amen.[1]

Εὐεργέτην τεκοῦσα,
τὸν τῶν καλῶν αἴτιον,
τῆς εὐεργεσίας τὸν πλοῦτον,
πᾶσιν ἀνάβλυσον·
πάντα γὰρ δύνασαι,
ὡς δυνατὸν ἐν ἰσχύι,
τὸν Χριστὸν κυήσασα,
θεομακάριστε.[2]

No topic is more definitive of Protestant theology than grace. No figure in Roman Catholic and Eastern Orthodox piety is more venerated than Mary, the mother of Jesus. Here I wish to conjoin topic and figure, to ponder the biblical cameos of Mary as a paradigm of grace in early Christian thought.[3] My aim is to reflect exegetically and constructively on seven New Testament pericopae,[4] with attention to their theological nuances both differing and convergent. To engage in depth the tradition of mariological doctrine beyond its biblical roots would trespass the bounds of my assignment and competence.[5] I shall suggest, nevertheless, that even a cursory review of the New Testament's depictions of Mary affords us much in our contemplation of God's grace: the wellspring of that "practical

33

divinity" expounded so eloquently, in life as in scholarship, by our friend and teacher Tom Langford.[6]

"The Mother of My Lord": A New Testament Conspectus

The Virgin Who Will Conceive God's Messiah (Luke 1:26-56)

Though not the earliest, canonically or chronologically, Luke 1:26-56 is the biblical presentation of Mary whose stamp on subsequent doctrine and piety has been most profound. For our purposes in this honorary volume, there is no passage more fruitful from which our own reflections may blossom. Examined exegetically, this text may be considered a balanced set of mirroring pairs: (a) the angel Gabriel's visitation to Mary of Nazareth (vv. 26-31); (b) Gabriel's canticle in praise of Jesus (the Annunciation, vv. 32-38); (a') Mary's visitation to her kinswoman, Elizabeth of Judah (vv. 39-45 + 56); (b') Mary's canticle in praise of God (the Magnificat, vv. 46-55). Such careful composition underscores Luke's primary themes.

Gabriel's visitation to Mary (1:26-31). The keynote of this pericope, as of the entire passage, is sounded by Gabriel's salutation of Mary (1:28): "Joyous greetings, she on whom great favor has been freely bestowed! The Lord [is] with you" (χαῖρε, κεχαριτωμένη, ὁ κύριος μετὰ σοῦ *chaire, kecharitōmenē, ho kyrios meta sou*).[7] No English translation can do justice to Gabriel's concise felicitations, which emphasize how Mary is viewed in God's eyes: *chaire, kecharitōmenē* ("Glad tidings,[8] she who has been regarded with high privilege!"). In both classical Greek and Jewish Greek of the diaspora, ἡ χάρις (*hē charis*, "grace" or "esteem") refers basically to what delights, bestirring in its beholder joy and, among the gods, the power to beautify that which evokes such favor.[9] The closest cognate in Hebrew embraces the same cluster of nuances: the essence of חנן (*ḥānan*) is at once beauty and a positive disposition to it (Ps 84:11; Prov 22:11; Sir 40:17, 22). Within this verbal family חן (*ḥēn*) characteristically refers to a human's deeply affectionate favor (Ruth 2:2, 10, 13; 1 Sam 16:22; 20:3; Esth 2:15, 17; 5:2); חנון (*ḥannûn*), to Yahweh as "gracious" (Exod 34:6; 2 Chr 30:9; Neh 9:17, 31; Pss 86:15; 103:8; 111:4; 116:5; 145:8; Joel 2:13; Jonah 4:2).[10] In both the OT (Gen 39:21; Exod 3:21; 11:3; 12:36) and classical Greek (Aristotle, *Rhetoric* 2.7.1385a), *ḥēn* and *hē charis* stress the favor of a superior that is utterly gratuitous and bestowed upon an inferior, apart from any merit of the beneficiary or expectation of reward.

The angel's greeting of Mary in 1:28, *chaire, kecharitōmenē* ("Hail, O favored one" [RSV]), includes Luke's first adoption of a term in the *charis* ("grace") family.[11] Another follows almost immediately, in 1:30: "Fear not, Mary, for you have found favor [χάριν *charin*] with God." Underpinning Gabriel's pronouncements are those Hebrew and Greek assumptions we have just noted. First, grace in Luke 1:26-31 is essentially God's delighted esteem (1:28, 30). Second, through direct intervention by a divine emissary (1:26, 28), that favor is bestowed at God's munificent initiative upon a "nobody": one Mary, from the Galilean backwater village of Nazareth (1:26-27; cf. John 1:46).[12] Mary's fullness of grace is by no means a prerequisite of her visitation by the Holy Spirit; rather, her miraculous conception will confirm that remarkable favor from God which she already enjoys (thus the aorist tense of the verb εὑρίσκω *heuriskō:* "for you *have found* favor"). Third, far from presuming on a privilege so wonderful, Mary responds with unspoken questions and visible terror (Luke 1:29-30*a*). Fourth, while uncoerced and uninvited, Gabriel's dispatch by God is right on time: six months into Elizabeth's pregnancy (1:24, 26, 36)—when her fetus has developed sufficient capability to leap for joy at Mary's forthcoming voice (1:44)—yet during Mary's betrothal, before its consummation (1:27, 34). The latter point signifies a fifth dimension of God's grace: its manifestation as powerful love, which will culminate in the conception and birth of a son to Mary, astonishingly independent of human impregnation.[13] Sixth, the name to be given that child, Jesus (1:31; a common form of the Hebrew name Joshua, "Yahweh saves"), like Joseph's membership in the house of David and the appearance of a divine envoy named Gabriel, implies an aspect of grace that for Luke is vitally important: though unique in its expression, God's affectionate esteem for Mary is consistent with the saving conduct of the Lord, who has always been with Israel as he is now with Mary (1:28; cf. Luke 1:7 with Gen 18:11; Luke 1:17 with Mal 4:5-6; Luke 1:19, 26 with Dan 8:16; 9:21; Luke 1:27 with 2 Sam 7:12-17; the narrative style of Luke 1:5–2:52 with 1–2 Sam and 1–2 Kgs). As a virgin—a young woman fully capable of childbearing—Mary of Nazareth also takes an unprecedented place amid a venerable succession of barren women who surprisingly gave birth to many of Israel's leaders: Sarah, to Isaac (Gen 18:9-15; 21:1-7); Rebekah, to Jacob (Gen

25:21-26); Rachel, to Joseph (Gen 30:1, 22-24); Manoah's wife, to Samson (Judg 13:2-25); Hannah, to Samuel (1 Sam 1:1-28); Elizabeth, to John the Baptist (Luke 1:5-25, 57-80).

The Annunciation (1:32-38) articulates the sheer magnitude of God's favor toward Mary, the astounding means of its accomplishment, and its varied corroboration. This peasant girl will beget more than merely a son. Jesus is destined for incomparable greatness, to be acclaimed "the son of the highest" (1:32*a;* see also 8:28; 9:35), to reign without end over the house of Jacob, in fulfillment of God's promise to David (1:33; see 2 Sam 7:16; Isa 9:7; Dan 7:14). When Mary replies that she has not been sexually intimate (Luke 1:34), Gabriel explains that she will conceive by dint of the Holy Spirit; precisely for that reason, "the child begotten will be called holy—Son of God" (1:35). The warrants for this promise are three, couched in reverberant language. (1) "Behold" (ἰδού *idou*)—Elizabeth, once called sterile, is now in her second trimester: evidence that "not anything said" (οὐκ...πᾶν ῥῆμα *ouk...pan rēma*) will be impossible with God (1:36-37). (2) "Behold" *(idou)*—Mary consents to her station as the Lord's obedient slave (ἡ δούλη κυρίου *hē doulē kyriou;* see also 1:48):[14] "May it be for me in accordance with what you have said" (τὸ ῥῆμα σου *to rēma sou*), expressing hope that lingers after Gabriel's departure (and with him, his assurance; 1:38). (3) The angelic confidence espoused by Mary—that with God anything is possible (1:37)—echoes an OT affirmation repeatedly hurled in the teeth of apparent impossibility (Gen 18:14; Job 42:2; Zech 8:6).

Though *charis* and its cognates do not appear in Luke 1:32-38, by implication this pericope teaches or reminds us of important characteristics of grace. Grace is God's radical, safeguarding, astonishing creation of new life where none existed.[15] The analogue for the Spirit's promised "coming upon" (ἐπελεύσεται *epeleusetai*) and "overshadowing" (ἐπισκιάσει *episkiasei*) the virgin (1:35) is not Zeus's rape of Leda—an episode justly arousing terror at violation, in stark contrast with the joy of healing (or salvation) of which Mary will sing (1:47). The proper biblical analogues include the cloud that protects mortals from the Almighty's dazzling presence (Exod 24:15-18; Luke 9:34) and the hovering of God's transformative רוח *rûaḥ* ("wind," "breath," "spirit") over the waters of chaos (Gen 1:2; Ps 33:6; Jdt 16:14; *2 Apoc. Bar.* 21:4) and Israel's faithful (1 Sam 16:13; Isa 32:15; Acts 1:8; 2:17). Correlatively, grace elicits trust from the Lord's slaves, both women

(Luke 1:38; Acts 2:18) and men (2:18). Among those chosen servants in Luke's Gospel is Jesus himself (Luke 22:27), whose receipt of David's throne from the Lord God is no less a gift (1:32; 22:29) than the grace of Mary's pregnancy. Jesus, like his mother, points us to God as the delighted, generous Giver (12:32).

By subtly echoing the elements of Gabriel's visitation to Mary, *Mary's visitation to Elizabeth (1:39-45, 56)* reinforces Luke's presentation of grace. An aura of breathless joy envelops the scene: Mary hastens (1:39); with delight the fetus jumps (1:41, 44); Elizabeth pours out a canticle of praise (ἀνεφώνησεν κραυγῇ μεγάλῃ *anephōnēsen kraugē megalē*, 1:42; cf. 1 Chr 15:28; 16:4, 5, 42 [LXX]). Confronted with the wonder of divine incursion, Elizabeth concedes her human inadequacy (Luke 1:43) while her unborn child leaps with gladness (1:44; see also Acts 2:26). The strength and percipience of Elizabeth's prophetic song (Luke 1:43-45) derive, not from her own power or discernment, but from her being filled with Holy Spirit (Luke 1:41; see also 1:67). The formulation of 1:43-45 is significant: phraseologically tied to Israel's past,[16] Elizabeth's blessings of her Lord and his trusting mother[17] proclaim that consummate, end-time joy has *now* broken into their human history (see also 4:21). Such grace explodes the ordinary calendar, creating its own season. In that eschatological light Luke's comment that Mary stayed with Elizabeth for another three months (1:56) is arguably more than a throwaway tag line: Mary remains with her kinswoman, far advanced in pregnancy, until Elizabeth's own time of deliverance is fulfilled (1:57).[18] In Luke's hands pregnancy and childbearing have become allusive signposts for the God-given preparation and completion of Israel's righteousness before God (see Luke 1:6, 14-17, 68-80).

The Magnificat (1:46-55), surely one of the loveliest specimens of biblical poetry, entwines the many threads of grace in Luke 1:26-45. The form of its rendition could not be more appropriate to its subject matter: before grace, in all its matchless beauty, prose will not suffice. Mary's affirmation is not an algebraic formula to be solved. It is, it must be, *an aria* to be trolled,[19] and the same could be said of the other canticles in Luke 1–2. Moreover, Mary's response is irreducibly one of *faith*. This canticle contains a single verb conjugated in the future tense ("[all] will call [me] fortunate" [μακαριοῦσιν *makariousin*], v. 48). Every other verb is conjugated in the present or, more frequently, the aorist (past) tense, referring to what God is doing or has already

begun to do. The specific activities for which Mary praises the Lord—
the scattering of the haughty (v. 51 *b*), the overthrow of sovereigns and
exaltation of the lowly (v. 52), the filling of the hungry with good
things and the sending of the rich away empty (v. 53)—are considered
faits accompli. Such is the language, not only of faithful hope (see Rom
8:24-25; Heb 11:1), but of a renewed confidence that God is *already*
transforming the values by which society conventionally operates (see
Rom 12:2).[20] In that connection there is no mistaking the *theocentric*
character of the Magnificat: from first to last, this is a song about what
God has done and may be trusted to continue. Correlative with his
portrait of Jesus (in my view), Luke's presentation of Mary is deliber-
ately crafted to point his reader to God.

That God, this hymn tells us, is the One who has "looked upon"
(ἐπέβλεψεν *epeblepsen*) a particular Nazarene girl, which harks back to
the ancient sense of *charis* or *ḥēn* as an affectionate, favorable regard
of someone. What God has done for Mary falls consistently, albeit
unexpectedly, in line with the help God has always promised and
supplied Israel, from Abraham (Gen 17:6-8; 18:18; 22:17) through David
(2 Sam 7:11-16) and beyond (Luke 1:54-55). Expressly acknowledged,
God's constancy is even more subtly suggested in Mary's song by its
saturation with OT expressions ("the Mighty One" [Luke 1:49], see Zeph
3:17; "great things" [Luke 1:49], see Deut 11:7; Judg 2:7; God's "strong
arm" [Luke 1:51], see Exod 6:6; Deut 26:8; Ps 89:10, 13) and motifs
("God my savior" [Luke 1:47], see Ps 24:5; Isa 12:2; God's "mercy" [Luke
1:50, 54], see Exod 34:6; 2 Sam 7:15; Israel as God's "servant" [Luke 1:54],
see Isa 41:8).[21] Like Hannah, whose canticle over Samuel's birth (1 Sam
2:1-10) is echoed by the Magnificat, Mary openly locates herself among
the lowly and the hungry (Luke 1:48, 52-53) who cannot rely on their
own strength but surrender their lives entirely to God's blessings. And
like Hannah, the pregnant virgin rhapsodizes her praise of God's holy
name (Luke 1:49; see also Ps 111:9). Mary's spirit (τὸ πνεῦμα *to pneuma*)
finds gladness in God; her inmost self (ἡ ψυχή *hē psychē*) magnifies the
Lord (Luke 1:46; see also Ps 69:30; Sir 43:31).

*The Concerned Yet Mistaken Parent (Luke 2:41-52; Mark 3:31-35;
John 2:1-12)*

The next three pericopae stem from different and probably independent[22] traditions about Jesus: his youth, his mature ministry, and

his passion. An intriguingly common denominator among them all, however, is the sketch of Mary by Luke, Mark, and John.

Luke 2:41-52, the conclusion of that Evangelist's infancy narrative, recounts the legend of young Jesus' discovery in the Temple by his distraught parents. So familiar is that story, so memorable its punchline ("Did you not know that I must be in my Father's house?"), that we might overlook Luke's interesting details about Jesus' parents, especially his mother.

That picture is complex, its brevity notwithstanding. Consistent with his earlier portrayals of Mary and Joseph (2:21-25, 39) and of Zechariah and Elizabeth (1:6, 59-64), Luke emphasizes that Jesus' parents were religiously observant and obedient to God's commands: thus, their visit to Jerusalem at Passover during Jesus' twelfth year is one of many that they customarily made every year (2:41-42).[23] Understandably, upon realizing that their child was not among them during their return home, they search for him: first, among the entourage to Nazareth (2:39, 44); eventually, back in Jerusalem (2:45). Thus far, Jesus' parents appear as dutiful as we have grown to appreciate them in Luke 1:26–2:40. But what kind of parents, we may justifiably wonder, would travel a full day before confirming that their (miraculously) firstborn and—so far as we can tell from Luke 2—only son was *not* among their caravan (2:44)? And, when they get back to Jerusalem, why does it take Jesus' parents *three days* of searching before they find him in the Temple (2:46)—whose environs, after all, child and parents would have visited, if their excursion's original purpose was celebration of the Passover? Upon recovering the lost child, they—Mary, in particular—express astonishment and torment by his conduct (2:47-48). By that time, however, Luke's readers may be forgiven for feeling somewhat the same about the parents.

Surprisingly, our doubts about their alacrity are corroborated by young Jesus himself. To translate 2:49 literally unto woodenness: "How is it that you sought me? You didn't know—did you?—that in the [matters] of my Father I must be." Contrary to conventional renderings of this verse, Jesus' question is framed by Luke in a way implying that he didn't expect his parents to be any more discerning than they turned out to be—nor, for that matter, more discerning than the Temple-teachers, amazed by Jesus' discernment and his answers (2:47). The parents' ignorance of their child's ultimate allegiance to God is in no measure dissipated by Jesus' questions of them: "Yet they did not understand the word [τὸ ῥῆμα *to rēma;* see also 1:37-38] that he spoke to them" (2:50). That the Evangelist means not to suggest sheer cockiness of a precocious youngster is immediately confirmed by Luke's affirmations of Jesus' obedience to his parents, and his progressive wisdom, maturity, favor—grace *(charis)*—among God and people (2:51*a*, 52; see also 1 Sam 2:26; Isa 11:1-2; Luke 1:80). That grace, however, does not depend on Mary's being an extraordinarily responsible, pious, or perceptive mother, without need of pondering "these things" (τὰ ῥήματα *ta rēmata,* 2:51*b;* see also 2:19). Indeed, one of the points made by Luke's narration of this remarkable story is that through Jesus God's grace is truly bestowed, from the beginning and consistently, on those who, like Mary, misunderstand or reproach it—who, in fact, tend to look for grace everywhere but where it must be found.

Mark 3:31-35 is another pericope about the family in search of Jesus (here, an adult). This story, like Luke 2:41-52, has been rubbed smooth by its familiarity. Standing outside his home, impeded by a great crowd, Jesus' mother and brothers[24] send for him. On being informed that they are seeking him, Jesus redefines his brother, sister, and mother as anyone who does the will of God.

What to us may ring as a charming religious platitude would have landed with a thud on first-century Jewish and Roman ears. No social unit of antiquity was more basic than the family, no ties more binding than those of kinship. Jesus' rebuff of his mother and brothers, instead esteeming strangers obedient to God's will, is reminiscent of young Jesus' reply to his mother that both she and his earthly father ought to expect finding Jesus involved in his (heavenly) Father's business (Luke 2:48, 49*b*).[25] In 3:31-35 Mark seems to go out of his way to distance Jesus from his family. The latter are said to be standing outside (ἔξω *exō,* 3:32)—the space occupied, as Mark's readers soon will learn, by those who see but do not see, who hear but do not understand (4:11-12). In 3:32 his mother and brothers are also reportedly "searching for" (ζητοῦσιν *zētousin*) Jesus. Those who do that in Mark usually have hostile intentions (see 8:11, 12; 11:18; 12:12; 14:1, 11, 55)—as sinister as "those close to him" (οἱ παρ' αὐτοῦ *hoi par' autou*), "his family" (NRSV), who in 3:21 set out to seize Jesus because they think him mad. If the family members in 3:31 are not identical with the posse in 3:20, Mark closely associates both groups, not only with each other, but also with the scribes from Jerusalem who consider

Jesus demonically possessed (3:22, 30).[26] For those opponents Jesus spins a web of parables, one of which envisions the collapse of a house divided against itself (3:23-26). Although they probably used Mark as one of their sources, Matthew and Luke were apparently troubled by this division of Jesus and his family: both the first and the third Evangelists soften the wording of Mark 3:31-35 (cf. Matt 12:46-50; Luke 8:19-21) and separate that story from the Beelzebul controversy (cf. Matt 12:22-32; Luke 11:14-23; 12:10).

Mark's intention is not scrupulously clear; Jesus is, after all, speaking parabolically (3:23). Read in the light of 6:1-6a, the only other passage in Mark referring to Jesus' mother and brothers (and sisters), 3:31-35 uncomfortably suggests that those seemingly closest to Jesus—hometown acquaintances, religious leaders, even his mother, siblings, and finally the Twelve (8:31-33; 9:32-41; 10:35-45)—are not thereby assured of understanding him. Prophets enjoy some honor, except among their relatives and in their own homes (6:4).

John 2:1-12. The miracle of the wine at the wedding in Cana is another episode in which the mother of Jesus (never named in John) plays a minor but complex role. Although the story begins as though Jesus' mother is going to be its principal antagonist, even by 2:1 the reader of the Fourth Gospel knows that characters like John the Baptist, priests and Levites, and the disciples are introduced for the purpose of pointing up Jesus' significance (see John 1:6-8, 15, 19-28, 29-34, 35-39, 40-42, 45-49). So too does Jesus' mother function in 2:1-12.

Perhaps the most intriguing feature of Mary's conversations with others in this passage is the repeated, odd disjunction between what she says and what is said to her. When the wine for the wedding guests is depleted, Jesus' mother does not explicitly request that he do anything about it; hers is the simpler observation, "They haven't got wine" (2:3). As is characteristic of Jesus in this Gospel (see, e.g., 4:10-14, 47-50; 16:16-19), his reply seems aloof, even irrelevant to his mother's statement: "What [is that] to me and you, woman? My hour has not yet come" (2:4). By different means, John creates a wedge of incomprehension between son and mother: Jesus' sovereign resistance to human, even maternal, claims on him, which we have also observed in Luke and in Mark. Instead of replying to her son, Mary says to the waiters, "Whatever he tells you, do [it]" (John 2:5): a command equally lacking clear justification. Jesus' instructions to the waiters are to fill some ritual jars with water, then to draw out some of that water for the headwaiter (2:6-8). The story ends, riddled with as many disjunctures as opened it. The servants know where the water came from, but it is not clear that *they* know of its transformation into wine (2:9). The headwaiter knows that he is tasting the best wine in the house, though *he* does not know where it came from (2:9-10*a*). The bridegroom's response to his wine-steward's compliment (2:9*b*-10) is left unreported, but from John's narration there is no reason to suppose that the groom knows what the headwaiter is talking about, or *anything* of what has transpired. The Evangelist's penultimate explanation—that Jesus' activity at Cana was the first of his "signs" (τὰ σημεῖα *ta sēmeia*) that revealed his "glory" (ἡ δόξα *hē doxa*, the property of divinity [2:11*a;* see 1:14; 12:41])—seems odd on its face: what should we make of a revelation that virtually no one has recognized? This tale's real conclusion, 2:11*b*-12, fits the critical pieces into place. Jesus' ambiguous signs have profoundly revelatory value *for his disciples:* those who believed in him and "abided" (ἔμειναν *emeinan*) with him (see also 1:12; 15:4-10). For those in John without faith in Jesus, his signs are not convincing (2:23-25; 11:47-48); for those who already believe—including John's readers—those signs evoke and corroborate their faith (4:50-54; 20:30-31).

In which camp does Mary stand? After 2:5 she disappears from the wedding gala. In 2:12 she reappears among Jesus' brothers and disciples who stay (or abide) with him in Capernaum. Her presence there is not unimpeachable testimony to her own faith in Jesus, since by 7:1-10 even his brothers do not believe in him. Yet John hints that Jesus' mother will fare better as a believer. Although it is not clear that she understands her son's reference to "his hour" (of crucifixion: 7:30; 8:20; 12:23, 27; 13:1; 17:1), that comment mysteriously prompts her to spur others to do whatever Jesus tells them. Since in John's Gospel the Son does nothing other than what he sees the Father doing (5:19), to do what Jesus commands is critically important for his disciples (15:10-17). Mary may no more comprehend Jesus as "the gift of God" (ἡ δωρεά τοῦ θεοῦ *hē dōrea tou theou*) than does the Samaritan woman at Jacob's well (4:10), but the subsequent reactions of both women to Jesus suggest an incipient faith in him capable of amplification (see 4:15, 19, 29; 19:25). And while John leaves unexplained the symbolism of so much wine ("twenty or thirty gallons," 2:6), Frank Kermode's suggestion is intriguing: "Perhaps it is the grace beyond grace [1:16], the messianic wine of being that replaces the inferior wine of the Torah, which [for John] is appropriate only to becoming."[27]

A Vulnerable Woman and Mother (Galatians 4:1-7; Matthew 1–2; John 19:25b-27)

The New Testament's remaining references to Mary are comparatively slender. In *Galatians 4:1-7* Paul contrasts the human condition of bondage to "the world's enslaving forces" (τὰ στοιχεῖα τοῦ κόσμου *ta stoicheia tou kosmou*), including the law, with that of liberation from it. At a time of divine selection, God broke into this disarrayed, oppressive cosmos through the agency of his own Son, to snap the shackles of our enslavement (4:4; see also Rom 8:3). God completed this invasion by sending his Son's own Spirit, to effect our adoption as "sons" (ἡ υἱοθεσία *hē huiothesia*): our transfer from this world's enslavement into a new life of incorporation into "the Son" (ὁ υἱός *ho huios*).[28] God's Son was himself "born of woman, born under law" (Gal 4:4): Jesus was fully human and utterly vulnerable (see also Phil 2:7), subject to all the tyrannies of this life—including death—experienced by every human "born of woman" (Job 14:1; 15:14; 25:4; Matt 11:11 = Luke 7:28). To draw from these metaphors an implication neither central nor foreign to Paul's argument: the woman by whom God's Son was born was herself "born of woman," equally enslaved as every human after the Fall and equally emancipated from that slavery by the grace of Christ in which redeemed humanity now lives (Gal 2:20-21).

Matthew 1–2. In the Lukan infancy narrative Mary is a primary actor and Joseph, her mute partner; in Matthew's birth narrative those roles are precisely reversed. Mary's function in Matthew 1–2 is twofold. First, in the genealogy of Jesus (Matt 1:1-17), she is identified as one among five women (vv. 3, 5a, 5b, 6b, 16a) in an otherwise conventional patrilineage.[29] Second, in the circumstances attending Jesus' conception and birth, Mary and her infant son constitute the silent center around which whirls a cyclone of legal obligations (1:18-20), angelic guidance in dreams (1:20-25; 2:12-15, 19-23), foreign homage (2:1-2, 9-12), celestial portents (2:2b, 9-10), political intrigue (2:3-4, 7-8, 13, 16, 22), and mass infanticide (2:16), all held together by scriptural fulfillment (1:22-23; 2:5b-6, 15b-18, 23b).[30]

43

As regards Mary, at least three themes recur throughout these joyous yet terrifying pericopae. First, by her appearance in Jesus' genealogy and her virginal conception of Christ through Holy Spirit, Mary exemplifies the *astonishing, personal novelty* with which God breaks into human history, along Israel's familiar paths in particular. Second, because of those irregularities, Mary is presented by Matthew as the last in a series of Hebraic-Jewish women who have been *threatening* to the conventional order of marriages and politics and have been *threatened* by it. The second part of that theme is most vividly dramatized by the "upright" (δίκαιος *dikaios*) Joseph and the murderous Herod, both of whom intend without success to dispose of Mary and her offspring in very different ways (1:19-20; 2:13, 16).[31] Third, while Mary and her child are repeatedly protected by God's agents, *divine providence comes at high cost.* The gifts lavished on the newborn Jesus by jubilant Gentile Magi (2:10-11) are mirrored by disconsolate Jewish mothers whose hands drip with the blood of their infant sons (2:16-17). Both these tableaux receive strikingly apt commentary in the two stanzas of Luke's Nunc Dimittis: in the child Jesus, devout Simeon sees the Lord's salvation of all peoples (2:25-32) and a sword that will slice through Israel, not excepting Mary's own soul (2:33-35).

Here we cannot review the history of exegesis of *John 19:25b-27*, much less resolve the perennial question of whom or what may be symbolized therein by Jesus' mother.[32] Since throughout the Fourth Gospel his mother (2:1-12) and the disciple whom he loved (13:21-30; 20:1-10; 21:7, 20-24) have neither name nor identity apart from their particular relation to Jesus, those figures at the foot of the cross are probably important for John's understanding of a new relationship created by the now crucified-glorified Christ. In 2:1-12, Jesus' association with his mother was attenuated because his hour had not yet come (2:4). From that it seems to follow that, in 19:25b-27, Jesus, "the one who comes from above" (3:31) whose hour of exaltation has arrived (3:13-15; 12:23; 13:1; 17:1), is revealing (ἴδε *ide*, "behold"; see also 1:29; 3:26; 19:14) his creation of a new family, transcending this world's kindred, whose essence is loving discipleship that abides in the Son and in the Father (12:32-33; 13:34-35; 14:20-21; 15:12-17).[33] The fourth Evangelist is not in the least interested to trace the development of faith within Jesus' natural mother. John is profoundly concerned with the one-of-a-kind Son who graciously reveals the loving Father who sent him, the God by whose will believers in Christ are begotten (1:12, 16-18; 3:5-8, 16; 5:19-24; 6:60-65; 10:11-18; 14:6-14; 17:20-26). Accordingly, in this Gospel Mary does not beget Jesus, who is "from above, not of this world" (8:23; see also 1:1-5, 9-14). The mother of Jesus, like all disciples, is herself begotten "not of blood, neither of fleshly will nor of man's will, but of God" (1:13).

Grace Viewed Through a Marian Prism

Across the history of Christian doctrine, the mother of Jesus has played many roles: immaculately conceived Daughter of Zion, ever-virginal Second Eve, Theotokos and Queen of Heaven, Paragon of Chastity, *Mater Dolorosa* ("Mother of Sorrows"), and Mediatrix, among others.[34] More recently, Mary has been viewed as the disciple par excellence,[35] the feminine essence of Holy Spirit enfleshed as a woman,[36] and a bridge-figure within the ecumenical movement.[37] Without intending to imply its superiority over all other estimates, how might we limn Mary's figure in the NT as an exemplar of grace? For convenience our conclusions may be categorized theologically and anthropologically.

The Truth About God

First, like other biblical personalities, Mary's experience reveals that *grace is the intrinsic nature of God:* God's utterly gratuitous disposition of merciful favor upon his creatures (Luke 1:28, 30; 12:32). For this reason, every passage examined in this chapter has been *theocentrically* oriented, concentrated on God's will (Mark 3:35), business (Luke 2:49), and magnificent works (Luke 1:46-55)—especially the sending of his Son for our redemption (Gal 4:4). Not Mary, not even Jesus, has been the focal figure in these vignettes: both the Son and his mother direct attention away from themselves toward God, who is supernally gracious (Matt 1:23; Luke 1:32, 45, 47; Gal 4:6).[38]

Second, grace is *an eschatological reality,* transcendently invading this world in God's own appointed time (Luke 1:26, 36, 43-45; John 2:4; 19:25*b*-27; Gal 4:4-7). Thus it is radically free from any human instigation (Luke 1:34-35), unfettered by the bounds of human possibility (Matt 1:11; Luke 1:37), and hostile to this world's enslaving powers (Gal 4:3) and wicked principalities (Matt 2:3-4, 13, 16, 22).

Third, all of these stories attest to *the coherence of God's favor toward Mary with that divine mercy that Israel's children have always known.* This, I think, holds even in pericopae suggesting that the law has been commandeered by nefarious forces (Gal 4:1-9; see also Rom 8:1-8) or superseded by Christ's coming (John 2:1-12). Nestled in the Temple (Luke 2:46-49) as the fulfillment of God's promises to Abraham's posterity (Luke 1:32-33, 43-45, 54-55), Mary's son is the saving climax to which Israel's history has always been unfolding (Matt 1:1-17, 22-23; 2:5, 15, 17-18, 23).[39]

Fourth, *God's grace is radically creative and magnanimously loving.* It preserves the Davidic dynasty from all threats to its continuance (Matt 1:11, 19; 2:13, 22), generating extraordinary life, holy and loving, in Mary's womb (Luke 1:32-38) and at Jesus' cross (John 19:25b-27). Grace has already subverted the norms by which this world lives (Luke 1:46-53; Gal 4:1-7). In an evil world that prefers a corrupted status quo, grace comes not without cost to Israel's children (Matt 2:16-18; Luke 2:34-35), including God's own Son (John 3:16).

The Truth About Ourselves

Mary's encounters with God's grace exemplify its incursion into human life. First, standing before God's unmitigated generosity toward us, we realize our basic frailty (Gal 4:4), poverty (Luke 1:49), and constant dependence on God for protection (Matt 1:20; 2:12-14, 20-22). That is how grace is recognized for what it truly is: no favor that we can curry, notwithstanding our delusions to the contrary, but God's unstinting care for us whose lives are as *radically dependent on divine mercy* as that grace is radically characteristic of God.

Second, *God's grace restructures human relationships and redefines our fundamental loyalties.* No longer are we enslaved to sin, death, and the powers of this age; we have been adopted by God and incorporated into his Son (Gal 4:1-7). This ontological shift means that the claims of our human families are subordinate to God's will and Christ's command of love among that new family of disciples created by his glorious death (Matt 1:18-19; Mark 3:31-35; Luke 2:41-52; John 2:1-4; 19:25b-27).

Third, like Mary, *our response to grace is inevitably ambivalent:* a tumultuous confusion of shock and acquiescence (Luke 1:29, 38), gladness and consternation (Luke 1:47; 2:48), remarkable faith and equally glaring presumptuousness (Luke 1:46-55; Mark 3:21, 31-32), unexpected insight (John 2:5, 11) and baffled rumination (Luke 2:19, 50-51). By its very nature God's grace does not depend on the resolution of our blessed perplexities. Through the Spirit God even unties our tongues to articulate our gratitude and continuing need for grace (Luke 1:41-42, 64-67; 2:27; Gal 4:6).

Fourth, and most essentially, grace means that *God esteems us,* as he regarded Mary, *with delight and deep affection* (1:28, 30). As God's creatures, each of us is as particularly remembered by the Creator as every ordinary male and extraordinary female in Matthew's genealogy (1:1-17). In God's eyes we are beautiful in our capacity to magnify the Lord (Luke 1:46); from the cross Jesus knows that our loving discipleship completes everything intended by God's own love for us (John 19:27-28).[40]

By Mary we are reminded that our inherent neediness is answered by God's intrinsic mercy; that our allegiance, like Israel's, belongs ultimately to God; that our bewilderment is a by-product of the new thing God is doing; that our loveliness never fades in the eyes of our Creator, who is creative love. In honor of Mary, who beside us reaches for God, the prayers of later piety may not, after all, be so far removed from her graceful image in scripture.

Hail Mary, full of grace, the Lord is with thee. Blessed art thou amongst women, and blessed is the fruit of thy womb, Jesus. Holy Mary, Mother of God, pray for us sinners, now, and at the hour of our death. Amen.	Having brought forth unto us the cause and giver of good, From your great abundance of kindness, Pour forth upon us all; For all is possible. For you who carried the Christ. Who is mighty in power: You, who are blessed of God.

Notes

1. *Saint Benedict's Prayer Book for Beginners* (York: Ampleforth Abbey, 1993), 108. A translation of this and the following epigram appears at the end of this chapter.

2. *The Service of the Small Paraklesis (Intercessory Prayer) to the Most Holy Theotokos* (Brookline, Mass.: Holy Cross Orthodox, 1984), 8.

3. This approach is hardly ragged from overuse. James Moffatt's classic study, *Grace in the New Testament* (New York: Long & Smith, 1932), mentions Mary only twice, in passing, with

references to "grace" (ἡ χάρις *hē charis*) in Luke 1:30 (p. 31) and "she who is highly favored"(κεχαριτωμένη *kecharitō menē*) in the *Odes of Solomon* 11.1-2.

4. Not included is Revelation 12:1-17, whose unnamed woman is now generally recognized as referring at best secondarily—but even then, uncertainly—to Mary. See Richard P. McBrien, *Catholicism: New Edition* (San Francisco: HarperCollins, 1994), 1080-81.

5. Hilda Graef, *Mary: A History of Doctrine and Devotion* (London: Sheed & Ward, 1985 [originally published in two parts, 1963 and 1965]), remains an indispensable sounding of this bottomless river of research.

6. See esp. Thomas A. Langford, *Practical Divinity: Theology in the Wesleyan Tradition* (Nashville: Abingdon Press, 1998).

7. Here and throughout, all translations are my own unless otherwise indicated.

8. It is debatable how *chaire* should be rendered: as forcefully as "Rejoice" (cf. Zeph 3:14 [LXX]; thus the NAB and Joel B. Green, *The Gospel of Luke*, NICNT [Grand Rapids: Wm. B. Eerdmans, 1997], 86-87) or as blandly as "Hello" (cf. Acts 15:23; 23:26; Phil 3:1; 4:4; Jas 1:1; so *Mary in the New Testament*, ed. R. E. Brown, K. P. Donfried, J. A. Fitzmyer, and J. Reumann [Philadelphia and New York: Fortress, Paulist Press, 1978], 130-32). Given the immediate context of Luke 1:28, within the light of that Evangelist's pervasive association of Jesus' advent with χαρά *chara* ("joy"; see 1:14; 2:10; 8:13; 10:17; 15:7, 10; 24:41, 52), I favor a translation inclined toward the first alternative, without pressing that sense to excess.

9. For documentation within relevant ancient sources, see Hans Conzelmann, "χάρις, κ.τ.λ.," *TDNT* 9 (1974): 373-76, as amended by John Nolland, "Grace as Power," *NovT* 28 (1986): 26-31.

10. For further information, consult D. N. Freedman, J. R. Lundbom, and H.-J. Fabry, "חָנַן," *TDOT* 5 (1986): 22-36.

11. Alone among the Synoptic Evangelists, Luke uses words from this group: thirteen occurrences in the Gospel (1:28, 30; 2:40, 52; 4:22; 6:32, 33, 34; 7:21, 42, 43, 47; 17:9), twenty-one in Acts (2:47; 3:14; 4:33; 6:8; 7:10, 46; 11:23; 13:43; 14:3, 26; 15:11, 40; 18:27; 20:24, 32; 24:27; 25:3, 9; 25:11, 16; 27:24).

12. Some strains of medieval mariology evolved to interpret κεχαριτωμένη *(kecharitō menē)* as implying Mary's possession of every secular and spiritual gift, an already realized perfection that acquitted her fit to conceive the Christ (see Graef, *Mary*, 1.170-73). By contrast, as Raymond E. Brown correctly observes, "For Luke Mary's special state is to be constituted by the divine favor involved in the conception of Jesus" (*The Birth of the Messiah: A Commentary on the Infancy Narratives in the Gospels of Matthew and Luke*, new updated ed., ABRL [New York and London: Doubleday, 1993], 326).

13. Patrick J. Bearsley's comment strikes the bull's-eye: "Mary's virginal conception attests to the omnipotence and transcendence of God, who does not need to work through human agency or in human ways to achieve His effects" ("Mary the Perfect Disciple: A Paradigm for Mariology," *TS* 41 [1980]: 461-504 [here, 496]).

14. In Acts (2:18; 4:29; 16:17) "slave" refers to any believer who serves under God's rightful authority. Accordingly, the term's application to Mary in Luke 1 by no means sanctions any general subjection of women to men. The exegetical issues here are finely discerned by Beverly Roberts Gaventa, *Mary: Glimpses of the Mother of Jesus*, Studies on Personalities of the New Testament (Columbia: University of South Carolina Press, 1995), 54.

15. As early as Psalm 136:1-9 and continuing through the rabbinic, medieval, and mystical traditions of Judaism, creation itself was regarded as an act of grace. See David R. Blumenthal, "The Place of Faith and Grace in Judaism," in *A Time to Speak: The Evangelical-Jewish Encounter*, ed. A. J. Rudin and M. R. Wilson (Grand Rapids and Austin, Tex.: Wm. B. Eerdmans, Center for Judaic-Christian Studies, 1987), 104-14, esp. 104-5.

16. "And it came to pass that as Elizabeth heard, . . . the baby jumped" (Luke 1:41: a familiar Semitic construction, especially prevalent in Luke 1–2); "Richly blessed are you among women" (1:42; see also Judg 5:24; Jdt 13:18).

17. Alongside Matthew 1:23, the implicit Christology of Luke 1:43 inches toward what would later become the personification of Mary as Theotokos, "the one who gave birth to the one who is God" (not simply *Mater Dei*, "Mother of God"). Neither Luke nor Matthew employs that Greek term, however. The earliest uses of Theotokos cannot be securely traced farther

back than the fourth century, when its conceptuality assumed importance amid the Arian controversy (Athanasius, *Orations Against the Arians* 3.29). Against the Nestorians, the Council of Ephesus (431) made it binding on all Christian faithful to acclaim Mary as Theotokos. For relevant primary documents, see *Creeds, Councils and Controversies: Documents Illustrating the History of the Church AD 337–461* (ed. J. Stevenson; rev. W. H. C. Frend; London: SPCK, 1989), 287-321.

18. For explicit analogies of end-time consummation with a birthing mother, see John 16:21-22; Rom 8:18-25.

19. Theology and musicology embrace in the remarkable study of Samuel Terrien, *The Magnificat: Musicians as Biblical Interpreters* (New York and Mahwah, N.J.: Paulist Press, 1995).

20. This point receives thoughtful exploration in Gail O'Day, "Singing Woman's Song: A Hermeneutic of Liberation," *CurTM* 12 (1985): 203-10.

21. Brown, *Birth of the Messiah*, 358-60, thoroughly tabulates the OT background of Luke 1:46-55. The fulfillment of God's promises and Israel's restoration are primary themes in the Magnificat and other canticles in Luke 1–2, as demonstrated by Stephen Farris, *The Hymns of Luke's Infancy Narratives: Their Origin, Meaning and Significance*, JSNTSup 9 (Sheffield: JSOT, 1985), esp. 151-60.

22. Mark 3:31-35 is probably the source of Luke 8:19-21. The traditions preserved in Luke 2:41-52 and John 2:1-12 are without parallel in the other Gospels.

23. Luke's last reference to Mary strikes the same chord: Jesus' mother and brothers remained in devoted company with the Eleven in Jerusalem, after Jesus' ascension (Acts 1:14).

24. In spite of tortured attempts by some commentators to translate οἱ ἀδελφοὶ αὐτοῦ *hoi adelphoi autou* as "his cousins" rather than "his brothers," Mark is obviously ignorant of the later doctrine of Mary's perpetual virginity.

25. More blatant and equally countercultural is Jesus' astonishing elevation of preaching God's sovereignty over a survivor's responsibility to bury his father (Matt 8:21-22 = Luke 7:59-60).

26. Many commentators interpret Mark 3:19b-35 as one of that Evangelist's characteristic "intercalations" or "sandwiches" of traditions. See, e.g., the discussion by Morna D. Hooker, *The Gospel According to Saint Mark*, BNTC (Peabody: Hendrickson, 1991), 114.

27. Frank Kermode, "John," in *The Literary Guide to the Bible*, ed. Robert Alter and Frank Kermode (Cambridge, Mass.: Belknap, Harvard University Press, 1987), 449. In support of Kermode's reading, see John 1:45 (Jesus as the fulfillment of Jewish tradition) and Jer 31:12; Amos 9:13-14 (abundance in the age to come).

28. For an incisive exegesis of Galatians 4:1-7, which discovers therein "nothing less than the theological center of the entire letter . . . , the good news of Paul's letter to the Galatians," consult J. Louis Martyn, *Galatians: A New Translation with Introduction and Commentary*, AB 33A (New York and London: Doubleday, 1997), 384-408 (here, 388).

29. The heavily controverted reasons for the inclusion of women in the Matthean genealogy are thoroughly explained and assessed by Brown, *Birth of the Messiah*, 71-74.

30. M. Eugene Boring, "The Gospel of Matthew: Introduction, Commentary, and Reflections," *NIB* 8 (1995), 151-54, offers a superb examination of Matthew's use of scripture.

31. On this point see the interesting discussion in Gaventa, *Mary*, 41-44.

32. The favorite proposals: New Eve, Lady Zion who begets a new people, Mother Church whose baptism begets Christians, Spiritual Mother of heavenly nurturance. For survey and assessment, consult Rudolf Schnackenburg, *The Gospel According to St John* (New York: Crossroad, 1987), 3:279-82; Raymond E. Brown, *The Death of the Messiah: From Gethsemane to the Grave*, ABRL (New York and London: Doubleday, 1994), 2:1021-25.

33. For extended defense of this proposal, see Barnabas Lindars, *The Gospel of John*, NCB (Grand Rapids and London: Wm. B. Eerdmans, Marshall, Morgan & Scott, 1972), 579-80; Schnackenburg, *The Gospel According to St John*, 3:274-79; Brown, *The Death of the Messiah*, 2:1019-26; Francis J. Moloney, *The Gospel of John*, SP 4 (Collegeville, Minn.: Liturgical Press, 1998), 503-4.

34. See Jaroslav Pelikan, *Mary Through the Centuries: Her Place in the History of Culture* (New Haven and London: Yale University Press, 1996).

35. Bearsley, "Mary the Perfect Disciple"; Bertrand Ruby, *Mary, the Faithful Disciple* (New York and Mahwah, N.J.: Paulist Press, 1985).

36. Carolyn Grassi, "Mary in Early Christian Community," in Joseph A. Grassi, *Mary, Mother and Disciple: From the Scriptures to the Council of Ephesus* (Wilmington, Del.: Michael Glazier, 1988), 45, 140-56; Tina Beattie, *Rediscovering Mary: Insights from the Gospels* (Ligouri, Mo.: Triumph Books, 1995).

37. David Flusser, "Mary and Israel," in David Flusser, Jaroslav Pelikan, and Justin Lang, *Mary: Images of the Mother of Jesus in Jewish and Christian Perspective* (Philadelphia: Fortress Press, 1986), 7-16; John Macquarrie, *Mary for All Christians* (Grand Rapids: Wm. B. Eerdmans, 1990).

38. In this estimate at least, some Roman Catholic and Protestant theologians appear to be converging in agreement: cf. McBrien, *Catholicism,* 1106-7, with Schubert M. Ogden, *The Point of Christology* (San Francisco: Harper & Row, 1982).

39. None of the Marian texts we have examined offers aid and comfort to modern Marcionites. The unity of grace and law in the OT is probed in J. M. Myers, *Grace and Torah* (Philadelphia: Fortress Press, 1975), and Ronald M. Hals, *Grace and Faith in the Old Testament* (Minneapolis: Augsburg, 1980).

40. See John Navone's *Toward a Theology of Beauty* (Collegeville, Minn.: Liturgical Press, 1996) for a thoughtful attempt to reclaim God's primary delight in creation's beauty as a basis for Christian theology.

THE ECONOMY OF GRACE:
Reflections on 2 Corinthians 8 and 9

BEVERLY ROBERTS GAVENTA

All is of grace and grace is for all.
—JAMES MOFFATT

This lean dictum stands at the heading of Moffatt's discussion of grace in the letters of Paul.[1] "All," that is, every single feature of the gospel and its workings in individuals and communities, stems entirely from God's gracious gift. And that grace extends to include "all," without reference to any barriers whatsoever. The dictum aptly summarizes the perspective on God's grace that permeates the Pauline letters, and yet the dictum is deceptive in that it offers no hint of the outrage that meets such radical grace.

The outrage generated by the second half of the dictum ("grace is for all") comes to elegant expression in J. Louis Martyn's essay, "From Paul to Flannery O'Connor with the Power of Grace."[2] Among the several contributions of that essay is the way in which the conversation Martyn arranges between Paul's apocalyptic viewpoint and the fiction of O'Connor illumines the radical inclusivity of grace. O'Connor's characters often experience grace as an invasion that demolishes the categories they have constructed for those humans whom they imagine to be "included" and those they deem to be "excluded." A particularly vivid incident occurs in the story "Revelation" when Mrs. Turpin, who occupies herself "at night naming the classes of people," experiences "abysmal life-giving knowledge" in the form of a disturb-

51

ing young woman.[3] Mrs. Turpin's final vision, in which people from all the "classes" together march up to heaven, ably paraphrases the "all" of Romans 3:22 as well as the insistence of Romans 5:6-8 that the gospel came about among the ungodly. To put it simply, "all" means "all."

The first part of the dictum, that "all is of grace," might appear to provoke less controversy, since it pertains not to the recipients of grace but to its workings. Yet here again qualifiers and constraints enter the conversation. A revealing story appears in the preface to Robin Scroggs's book, *Paul for a New Day*. Scroggs recalls an occasion when he gave a series of lectures on Paul for a conference of ministers. The first presentation sketched out Paul's understanding of God's action in justifying humankind and ushering in a new existence, but in the discussion period afterward the questions focused entirely on the necessity of human action rather than on God's gracious initiative.[4] Variations on this scenario recur often in the classroom and elsewhere—discussions of Paul's gospel of God's radical intervention on behalf of humankind prompt, not a singing of the doxology, but the question of Peter's addressees in Acts 2:37, "What should we do?" To the answer that, for Paul, "all is of grace," comes the immediate suspicion that grace has been cheapened.

Is it indeed the case that "all is of grace," or is there some limit to the "all"? In my judgment, Moffatt's dictum has it right. For Paul, the "all" in this half of the dictum is as inclusive as the "all" in the second half; human beings do nothing that puts them in right relationship with God, keeps them in relationship with God, enhances that relationship, or bolsters it. Everything, *even that which appears to be a response to grace*, still comes from grace. I want to explore that notion in 2 Corinthians 8–9, Paul's most extended discussion of the collection for the "saints" in Jerusalem. I shall argue that precisely in this passage, where an urgent "practical" problem might lead Paul to emphasize human initiative and responsibility, he instead depicts an economy of grace, in which even the most impressive act of human generosity exists merely as a frail symptom of God's grace.[5]

In 2 Corinthians 8 and 9, Paul appeals to believers in Corinth for their support of the collection for Jerusalem Christians. That the collection plays an important role in Paul's ministry is clear from the number of times he refers to it in his letters. In Galatians, Paul recalls his second visit to Jerusalem and the agreement regarding his apostleship among the Gentiles, an agreement that carried the stipulation that Paul should "remember the poor" in his work (Gal 2:10). In 1 Corinthians 16, Paul has already asked the Corinthians to put aside something every week, but the fact that he must return to the collection in 2 Corinthians, and with such care, suggests that the Corinthians have been less than enthusiastic in their response. Romans 15 indicates Paul's plans for taking the collection to Jerusalem and also his anxiety that he may not be well received in that city (vv. 25-28, 31).[6]

The importance of the collection comes into view not only in the number of these references to it but also from the variety of arguments employed in 2 Corinthians 8–9. First, Paul introduces the God-graced generosity of Macedonian believers as an example (8:1-7). He then appeals to the grace of Jesus Christ and its relationship to human generosity and mutual support (8:8-15).[7] Following these direct appeals to generosity, Paul defends the role of Titus and others in protecting the collection from any accusation of fraud or misappropriation (8:16-24). He then makes another appeal for the collection as a way of avoiding shame, either the shame of Corinthian believers or that of Paul's own ministry (9:1-5). A final collection of sayings on generosity in relationship to God brings the discussion to a close (9:6-15).

Although the scholarly literature by no means neglects these two chapters, much of that literature addresses itself primarily to the historical circumstances surrounding the collection and the significance of the collection for Paul's apostleship.[8] Keith Nickle, for example, endeavors to tease out from the scattered remarks in Acts and in Paul's letters the historical events connected with the collection and looks for analogies in early Judaism.[9] That Dieter Georgi's study operates with the same concerns is clear from its subtitle, *The History of Paul's Collection for Jerusalem.*[10] The theological dynamics of the passage have received significantly less attention, probably because the collection is assumed to be a "practical" rather than a "theological" matter, but such distinctions are noticeably absent from Paul's letters.

With respect to the topic at hand, the first thing to notice is simply the density of grace language in these chapters. Translations routinely obscure that density, as when the NRSV renders *charis* as "privilege" (8:4), "generous undertaking" (8:6, 7, 19), "generous act" (8:9), "thanks" (8:16; 9:15), and "blessing" (9:8) rather than "grace." Such variation in the translation of *charis* assists readers in sorting out Paul's assertions about the collection, yet it prevents readers from recognizing that only Paul's letter to the Romans employs the language of grace with more frequency and more variety than does 2 Corinthians.[11]

Precisely because the word *charis* figures in a variety of ways in this passage, discerning exactly what role grace plays in Paul's appeal is a complicated matter. It will be instructive to linger over the particulars.

Grace That Stems from God

Explicit references to God in relationship to grace both open (8:1) and conclude (9:14-15) this passage. Paul introduces the topic of the collection by invoking the example of the generosity of believers in Macedonia, clearly as a spur to the conscience of the Corinthian congregation. Not only have the Macedonians already made a contribution, but they did so in distress, from their poverty, and urging that they be included in the gift (Gk.: *charis*). Yet it is important to notice that Paul begins this move by reference, not to the Macedonians themselves, but to "the grace of God that has been granted to the churches of Macedonia."[12] The relationship between verse 1 and verses 2-6 is crucial for understanding the argument. As elsewhere in Paul's letters, "we [or I] want you to know" introduces the topic at hand (e.g., 1 Cor 12:3; 15:1; Gal 1:11). Importantly, Paul identifies the topic at hand as God's grace rather than the collection itself or even the benevolence of the Macedonians.

He then moves on to explain what "grace of God" has been given to the churches of Macedonia, namely, their contribution to the collection. Verses 2-6, which are grammatically closely connected to verse 1,[13] elaborate the activity of the Macedonians. They have been generous despite their own unstated affliction (v. 2). They gave beyond their ability and indeed urged that they be included in the gift (vv. 4-6). Somehow, all of these actions describe the grace of God rather than an activity for which the Macedonians themselves might deserve to receive praise. The actions of the Macedonians, while exemplary, result from God's own grace.

Paul refers explicitly to God's grace again in 9:14. As he brings his appeal for the collection to a close, he anticipates the Corinthians' "obedience" and "generosity." The Jerusalem saints will, in turn, "long for you and pray for you because of the surpassing grace of God that he has given you." In context, the "surpassing grace of God" is not a general reference to God's gifts but a specific reference to the Corinthians' own anticipated participation in the collection. It is God who makes this gift of theirs possible. The entire appeal of chapters 8 and 9 ends as it began, identifying the generosity of believers as originating with the grace of God (in this case, the generosity he anticipates from the Corinthians rather than that already demonstrated by the Macedonians).

God's generosity also comes into view in verses 8-10, although the word *charis* does not appear here. God is "able to provide you with every blessing in abundance, so that by always having enough of everything, you may share abundantly in every good work." Frances Young and David F. Ford have rightly noted the extravagance of such claims, particularly in a world known more for scarcity than for abundance.[14] That God's grace stands behind the collection itself presumes that God is able to be gracious.

The emphasis in this discussion on the grace of God coheres entirely with the preceding chapters of the letter. As early as 1:12, Paul claims God's grace as that which enables his own ministry; it is God who makes the apostles "competent" for their work (3:4-6). And in 4:15, he speaks of grace extended "to more and more people" so that it increases "thanksgiving, to the glory of God." The claims of 9:8 and 13 that God both enables generosity and receives thanksgiving through human generosity find their antecedents earlier in the letter.

The role of God's own grace receives little attention in many treatments of this passage. For example, although H. D. Betz draws attention to God's grace in 8:1 and rightly notes the semantic range of *charis* both in Paul's letters and elsewhere in Greek literature, he does not connect the generosity of the Macedonians with God's grace.[15] Apparently, he understands these references to God's grace to have little substantive role in the appeal. However, their strategic location at the beginning and end of this appeal for the collection suggests a more specific function: the collection itself—on the face of it a human endeavor—has its origin and energy in God's grace.[16] As Jerome Murphy-O'Connor puts it, Paul understands the collection to be "a channel of divine aid."[17]

The Grace of Jesus Christ

In addition to framing the appeal by reference to God's own grace, Paul writes in 8:9 about the "grace of our Lord Jesus Christ."[18]

Although Paul elsewhere refers to grace "from the Lord Jesus Christ," elsewhere it appears in salutations (Rom 1:7; 1 Cor 1:3; 2 Cor 1:2; Gal 1:3; Phil 1:2; Phlm 3) and in letter closings (2 Cor 13:13; Gal 6:18; Phil 4:23; 1 Thess 5:28; Phlm 25). Only here does it carry with it an explanatory statement.

Our examination of this statement will profit from rendering it somewhat more literally than does the NRSV, as well as by depicting the translation schematically so that the parallel emerges clearly:

For you know the grace of our Lord Jesus Christ, since

| on your account | he became poor | although being rich |
| in order that you | by his poverty | might become rich. |

Particularly when the parallelism of the statement is recognized, Christ's *charis* consists of his purposely taking on of "poverty" in order to "enrich" the Corinthians.[19] Notice that the parallelism is not complete. If it were, we would expect

| on your account | he became poor | although being rich |
| in order that you | *although being poor* | might become rich. |

This slight "flaw" in the parallelism prevents Paul from drawing attention to the poverty of the Corinthians. Even if the poverty he has in view here is not material poverty, Paul is not inclined to hand the Corinthians an excuse for withholding funds from the collection. More important, Paul's wording draws attention to the "poverty" of Jesus Christ.[20]

Taken by itself, the logic of verse 9 seems straightforward: the grace of Jesus Christ consists in his self-impoverishment for the sake of enriching others. The problem arises when we ask how that statement about the grace of Jesus Christ functions in the appeal. Paul gives few clear signals, apart from the "for" (Gk.: *gar*) that introduces verse 9 and thereby connects it grammatically with verse 8. Nothing in the statements surrounding this verse depends on its content, however. Indeed, it would be entirely possible to read verse 8 and then move directly to verse 10, skipping over verse 9 entirely.

Implicitly at least, Paul appeals to the grace of Jesus Christ in order to encourage a form of mimesis. Just as the liberality of the Macedonians has offered an example, so now Jesus Christ's self-imposed poverty offers an example which Paul invites the Corinthians to imitate—at least to a limited extent.[21] Paul does not imagine that humans can duplicate Jesus' actions fully.[22] In that sense, the logic of 8:9 anticipates that of Philippians 2:5, which introduces the Philippians hymn, "Let the same mind be in you that was in Christ Jesus." Neither passage anticipates that believers will become like Jesus, either in their poverty or in their exaltation, yet they may share his "mind," they may share his generosity. Elsewhere, of course, Paul does explicitly appeal to the imitation of Christ (1 Cor 11:1; cf. 1 Cor 4:16; 1 Thess 1:6).

Yet it is important to see that here there is no direct command that the Corinthians should imitate Christ. Indeed, both verse 8 and verse 10 eschew "command" language.[23] Instead of arguing that believers must support the collection as imitators of Christ, Paul invokes the gracious act of Jesus Christ that may be emulated. The self-impoverishing grace of Jesus Christ has brought about the enriching of the Corinthians, an enriching that makes it possible for them also to behave graciously.

Perhaps the closest analogy to this appeal to Christ's poverty comes, not in ethical exhortations or even in other passages that urge imitation, but in 2 Corinthians 5:14-15:

> For the love of Christ urges us on, because we are convinced that one has died for all; therefore all have died. And he died for all, so that those who live might live no longer for themselves, but for him who died and was raised for them.

The "love of Christ" does not become here an ethical standard to be achieved, either as a condition for incorporation into the community or as a response to God's action. Instead, Christ's death has objectively changed things, so that those who are "called" are also changed. Similarly, the grace of Christ's poverty has, in Paul's view, created generosity among believers as well.

The Grace of Believers

One unusual feature of 2 Corinthians 8–9 is its reference to *charis* in connection with believers, since in the Pauline letters human beings do not normally serve as dispensers of grace.[24] Perhaps that feature of the passage seems less odd given the context; after all, Paul writes this entire section of the letter with a view to eliciting a contribution from the Corinthians. It is their *charis*, their gift, that Paul urgently desires. Three times in this passage he uses the word *charis* in relationship to the Corinthians (NRSV: "generous undertaking"). In 8:6, he reports that he has urged Titus to complete "this grace" among the Corinthians, and in 8:7 he urges the Corinthians to abound in "this grace." Second Corinthians 8:19 speaks of Titus traveling with Paul while carrying out the collection of "this grace" for the glory of God. In addition, terms other than *charis* also refer to the gift Paul seeks: sharing (*koinonia*, 8:4; 9:13), ministry (*diakonia*, 8:4; 9:1, 12, 13), rendering (or service, *leitourgia*, 9:12).

The relationship between this gift of believers, on the one hand, and the *charis* of God and of Jesus Christ, on the other, lies at the heart of this essay. Does Paul's appeal assume that the *charis* to be offered by believers comes about by their own decision to respond? Or is even their gift to the collection an instance of God's gracious action in the gospel of Jesus Christ? To put the matter succinctly, is the *charis* of the Corinthians their own action or is it God's? (Is it "all of grace" or not?)

Despite the abundance of language here for the gifts of believers, there are indications *even in the way in which these gifts to the collection are described* that they are subsidiary in nature; believers give only as they have already received from the gracious actions of God and of Christ. Early in the discussion, Paul itemizes those things in which the Corinthians already excel ("in faith, in speech, in knowledge, in utmost eagerness, and in our love for you"), and then urges them to excel also in their gift for the collection (8:7). Remarkably, the other items Paul refers to here appear elsewhere in his letters as gifts from God (see especially 1 Cor 1:4-7), which would strongly suggest that the "gifts" bestowed by the Corinthians themselves also stem from God's own gifts to them.[25] In addition, the appeals in 9:6-15 play on this conviction, for it is God who provides "every blessing" so that believers may share with others.

The Economy of Grace

How do these three "graces" come together—that of God, of Jesus Christ, and of believers?

In this discussion of an urgent "practical" need, that of contributions for the collection, Paul avoids the language of commandment. Instead, he opens and closes his appeal by reference to the grace of God (8:1; 9:15). The grace of Jesus offers an example that believers may emulate (8:9). Even the "gift" Paul anticipates from the Corinthians he classifies among things they have received rather than things they have cultivated (8:7). All of this indicates that even here, where Paul urgently needs to make the case for compliance with the collection, he does so on the assumption that this most pragmatic of actions stems from a divine gift.

The study of 2 Corinthians by Frances Young and David F. Ford helpfully draws our attention to the way in which Paul employs theological language to talk about money and economic language to talk about God.[26] Paul's discussion here bursts wide open the sense of economy as the efficient, thrifty use of resources, for God is the antithesis of thrift. More important for the question of this essay, God's economy is not one in which the sum needed for salvation comes from a contribution from God (however large) and another contribution from humanity (however small). Everything in this economy comes from a single source, that of God's grace.

Afterthoughts

Admittedly, this essay has considered only one passage in the Pauline corpus. Yet it is instructive to notice how often those Pauline texts understood to be "ethical" or "exhortative" contain within them indications that the behavior called for actually results from God's own actions rather than any willing or doing of humankind. For example, 1 Thessalonians 5:12-22 consists of instructions regarding community life, most of which are framed as commandments (e.g., "Respect those who labor among you," "Admonish the idlers," "Abstain from every form of evil"). Yet this catalog of instructions culminates in a prayer-wish that identifies God as the one who is able to sustain believers in these practices:

> May the God of peace himself sanctify you entirely; and may your spirit and soul and body be kept sound and blameless at the coming of our Lord Jesus Christ. The one who calls you is faithful, and he will do this.
> (1 Thess 5:24; cf. 1 Thess 3:11-13; Rom 15:5-6, 13)

It would be a simple matter to dismiss such theological assertions as empty verbiage, even as manipulation.[27] And, indeed, in 2 Corinthians 8–9 Paul is attempting to move the Corinthians to do a very particular thing. Yet even his profound concern about the collection does not cloud over his insistence that human *charis* is but a frail reflection of God's own *charis*.

For Paul, everything comes from God's free gift, just as Moffatt's dictum recalls. That gift continues to be experienced as an invasion in a world that treasures the illusion of independence and self-control. Even the confession that "all is of grace" consistently generates equivocation and hostility, precisely because it acknowledges that God alone is God.[28]

Notes

1. James Moffatt, *Grace in the New Testament* (New York: Ray Long and Richard R. Smith, 1932), 131.
2. J. Louis Martyn, *Theological Issues in the Letters of Paul* (Nashville: Abingdon Press, 1997), 279-97.
3. "Revelation," in *The Complete Stories of Flannery O'Connor*, pp. 488-509 (New York: Farrar, Straus, Giroux, 1971), 491, 508.
4. *Paul for a New Day* (Philadelphia: Fortress Press, 1977), viii.
5. My title plays on the subject matter of 2 Corinthians 8–9; it is also influenced by the discussion of "the economy of God" in Frances Young and David F. Ford, *Meaning and Truth in 2 Corinthians* (Grand Rapids: Wm. B. Eerdmans, 1987), 166-85. Paul's understanding of grace has received relatively little scholarly attention; among the more important contributions are the following: G. P. Wetter, *Charis: Ein Beitrag zur Geschichte des ältesten Christentums* (Leipzig: Hinrichs, 1913); Moffatt, *Grace in the New Testament;* Rudolf Bultmann, *Theology of the New Testament*, vol. 1 (New York: Scribner's, 1951), 288-92; Conzelmann, "charis," *TDNT* 9:372-402; Darrel J. Doughty, "The Priority of *CHARIS*" *NTS* 19 (1972–73), 163-80. The recent dissertation of J. R. Harrison ("Paul's Language of Grace in Its Graeco-Roman Context," Macquarie University, 1996) has been unavailable to me (see the discussion in J. D. G. Dunn, *The Theology of Paul the Apostle* [Grand Rapids: Wm. B. Eerdmans, 1998], 321).
6. Concern with the collection and other financial matters is not a trivial matter. Mark Kiley notes that all of the undisputed Pauline letters contain some reference to financial transactions on behalf of his work and suggests that the absence of such references from the other letters attributed to Paul be regarded as a factor in favor of their pseudonymity (*Colossians as Pseudepigraphy* [Sheffield, England: JSOT Press, 1986], 47).
7. The relationship between Christ's generosity and the appeal to human generosity is a complex matter; see the discussion to follow.
8. Scholarly debate regarding the integrity of 2 Corinthians is extensive, and some scholars would not discuss chapters 8 and 9 together because they regard them as separate compositions. In this essay I assume that two letter fragments constitute canonical 2 Corinthians. Chapters 1–9 constitute the bulk of one letter (minus the interpolation of 6:14–7:1), and chapters 10–13 constitute most of a second, probably later, letter. For a clear and thorough review of the literature on this question and a defense of the position

followed here, see Victor Paul Furnish, *II Corinthians* AB 32A (Garden City, N.Y.: Doubleday, 1984), 30-41.

9. *The Collection: A Study in Paul's Strategy* SBT 48 (London: SCM, 1966).

10. Dieter Georgi, *Remembering the Poor: The History of Paul's Collection for Jerusalem* (Nashville: Abingdon Press, 1992).

11. That variety itself makes it difficult to settle the scholarly debate over whether *charis* in Paul's vocabulary has to do primarily with God's power or with the event of salvation (see Doughty, "The Priority of *CHARIS*," and Hendrikus Boers, "*Agapē* and *Charis* in Paul's Thought," (*CBQ* 59 [1997], 693-713). That variety, however, does not answer the question of this essay, whether "all" is indeed "of grace."

12. Technically, it is possible to translate the churches of Macedonia as an instrumental dative, so that God's grace was given by the churches of Macedonia, but it is difficult to imagine anything in Paul's letters that would support such a translation.

13. In Greek the connection is clearer than in the NRSV. Both v. 2 and v. 3 begin with the conjunction *hoti*, which subordinates these statements to the introductory statement of v. 1.

14. Young and Ford, *Meaning and Truth in 2 Corinthians*, 172-74.

15. H. D. Betz, *2 Corinthians 8 and 9* Hermeneia (Philadelphia: Fortress Press, 1985), 42.

16. Furnish puts the matter rightly: "Here Paul eases himself into the subject of his collection . . . by describing the enthusiastic participation of the Macedonian churches in the project. But it is significant that he describes their participation first of all as an act of divine grace (v. 1)" (*II Corinthians*, 413).

17. Jerome Murphy-O'Connor, *The Theology of the Second Letter to the Corinthians* (Cambridge: Cambridge University Press, 1991), 81.

18. I treat God's grace and that of Jesus Christ separately because they appear separately in this text. I do not thereby suggest that the two are unrelated agents, still less that they are already in Paul's letters two persons of the Trinity.

19. The quotation marks convey my understanding that the poverty and riches being spoken of here are metaphorical (so also Furnish, *II Corinthians*, 417). G. W. Buchanan, by contrast, argued that this statement refers to the actual poverty of Jesus of Nazareth ("Jesus and the Upper Class" *NovT* 7 [1964], 195-209).

20. Perhaps the emphasis on Jesus' poverty serves to encourage the Corinthians to identify Christ's poverty with that of the Jerusalemites, although it is noteworthy how little the argument in 2 Corinthians 8–9 depends on a presentation of the actual needs of those in Jerusalem.

21. Vv. 13-15 seem designed to assure readers that they are not expected to impoverish themselves.

22. It seems to be for this reason that Furnish argues that Jesus does not here serve as an example (*II Corinthians*, 418).

23. Furnish rightly characterizes this appeal as Paul's "counsel," rather than his "order" (*II Corinthians*, 409).

24. First Cor 16:3 does speak of "your *charis*," but there as well the reference is to a gift for the collection. If Gordon Fee is correct, the "double favor" (literally, "second grace") of 2 Cor 1:15 refers, not to the gift the Corinthians will receive from another visit from Paul, but to a second opportunity to contribute to the collection; see "*CHARIS* in II Corinthians 1.15: Apostolic Parousia and Paul-Corinth Chronology" (*NTS* 24 [1978], 533-58).

25. So also C. K. Barrett, *The Second Epistle to the Corinthians* Harper's New Testament Commentaries (New York: Harper and Row, 1973), 222.

26. *Meaning and Truth in 2 Corinthians*, 69-71.

27. The charge of Graham Shaw (*The Cost of Authority: Manipulation and Freedom in the New Testament* [Philadelphia: Fortress Press, 1982], 115-19) that Paul is merely engaged in manipulating his correspondents for the sake of enhancing his own authority is difficult to assess. Because the interpreter has no access to Paul's internal motivation (an observation that appears to have escaped Shaw), it is more profitable to examine the

theological and rhetorical construction of the argument, leaving judgments about sincerity to God.

28. I am grateful to Matthew Skinner for research assistance with this essay and to professors C. Clifton Black, Nancy Duff, and Donald H. Juel for constructive conversations along the way.

GRACE IN THE OLD TESTAMENT

ROLAND E. MURPHY

It is surely significant that the term "grace" appears so frequently in the recent study by Kenneth J. Collins, *The Scripture Way of Salvation: The Heart of John Wesley's Theology* (Nashville: Abingdon Press, 1997). Five of the seven chapters have "grace" in their titles. Since Collins' book is primarily a study of Wesley's theology against the background of Christian belief, it is not surprising to see that his "Explanatory Notes Upon the New Testament" are cited, but not his "Explanatory Notes" for the Old Testament. The following reflections on grace aim to provide a partial biblical base for the development of this notion in the Christian tradition, and also to honor Thomas Langford, who has distinguished himself in theological and Wesleyan studies.[1]

Key Texts

These reflections will only sketch the highlights of what is worthy of several volumes.[2] We limit ourselves to three biblical terms: *ḥesed, ḥannûn* (also the noun, *ḥēn*), and *raḥûm.*[3] These three terms occur together in the fundamental affirmation of Exodus 34:6, which may be considered a creedal summary, although spoken by the Lord, no less: "The LORD, the LORD, a God merciful and gracious *('el raḥûm wĕḥannûn),* slow to anger, and abounding in steadfast love *(ḥesed)."* The adjectives appear as verbs in the mysterious words of the Lord in Exodus 33:19: "I will be gracious *(ḥnn)* to whom I will be gracious, and will show mercy *(rḥm)* on whom I will show mercy." The English word, "gracious," does not convey the strength of the Hebrew root *ḥnn*. This has little to do with social graces; it designates favor bestowed upon another. It receives a certain nuance from the word that accompanies it, *rḥm*, which is associated with the womb of a mother, and the inexpressible tenderness of motherly love. This aspect is more fully brought out by the continuation of 34:6, "slow to anger, and abounding in steadfast love and faithfulness *(ḥesed we'ĕmet)*, keeping steadfast love for the thousandth generation, forgiving iniquity and transgression and sin, yet by no means clearing the guilty" (34:6-7a). It may be noted that this affirmation stands behind the well-known "Allahu akbar" confession of Islam.

The importance of Exodus 34:6 is borne out by its frequent appearance in the rest of the Old Testament: three times quoted in Psalms (86:15; 103:8; 145:8), and alluded to in 111:4 and 116:5. It occurs also in Joel 2:13 where it is a motive for sincere conversion in a penitential rite, and also in Jonah 4:2, and it is quoted in the great confession led by Ezra (Neh 9:17; see also v. 31). Hezekiah alludes to it in his summons to the tribes to celebrate the Passover (2 Chr 30:9). The use of the text in Jonah 4:2 is particularly telling. It will be recalled that Jonah is a disobedient prophet who attempts, unsuccessfully, to flee from the Lord. The reason why he tries to refuse the divine commission is revealed in 4:2. He knew that the Lord was a merciful God (Exod 34:6), even to the extent of showing such favor to the dreaded Assyrians, and he refused, initially, to cooperate by announcing a warning to the Assyrians—witness his anger in 4:1.

The other key text, Exodus 33:19, employs the words "favor" and "mercy" *(ḥnn* and *rḥm)*, but translations differ. For example the *Tanakh* renders it: "I will proclaim before you the name LORD, and the grace that I grant and the compassion that I show." The expression is called an *"idem per idem"* construction, literally, "I will be gracious to whom I will be gracious, and will show mercy to whom I will show mercy." This is usually taken to indicate the freedom of the Lord in bestowing grace and mercy, the utter gratuity of the gift in every respect, whether time or place. That is quite correct, but there may be an added nuance to the mystery of the divine generosity: to close a conversation.[4] In any case, there is no example in the Bible where favor-mercy can be compelled and still remain what it is. Grace comes before the Law is given at Sinai. The Lord chose as a particular people the descendants of the patriarchs, upon whom the promises of a future were mysteriously but freely bestowed. As the Deuteronomic exhortation puts it, "It was not because you were more numerous than any other people that the LORD set his heart on you and chose you—for you were the fewest of all peoples. It was because the LORD loved you and kept the oath that he swore to your ancestors" (Deut 7:7-8*a*).

Key Words

The noun, *hēn* ("grace" or "favor"; *charis* in LXX), appears 67 times in the OT, and it indicates the favorable attitude of someone to another; this leads to an action or deed that concretizes the subjective attitude. It is frequently associated with the eyes of another ("find favor in your eyes"). It is the face (Heb. *panim*) that betrays favor or disfavor. If the Lord turns the face, favor is shown to a person. On the contrary, if the Lord hides the face there is no favor, and indeed the situation is viewed as critical. The hiding of the divine face occurs well over 20 times in the OT to indicate divine disfavor (Isa 8:17, hiding the face from the house of Jacob), and especially in the psalms (e.g., Ps 44:25). The association of face and grace appears also in the parallelism of verbs in the famous priestly (Aaronic) blessing: "[May] the LORD make his face to shine upon you, and be gracious (the verb, *hnn*) to you" (Num 6:25). Acceptance of another is displayed by a (smiling) reaction. It is paradoxical that the Lord hides the face, but nonetheless there is nothing hidden from God, as in Hosea 5:3, "Israel is not hidden from me." What is the "grace" *(hēn)* that is activated and shown to another? It is shown by concrete events. Mortals know it by some tangible expression, such as an improvement in one's situation, a concrete "blessing" in the form of prosperity, health, wealth, deliverance, life, and salvation.

It is significant that the basic meaning of *rhm* has to do with "womb," and the plural of the noun emphasizes emotion in a display of mercy. A striking use of the verb occurs in the twofold appearance in Psalm 103:13: "As a father has compassion for his children, so the LORD has compassion for those who fear him." The adjectival form appears in the formula we have seen in Exodus 34:6, and juxtaposition of these two terms appears 11 times in the OT, and always referring to God. As we shall see, it is also frequently joined with *hesed,* or loving-kindness.

The word *ḥesed* appears in the Hebrew Bible about 245 times, and half of these are in the psalter (127 times).[5] The frequent appearance is due to the fact that it indicates a relationship between humans, and especially between humans and God. In general it is more than an attitude; the "kindness" is objectified in some action toward another. For our purposes, the divine-human relationship is important, because here *ḥesed* can be properly seen as a "grace," whereby the Lord acts in favor of the nation, or of an individual, freely and also in response to a desperate appeal. A striking use of the plural form, indicating divine interventions, occurs in Psalm 89:1, "I will sing of the loving kindnesses of the Lord." The rest of the psalm indicates how broadly the term is understood by Israel. It especially includes the covenant, both the Sinai pact (conditional for Israel), and the covenants with Abraham and David (unconditional promises of divine commitment). This is true of other uses as well.

Evidence from the Psalter

We will take a lead from the statistical information mentioned in the preceding paragraphs, and will concentrate on the psalter to develop the notion of (divine) grace. Particularly here can one recognize the truth of the old saw attributed to Prosper of Aquitaine, "The rule of praying establishes the rule for belief "—"legem credendi lex statuat supplicandi"; prayer and belief come together. Moreover, the chronological spread of the psalms is an indication of the life and permanence of this grace.

A preliminary remark about the psalms is in order. It might appear from the bold remarks of the psalmists that the Lord is being coerced, that the element of free grace and favor is lacking. There is a remarkable freedom in addressing the divinity. Patrick Miller comments:

> God may not be coerced, but God can be persuaded. The prayers do not assume that things are cut and dried, either God answers prayer or does not. They seek to evoke a response . . . especially those sentences and clauses that suggest reasons why God should act. . . . It is important, however, to keep in mind the nature of the arguments. They appeal to God to be and to act as God would be and act. . . . The motive clauses are, in effect, a way of indicating that God's response to the cry for help should be a manifestation of mercy and love, a demonstration

of God's just dealings in the world, a compassionate response to the sufferer in pain.[6]

In the psalter there are many telling associations of *rhm* and *hsd,* as in Psalm 25:6 (and cf. Isa 63:7): "Remember your (acts of) grace, O Lord, and your (acts of) loving kindness, for they have been from of old." In the context the psalmist is asking for forgiveness from sin, that the Lord *not* remember sins of youth, but remember him in the light of the divine loving-kindness (v. 7). The situation in Psalm 40:12-13 is similar. The opening line of the famous prayer attributed to David, Psalm 51, is an appeal for mercy *(hnn):* "Have mercy on me, O God, according to your steadfast love; according to your abundant mercy blot out my transgressions." Psalm 69, which is cited so frequently in the New Testament, contains the appeal: "Answer me, Lord, according to your generous kindness; turn to me in accordance with the abundance of your grace." The Israelites are assured that they are surrounded by steadfast love and grace (Ps 103:4). The long confession of Israel's sinful history in Psalm 106:45-46 culminates in the claim that the Lord "repented," after remembering the covenant, according to his abundant kindness and showed grace to Israel.

It has already been indicated that *hesed* or loving-kindness is particularly frequent in the psalter. Perhaps the most striking usage is in the liturgical affirmation that punctuates the historical summary in Psalm 136 (cf. 118:1-4, 18): the Lord's *hesed* endures forever. That characteristic is a radical part of the Lord; it is ages old (Ps 25:6), as God is. In fact, this steadfast love (not only the glory of the Lord as in Isa 6:3) "fills the earth" according to Psalms 33:5 and 119:64. Such a statement is entirely open-ended, and is never the object of direct analysis, unless perhaps Psalm 33 serves as a comment since it finishes with an invocation that this love be upon the community (v. 22). It is to be pondered (48:10) and praised (59:17).

In Exodus 34:6 *hesed* is paired with faithfulness (*'ĕmet* and its cognates), and this connection is repeated frequently in the psalms. Perhaps the most striking personification of these attributes occurs in Psalm 85:11, "Steadfast love and fidelity meet; justice and peace kiss." Nowhere is the pairing more conspicuous than in Psalm 89 (cf. 61:8), where it appears in the opening declaration and is repeated in the next verse, proclaiming the steadfast love and faithfulness (i.e., fidelity to the promise) of the Lord. The apparent serenity of this psalm continues; in verse 15 the twin characteristics are personified as servants standing before the Lord; in verse 25, they are the divine gift that will be with David; in verse 29 the *ḥesed* is parallel to the covenant that the Lord made with David; in verse 34 there is another statement that the two divine gifts will always remain with David. At that point the mood of the psalm changes. In view of what has happened to the line of David's descendants, the lament is now made. The Lord is accused of going back on his word and repudiating the covenant with David: "O Lord, where is your steadfast love of old that you swore to David in your faithfulness?" The two divine virtues are to be praised day and night. That means true life, because the exact opposite is the fate of residents in Sheol, as the psalmist challenges the Lord: "Is your love proclaimed in the grave, your fidelity in the tomb?" (88:12). One is never more alive than when one is praising God, and never more dead than when such an opportunity does not exist.

Perhaps one might not expect the acrostic Psalm 119, which is so concerned with the statutes and precepts of the law, to be pertinent to our topic, but notice that fidelity, steadfast love, and mercy are bunched together in verses 75-77, where it is also said that the Torah is a delight; it is the gift of God to Israel. "Let your mercy *(rḥm)* come to me that I may live; for your law is my delight" (v. 77). Observance of the law is not a rigorous *quid pro quo.* No material reward can compare with the Law: "Teaching from your lips is more precious to me than heaps of silver and gold" (119:72). "Life," in the full meaning of the word, is mentioned about a dozen times in connection with the energizing that the Law provides. This leads into another aspect of grace in the Old Testament. Thus far we have dwelt mainly on the subjective side of grace and mercy, how they are characteristic of the Lord. But is there an objective meaning, something given to the Israelites because of these divine attributes? Yes, there are, but they are expressed by other terms. Throughout the Hebrew Bible, the choice of Israel and the expression of this in the Mosaic covenant, as well as the promise to David (2 Samuel 7), are all understood as works of divine favor. These truths undergird the appeals for objective signs of divine favor in the psalms, for example, 22:5-6.

The various types of psalms exemplify the objective manifestations of divine grace. They can be praised (Ps 89:1), and be the reason for thanksgiving (Ps 30). These are praised in Psalm 67:2, which begins with a reminiscence of the priestly prayer in Numbers 6:22-27, "May God be gracious to us and bless us; may God's face shine upon us." The blessings are those of the harvest, a blessing for the earth—of Israel, but also of the nations (vv. 3-4). But it is in the laments and psalms of trust that they appear most frequently, since the psalmists are in need; they have recourse to the Lord for interventions, as indications of the divine attitude. It is paradoxical that these psalms rarely describe the concrete situation of the psalmist. The language is so extreme and metaphorical: the waters of chaos, the "hand" of Sheol, the poison of enemies. But there is an advantage to that for modern readers: we are not locked into the humdrum details of the complaint. Indeed the highly metaphorical language (e.g., Ps 22:1-22) enables the modern reader to apply the psalms to the most varying circumstances. The situation is similar with respect to the description of the gracious interventions of God. Usually these are not specified, although there is often the implication that sin has been forgiven and the corresponding punishment (such as sickness, Pss 38; 41) removed. Usually the divine grace is manifested in the broadest terminology: peace or well-being, life, salvation, and so forth. At times, it is mysteriously absent; that is, only the joyous and triumphant cry of the psalmist is registered: "The Lord has heard my cry." This reaction has been described as "the certainty of having been heard" (e.g., Pss 6:8*b*-9*a*, "The Lord has heard the sound of my weeping. The Lord has heard my supplication"). The question has been raised: What precipitated such assurance? A psychological answer, to the effect that this is an exaggerated statement of confidence, is hardly adequate; there are many measured expressions of trust that do not cross the line to certainty. Nor is there any sign that two psalms have been joined together, a lament and a thanksgiving song. The likely answer is that an "oracle of salvation" has intervened.[7]

This solution is without any explicit description of such an "oracle" within the Bible. Its existence has been inferred in order to account for the sudden change in mood. But the inference is not without solid reasons derived from the psalter and other books. Thus, in a context of certainty of being heard, the "I" of Lamentations 3:57 cries out, "You came near when I called on you; you said, 'Do not fear.' " "Do not fear!"—the phrase is repeated in Isaiah 41:10 along with the comforting assurances, "I am with you" (cf. 43:5) and "I am your God"; in 41:13-14, "Do not fear, I will help you." How do such statements fit into the psalms? Psalm 35:3 provides an example: "Say to my soul, 'I am your salvation.' " The psalmist awaits those words. Psalm 91 contains a powerful assurance to the worshiper; it comes to a climax with a quotation of God: "Those who love me, I will deliver; I will protect those who know my name. When they call to me, I will answer them; I will be with them in trouble, I will rescue them and honor them. With long life I will satisfy them, and show them my salvation." It is such words as these that the author of Psalm 130 awaits: "I wait with longing for the Lord, my soul waits for his word" (v. 5).

The term "salvation" is to be taken in the broad sense of deliverance, indicating a change in the situation of the person who prays. Now well-being or shalom has been attained. Within the Hebrew Bible it refers to national or individual deliverance. Another frequent term is "life." This of course refers to the blessings that the Lord has bestowed, the material blessings of a family, a prosperous farm, prestige in the community, and so on. Let it not be thought that this is materialism. One indication of this is the statement in Psalm 63:4, "Your love *(ḥesed)* is better than life." One paradox of the psalter is that though it lacks any clear eschatological hope of life with God after death (even in Pss 49 and 73), it has been the favorite deathbed book for those Christians who do believe in a future with God. Again, the open-endedness of the psalms!

Concluding Remarks

This treatment of the ramifications of the terminology relative to the Old Testament antecedent to the *charis* of the New Testament needs to be balanced against other biblical views of the Lord. In particular, there is the wrath of God, of which there is plenty of evidence in the Bible. One cannot dismiss the horrific description of the wrath of the Lord in Isaiah 30:27-33. In this case, it is directed against the nations, but Israel in its history has also experienced the Lord's anger. It explained the suffering that afflicted the psalmist (e.g., Ps 6:1; 40:11-12), and it explained national calamities, such as the treatment of the anointed of the Lord and the destruction of Jerusalem (Ps 89:38-45). Against this one might balance the remarkable claim in Hosea 11:8-9, "How can I give you up, Ephraim . . . for I am God and not a mortal . . . and I will not come in wrath." But that is the point: the danger of selectivity, a common biblical "disease."

The Bible is full of tensions, and many of these are centered in the portrayal of God. This fact is a benefit, not a drawback. It provides us with a healthy antidote to any Christian complacency. Exodus 34:6 could not become a security blanket. "Grace" is also conditioned by the often mysterious will of the Lord. There is an inescapable tension between human despair (articulated in Ps 88) and trust (which abounds in the psalms). The covenant lawsuit reflected in Psalm 50 contains a stern warning. Israel is told (vv. 14-15): "Offer praise as your sacrifice to God; fulfill your vows to the Most High. Then call on me in time of distress; I will rescue you, and you shall honor me."

Notes

1. The author taught at Duke University during Professor Langford's enlightened leadership as head of the department of religion and also as dean of the Divinity School.
2. Among others, see Ronald Hals, *Grace and Faith in the Old Testament* (Minneapolis: Fortress Press, 1980).
3. These terms are treated in the various theological dictionaries, such as *TDOT, TLOT, TDNT.* Particularly helpful is John Kselman in AB 2, 1085-86.
4. J. Lundbom, "God's Use of the *idem per idem* to Terminate Debate" *HTR* 71 (1978): 193-201.
5. Cf. H.-J. Zobel in *TDOT* V, 44-64, esp. p. 45. All references to psalms follow the numbering of the verses in the Masoretic text.
6. Patrick D. Miller, *They Cried to the Lord: The Form and Theology of Biblical Prayer* (Minneapolis: Fortress Press, 1994), 126.
7. Miller provides an excellent treatment of this phenomenon in *They Cried to the Lord*, 153-77.

PART II:
HISTORICAL ESSAYS

REFORMATION AND GRACE

DAVID C. STEINMETZ

The Reformation began, almost accidentally, as a debate over the meaning of the word "penitence." I say "accidentally" because the controversy over indulgences that set in motion the first stirrings of the Protestant Reformation seemed at the time far too limited and restrictive an issue on which to hang an entire program for the reform of the church. Only the year before in 1516 Luther had composed a probing series of propositions on the hopeless condition of the human will without grace. He had followed it up in 1517 with a stinging barrage of ninety-five theses against scholastic theology, theses that questioned with inescapable directness the church's use of the philosophy of Aristotle. But when the reform began, it was not Luther's attack on the method and conclusions of German academic theology, but his criticism of the medieval theory of penance that captured the imagination of Europe.[1]

Luther may only have intended to attack the extravagant claims that were being advanced by the Dominican, John Tetzel, who was selling indulgences across the river in the part of Saxony under the jurisdiction of Duke George. But when Luther sat down at his desk to draw up his theses for debate, he found that he could not direct his criticisms against the narrower issue of indulgences without discussing the far broader question of the meaning of penitence.

The first thesis touches the central issue. Jesus Christ announced the imminent coming of the kingdom of God and invited his listeners to repent. What exactly, Luther asked, did he have in mind? Did he mean to urge submission to the sacrament of penance? The Latin text of the New Testament with its translation of the words of Jesus as *penitentiam agite* ("do penance") certainly could give that impression. Underneath the Latin formula of the Vulgate, however, was the original Greek verb with its Hebrew antecedents. What was demanded by the preaching of Jesus was a "conversion," a "return," a "change of mind or intention," a fundamental turning of one's life to God, which begins but does not end with the first assent of the will to the gospel.

Debate over the meaning of repentance is basic to Protestantism. From the early and formative decades of the Protestant Reformation through the evangelical awakening of the eighteenth century to the Bangkok Assembly in 1973 and the Lausanne Covenant of 1974, Protestants have returned again and again to the theme of penitence and conversion.

American Protestants are, of course, familiar with the tradition of the Evangelical Awakening, which has left its mark on American churches from the time of Edwards and Asbury to the present. Less well known, but no less important, are the reflections of the Protestant Reformers on the subject of repentance. Although John Cotton would "sweeten his mouth" with a passage from John Calvin before retiring, most American Christians are more familiar with Calvinism than with Calvin. American evangelism has been molded more by Edwards, Finney, Moody, Sunday, and Graham than by the theology of the sixteenth-century reformers.

I

Common to almost all early Protestant discussions of repentance is a barely disguised hostility to every theory of conversion that stresses proper preparation for the reception of grace. Opposition to the notion of preparation for grace led Protestants inevitably to reject all medieval theologies of penance, the most Augustinian and restrained as well as the most Pelagian and careless. Nevertheless, it is fair to state that the form in which Luther first encountered a theory of preparation for grace was the form in which it was elaborated by Gabriel Biel in his *Collectorium* on the Sentences of Peter Lombard.[2]

Biel was the first professor of theology at the University of Tübingen, a university founded in the last quarter of the fifteenth century. Biel was balanced, judicious, immensely learned, and deeply spiritual. He was famous not only inside Germany but outside it as well; his works appeared in French as well as in German editions. But his understanding of repentance, about which he wrote learnedly and at great length, was fundamentally defective from Luther's point of view.

It was not that Biel failed to ground his arguments in the Bible or in the Augustinian tradition of the Western church. Indeed, Biel's ruminations on penitence are laced with frequent quotations from the Bible: James 4:8; Luke 11:9; Jeremiah 29:13; and above all, Zechariah 1:3: "Turn to me, says the Lord of Hosts, and I will turn unto you." This text from Zechariah summed up in the briefest possible scope the essence of Biel's theology of penance.

Biel argued that the notion of covenant was fundamental to a right conception of the sinner's relationship to God. God has established a covenant, the terms of which are proclaimed by the church in the gospel. God has promised to give saving grace to everyone who meets the conditions of that covenant. What is demanded of the sinner, quite simply, is that the sinner love God above everything else. Sinners can do this because, while sin has damaged their capacity for loving God, it has not obliterated it. To put it in its crassest form, grace is a reward for exemplary moral virtue, a virtue that Biel, like Kant, thought lay in the power of the unconverted will.

Luther rejected categorically this understanding of preparation for grace. Morally good acts do not have a claim on the favor of God. The real preparation for grace, if one can use this language at all without occasioning misunderstanding, is the preparation that God has made by his election, calling, and gifts. Luther agreed with Biel that God has established a covenant, but it is a covenant whose basis is diametrically opposed to the covenant recommended by Biel.

God promises to give his grace to "real sinners." "Real sinners" are people who are not merely sinners in fact (everyone, after all, is a sinner in that sense), but who confess that they are sinners. "Real sinners" conform their judgment of themselves to the judgment of God over them and by doing so justify God in his Word of judgment and grace. Paradoxically, it is the "real sinner" who is justified by God and who knows both theoretically and experientially what repentance offers and demands. The gospel as Luther conceived it is both easier and harder than the gospel that Biel offered. Being a real sinner is a condition that, on the face of it, anyone can meet; but it is harder because it demands rigorous honesty in the face of the truth. Penitents cannot prepare themselves for grace because they must be crucified by the Word of God's judgment and die. Repentance has to do with death and life and not merely with the resolute decision of an already good person like Biel to improve his frankly unimpeachable character.

Luther's objection to Biel's theory is not merely that it harbors a thoroughly unrealistic view of human nature, though that is part of his objection. Even more important for Luther than the fact that no one can live up to Biel's theory of repentance is the fact that no one is expected to. The gospel does not demand moral virtue as the preparatory stage of conversion. Biel's view of the matter is not only unworkable; it is irrelevant. The sole precondition for authentic conversion is real sin; the sole preparation that matters is the preparation that God has made in the gospel.

The saying of Jesus that the whole have no need of a physician is a saying that the church has always had great difficulty assimilating. It seems so much more reasonable to believe that God will be merciful to those people who meet certain prior expectations: the right ideology, the right sex or race, the right degree of devotion to the causes currently supported by the right elements in society. "But when we were right," Luther observed in one of his earliest writings, "God laughed at us in our rightness."[3] God's quarrel is with the whole human race and not merely with certain factions in it. Judgment falls not only on the theologically heterodox but also on the theologically pure. The one absolutely indispensable precondition for the reception of grace is not to be right—not even in the sense of theological orthodoxy—but to be sick. The gospel is for real sinners.

II

The church provides the context within which authentic repentance can take place. It may seem surprising to lay so much stress on the church in early Protestant thought, since Protestants have often been regarded as religious individualists who affirmed the right of private judgment against the corporate power of the late medieval church. But in point of fact the late medieval church was the home of a private and individualistic piety, while Protestantism has been hopelessly social from the beginning. Whether talking of ordination or of eucharistic theory, Protestants have focused on the congregation rather than the individual as the fundamental reality from which theological reflection must proceed. Critics may accuse Protestants of talking about the church too much or of talking about it in the wrong way, but not of neglecting it.

The church can, of course, stand in the way of authentic conversion, and in his *Reply to Sadoleto,* Calvin accused the late medieval church of doing precisely that. In a lengthy bill of particulars Calvin charged the late medieval church with keeping people from repentance by the disunity of its life and the disorder of its teaching. In particular the church had urged upon the faithful a duty of implicit faith in its own teaching authority, while, to use Calvin's vivid language, the "leaders of faith neither understood [the] Word nor greatly cared for it" but taught "doctrines sprung from the human brain." Not surprisingly this "supine state of the pastors" led swiftly to the "stupidity of the people" who thought that the "highest veneration paid to [the] Word was to revere it at a distance, as a thing inaccessible, and abstain from all investigation of it."[4] Reverence for the church—any church—in its unreformed state can only impede progress toward the radical change of direction that is demanded by Jesus in the Gospels.

Even in the worst of times the church is, to use Calvin's favorite imagery, a mother and school, which nurtures and instructs men and women in the Christian faith. When confronted by the quotation from Augustine, "I would not have believed the gospel if the authority of the church had not moved me," Calvin agreed with it, much to the surprise of his conservative critics. The important thing, however, is not to quote Augustine—anyone armed with the *Milleloquium* can do that—but to know what he meant.[5]

It is obvious what he did not mean. Augustine did not intend to teach that the authority of the church is so great, so metaphysically higher in the scale of being, that the gospel derives its authority in a secondary fashion from the prior and more encompassing authority of the church. Augustine said that he would not have believed the gospel if the authority of the church had not moved him; he did not say, or mean to imply, that he would not have believed the gospel if a committee of bishops had not approved it. The authority of the gospel is primary and the authority of the church is secondary and derivative.

The authority of the church to which Augustine alluded is the authority of the holiness of its life and the faithfulness of its witness. In a word, Augustine was moved to trust the gospel because he first trusted the people who told him about it. The gospel is better than the church, but it is never found except in the human and therefore touching witness of the church. The church, like the Samaritan woman, tugs at the sleeve of the unbeliever and says, "Come, see a man, which told me all things that ever I did: is not this the Christ?" (KJV). That is the authority of the church, the authority of a faithful and self-effacing witness.

To this church has been committed the power of the keys, the power to bind and loose the penitent from their sins. Yet it is a power that the church does and does not have. It does not have it in the sense that it is not a power that inheres in the community as a group, as color, weight, texture are qualities of an object. But it does have it in the sense that as a community it proclaims by word and deed the authority of the gospel. The gospel binds and looses from sins, not the church, and yet it does not do so apart from the church that bears it and bears witness to it.

Repentance—at least repentance in the sense in which it is recommended in the New Testament—is not a spontaneous religious emotion that springs up in the human heart without prior sufficient cause. It is a response to the message of God's judgment and grace, a message proclaimed by the church, the community established by God in which faith is formed. Although the gospel can and does reach outside the church and though God is never limited in achieving his purposes to any instrumental means, nevertheless, the church is the principal sphere and context for authentic conversion. Repentance is, if you will not misunderstand me, a churchly function. Indeed, it is the perpetual activity of a church reformed by the Word of God.

It would be an exaggeration to say that the Reformation grew out of a desire on the part of laity for good preaching, but it would not be entirely false. Although it was not the case in the late Middle Ages that there was absolutely no preaching at Sunday mass, it was not an activity very much done by local parish priests. Preaching was done of course by members of mendicant orders—orders like the Dominicans, Franciscans, Augustinians, and Carmelites—either in the local chapel of the order or in some village church. But preaching was not the central act of Christian worship. The central act of Christian worship was the celebration of the Lord's Supper in a special, highly ritualized, and very dramatic way. To become a priest was primarily a matter not of learning how to talk to a large group of laity about the

Bible, but of learning how to celebrate the sacraments of baptism, penance, eucharist (or Lord's supper), matrimony, and extreme unction. The priest was not primarily an explainer of texts, but a celebrator of mysteries.

Preaching played for early Protestants a role reserved for sacraments in the medieval church. Heinrich Bullinger spoke for a large consensus of early Protestants when he wrote in the Second Helvetic Confession (1562–66): Praedicatio verbi Dei est verbum Dei—"The preaching of the Word of God is the Word of God." Bullinger did not say that the preaching of the Word of God signifies the Word of God or that the preaching of the Word of God is a witness to the Word. Preaching is more than a witness to God's Word; insofar as it is an event in which the voice of God is heard again, it is the Word of God. The operative word is *est* or "is" and not *significat* or "signifies." What this means in its sixteenth-century context is that just as Catholics believe that, when mass is said, Christ is really present in the creaturely elements of bread and wine, so Protestants now claim that when a sermon is preached, the life-giving Word of God is really present in the creaturely elements of human speech. The Word of God is present because through culturally determined human language God again speaks a culturally transcendent Word. God speaks not *Heissel-Wörter* (or naming Words), words with which he simply names things that already exist; God speaks a *Thettel-Wort* (or deed Word), a Word that transforms the current state of affairs so that things cannot remain the way they were before. Preaching is not just a report of something happening elsewhere or of something which happened two thousand years ago. As Luther understands the concept of the Word of God in preaching, it is not just an act in which Ezekiel's oracles, which were once a living Word, are recollected. Rather at the hands of the preacher, Ezekiel's oracles become again the Word of God, powerful and life-giving in the time and place of the preacher and his congregation.

Bernard Lord Manning once defined a sermon, properly done, as "a manifestation of the incarnate Word from the written Word by the spoken Word." That is more or less what Luther also had in mind. The incarnate Word is offered in the text of Scripture. When the preacher bears witness to Christ the incarnate Word, he or she is not bearing witness to something else, something alien, something other, but to the Word as flesh in the Word as written by the Word as spoken.

Preaching is the Word of God in no less a sense than the Word spoken by God in creation. Through human preaching God once again does his unfinished work of grace and judgment, of creating and destroying. Christians must therefore be very careful how they use the Bible. When dealing with the Word of God written and spoken, they are dealing with something extremely powerful. With such a Word God created the world out of nothing.

III

The repentance to which a Christian is called is a continuous and lifelong process. While conversion begins, as everything in history does, at some point in time, the process of conversion is not completed until every aspect of the human personality is driven out into the light of God's severe mercy, judged, and renewed. Conversion proceeds layer by layer, relationship by relationship, here a little, there a little, until the whole personality and not merely one side of it has been re-created by God. Conversion refers not only to the initial moment of faith, no matter how dramatic or revolutionary it may seem, but to the whole life of the believer and the network of relationships in which that life is entangled: personal, familial, social, economic, political.

That is why the church is called a school. Faith is not only something one has; it is something one is learning. Mastery of the Greek alphabet is not the same thing as mastery of the *Odyssey;* yet mastery of the one proceeds from mastery of the other. The first moment of penitence initiates one into the school of faith, but the lessons to be learned can only be grasped by long and patient experience. Conversion, to change the metaphor, is not only the little wicket gate through which John Bunyan's pilgrim quickly passes as he abandons the City of Destruction; it is the entire pilgrimage to the Celestial City.

No aspect of Reformation teaching on penitence is more foreign to the American evangelical experience of the past two centuries than the stress on conversion as a process rather than as a crisis in human life. Evangelicals have always emphasized the initial moment of faith in which one passes from death to life, from darkness to light. This is a moment celebrated, recalled, and, when the experience fades, recaptured. While sanctification may be a process, conversion is the work of a moment.

The Protestant Reformers did not agree, but that was not because they despised the first stirrings of faith or the resolute convictions of people who bore witness to what they had seen and heard. They did not agree because they had a somewhat different doctrine of sin and were convinced that sin was such a complex phenomenon and so intricately embedded in human thinking and willing that only a thousand conversions would root it out.

Or maybe I have put that too negatively. The Reformers were convinced that only those who love God can hate sin. Thoroughly unconverted sinners are perfect children in their knowledge of sin. Only a saint knows what sin is and therefore only a person who has progressed in the love of God can see with sufficient clarity what exactly is the character of the sin that is distorting human life. It requires some growth in grace to repent properly. The more one grows in the love of God, the more perfect one's repentance. Mourners sitting on the anxious bench or filing into an inquirer's room have, unfortunately, only a child's eye view of their own sin. Real repentance, real conversion of life, is an activity of the spiritually mature.

Repentance is consistently portrayed by the Reformers as a return to baptism, a return to the foundation of God's gifts and promises, which are generous enough to sustain us throughout our whole life. They must be reappropriated, reaffirmed; they cannot be superseded. By the process of repentance, of continuous conversion, Christians appropriate the mercy and gifts of God at a deeper level than they have ever experienced them before.

Perhaps the most striking image of baptism in early Protestant literature is the one offered by Ulrich Zwingli. Baptism is like the cowl or uniform that is given to a novice in a mendicant order. The young boy of twelve is a Franciscan or a Dominican from the very moment he accepts the uniform and the obligations that wearing it entails. But he is not a Franciscan in the same sense as an old brother of eighty-two, who has worn the brown robe of St. Francis all his long and varied life. The young novice must grow up into the uniform he has been given. So, too, baptism is the Christian's uniform; believers must grow up into it. It is cut for a far more generously proportioned figure than the slight and insubstantial figure of mere beginners. But beginners will grow up into it as they are continuously converted at ever deeper levels of their personalities by means of the Word of God. Conversion does not bypass baptism; it fits believers to it, so that they take all that is offered and become all they profess.

IV

Every conversion has a price. Something is gained, but something is lost as well, and the loss may prove to be painful. There is a tendency in certain circles of American evangelicalism to offer the gospel as the solution for pressing human problems without mentioning that there is another side to the question. The gospel not only resolves problems that trouble the newly converted; it creates problems they never had before and would, if possible, gladly avoid.

Sometimes the problems are vocational. In his Preface to the *Commentary on the Psalms,* published in 1557, Calvin, who was generally reluctant to offer any information about himself in his published works, broke his silence to talk about his sudden and unexpected conversion to Protestantism. In a brief passage of unusual candor Calvin confessed that his principal ambition both before and after his conversion was to lead the quiet life of a humanist scholar, alone with his books, his commentaries, and his grammars. Against his own personal preferences he was driven by God to assume a role in shaping history.

Sometimes life itself is at stake. It makes sober reading to examine the pages of the *Martyr's Mirror* and to realize that almost none of the first generation of leaders of the Anabaptist moment lived to see that movement reach its tenth anniversary. Not all the martyrs were Anabaptist; certainly not all were Protestant. From William Tyndale to Edmund Campion, from Robert Barnes to Thomas More, from Hugh Latimer to John Fisher, conversion to Christ in the sixteenth century could entail the loss of one's own life. The age could, and frequently did, exact a grisly price for heeding the radical call of Jesus to turn about in one's tracks and head in a diametrically opposite direction.

Yet most frequently the problems are what one might loosely call moral problems. Every human decision has its moral aspects and since every human decision is qualified by obedience to the demand of the gospel for repentance and conversion, human life is somewhat more complicated than it was before. It is no longer possible simply to adopt the customary attitudes toward war or race or business or marriage or abortion or any other question that affects individual or corporate life. Every decision stands under the question posed by the words of Jesus: "Repent, for the kingdom of God is at hand!"

Calvin describes the life of the converted by two ponderous phrases: mortification of the flesh and vivification of the Spirit. The first phrase is clear enough; it means death to the old way of thinking and acting. But the second phrase is the one not to be lost sight of. The death of the old is for the sake of the birth of a new reality.

Luther was fond of talking about the strange and proper work of God. The strange work of God refers to the work of wrath and judgment; the proper work designates the work of mercy and renewal. Both were spoken of in the Bible but they were not given equal emphasis. Their relationship is dialectical. God does the strange work of judgment and destruction for the sake of the proper work of mercy and love. The old, unrepentant, faithless, unconverted reality must be destroyed, but not as an end in itself. God destroys the old decadent self in order to create in its place a new reality almost too glorious to be imagined. Suffering is for the sake of joy.

V

These four themes from early Protestant thought—the denial of the possibility of preparation for the reception of grace, the insistence on the church as the context in which genuine repentance takes place, the description of conversion as a continuous and lifelong process, and the warning that there is no conversion that does not exact a price from the penitent—are certainly not the only themes that need to be considered by the church in the present as it ponders its own evangelistic mission. Indeed, they may even need to be corrected by insights derived from the Bible or other voices in the Christian tradition. But they are insights that cannot be lightly set aside. As Calvin observed, when we deal with repentance and the forgiveness of sins, we are dealing with "the sum of the gospel."[6]

Notes

1. This essay is a revision and expansion of an earlier essay written while Thomas Langford was Dean of the Duke Divinity School.
2. Next to the glossed Bible the *Four Books of Sentences* of Peter Lombard was the central theological textbook for generations of students from the twelfth through the sixteenth

centuries. All medieval theological teachers used this book as the basis for their lectures on dogmatic theology. The *Collectorium* was the commentary on the *Sentences* prepared by Gabriel Biel (d. 1495), a theologian at the University of Tübingen whose writings were especially important for the theological development of the young Martin Luther.

3. *D. Martin Luthers Werke: Kritische Gesamtausgabe* 56 (Weimar, 1883): 449.1-6.

4. John C. Olin, ed., *John Calvin and Jacopo Sadoleto: A Reformation Debate* (New York: Harper & Row, 1966), 82.

5. The *Milleloquium divi Augustini* was an anthology of quotations from the writings of Augustine prepared in the later Middle Ages by members of the Order of the Hermits of St. Augustine, the order Luther joined in 1505. It was regarded by theologians inside and outside the Order as an immensely useful reference tool.

6. John Calvin, *Institutes* III.iii.1.

GOD WITH US:
Grace and the Spiritual Senses in John Wesley's Theology

RICHARD P. HEITZENRATER

John Wesley's understanding of grace is central to his theology, though Wesley seldom reflected on its definition. He is in good company; theologians make frequent references to "grace" and assume that the reader or listener knows what it means. Any examination of Wesley's various references to grace in his theology would benefit from an attempt to formulate a view of grace that is consistent with his own apparent understanding and usage of the concept.

Wesley is never inclined to present a full list of beliefs or a careful definition of each of his theological concepts. He was not a systematic theologian. So it is difficult to find in Wesley's writings a full-fledged definition of what "grace" is, as distinguished from what it does.[1] But, as several recent scholars have pointed out, Wesley was operating upon a fairly consistent set of theological assumptions and beliefs that can be discerned from a careful reading of his writings.[2] Instead of delineating in detail the true beliefs of a Christian, he was more inclined to describe Christian truths in terms of true Christians who "had the mind of Christ and walked as he walked." Wesley's writings have many more descriptions of the results of God's grace upon and in the lives of believers than philosophical or theological definitions of the precise nature of grace. But from the various descriptions of the action of grace in the divine-human relationship, one can piece together Wesley's understanding of the nature, role, and effects of grace.

Wesley assumes that his Anglican heritage provides a coherent system, an adequate matrix upon which he can embroider his personal theology. His training and development as a theologian formed Wesley in the English religious heritage. Even though his own theological expression assumes a distinctive shape, when Wesley delves deeply in the early church or wanders into medieval Pietism or borrows from Roman Catholic mysticism or ties together theological reflection and holy living, he exhibits the *via media* methodology of his own tradition.[3] Wesley's understanding of grace must therefore be seen in relation to the doctrinal position of the Church of England in the eighteenth century.

God's Grace and the Church of England

Wesley's explanations of the nature and function of grace are basically Anglican, which is to say that his theology of grace is in keeping with the doctrinal standards of the Church of England. But Wesley's understanding of the perceptibility of grace gives his doctrine a distinctive twist that distinguishes him from the typical Anglican clergyman of his day. By his own testimony, Wesley declares himself a thoroughgoing Anglican. When asked by a "serious" clergyman in 1739 in what ways the Methodists differed from the Church of England, he answered, "To the best of my knowledge, in none. The doctrines we preach are the doctrines of the Church of England; indeed, the fundamental doctrines of the Church, clearly laid down, both in her Prayers, Articles, and Homilies."[4]

Those documents, forged in the heat of sixteenth-century reform to present the standards of doctrine for the Church of England, were of course subject to interpretation two centuries later. The church in the eighteenth century, in spite of strict laws of uniformity and tight legal restrictions on "toleration," comprehended persons whose views ranged from deistic to evangelical. From within this heritage, one could cite Baxter, Laud, Toland, or Tillotson as readily as Cranmer and Hooker. And the catholic sense of the Church would allow for Augustine and Anselm, or Chrysostom and Kempis, to have an equal voice in the tradition. So for Wesley to see himself as a faithful son of the Church provides no more self-evident definition of his particular theological ideas than does Luther's or Calvin's claims to be faithful sons of the Roman Catholic Church.

With such a variety of theological positions evident within the church, Wesley chose explicitly to use the church's doctrinal standards as the official referent for his positions and tried to claim a close adherence to those standards. Some of his critics recognized that such an affirmation did not stop him from moving beyond that base.[5] The Thirty-nine Articles have no article on grace as such, but most of the references to grace therein (within seven of the articles) relate to the process of salvation. In that context, grace is seen as God working in three particular ways—the grace of God preventing us, justifying us, and working with us.[6] But the Articles never define precisely what that grace is, only implying that it has something to do with "God's good-will towards us,"[7] and that "the grace of Christ" is linked with "the inspiration of his Spirit."[8]

In fact, a large proportion of writers, from biblical times to the present, use the term "grace" without providing a careful philosophical or theological definition. Grace is often described by such terms as free, or unmerited, or prevenient, or justifying, or sanctifying, or saving, as if those adjectives determine or define the nature of grace. Grace is portrayed as a gift, but it is also seen as bestowing gifts. It is the source of salvation but also the consequence of salvation. God's grace is often equated with God's favor, God's mercy, God's pardoning love, the power of the Holy Spirit, or various virtues infused in the soul. In the Bible, familiar phrasing comes in two familiar forms: "the grace of God," "the grace of our Lord Jesus Christ." And the verbs associated with the work of grace tend to confuse the picture even further—in the passive sense, grace is given, bestowed, showered. Such descriptions seem to imply that grace is a "thing" that can be distributed, but what is "it" that is being dispensed in such ways? In the active sense, grace "descends," "works," "subdues," "justifies," "sustains," "comforts," "follows," "restrains," "renews," "enables." Other terms further confuse the picture: references to a "state of grace," "grace upon grace," "mere grace," being "under grace," "growing in grace," having "more grace" or "less grace." And to further cloud the picture, the term is sometimes found in the plural, such as "passive graces," "constellation of graces," "queen of all graces," "ordinary graces," "gifts and graces," and "the whispers of his graces."

Richard Hooker at times speaks only of God's "precedent" ("preventing") and "subsequent" ("helping") grace. But, like the Articles, he also speaks at times of "three kinds of grace," with a slightly different twist: "the grace whereby God doth incline towards man, the grace of outward instruction, and the grace of inward sanctification."[9] At one point, he even comes close to a definition of grace:

> By grace we always understand, as the word of God teacheth, first, his favour and undeserved mercy towards us; secondly, the bestowing of his Holy Spirit which inwardly worketh; thirdly, the effects of that Spirit whatsoever, but especially saving virtues, such as are faith, charity, and hope; lastly, the free and full remission of all our sins.[10]

With a slight alteration of Hooker's order (making the last item the second), this combination of descriptive comments provides the beginnings of an outline of how we might differentiate four categories within which grace can be understood in the Anglican and the Wesleyan traditions.

1) Grace as God's favorable inclination toward humankind
2) Grace as God's love manifest in acts of salvific assistance for humankind
3) Grace as God's continuing presence within humankind
4) Grace as the beneficial effects of God's relational activity for and with humankind.

These categories might never be spelled out as such in Wesley or the Articles, but they are certainly consistent with Anglican and Wesleyan thinking on the matter of grace. There is, however, a slight distinction that must be made within the list. The first three of these categories speak to *nature* of the single reality that is subsumed in the concept of "grace." The latter category is in a sense derivative, in that it speaks of the *results* of grace in humankind.[11]

Certain significant characterizations can be made about these categories in terms of the nature and work of grace, as well as its results and our perception. The *nature* of God's grace is understood to be relational, active, and powerful. The *work* of this active relational power of God is to enlighten, liberate, and empower humankind; the *result* of which is that these transformed persons are given knowledge, liberty, and power. In all these senses, God's grace is essentially tied to God's active presence and power in human existence. Our *perception* of God's grace (God's active presence and power) results from our use of grace-given spiritual senses.

This language and these categories and characterizations are not necessarily Hooker's or Wesley's, but they are consistent with their thought and can provide a framework within which we might understand conceptually what they are talking about when they use the term grace.

The Nature of God's Grace as Active Presence-Power-Influence

Whatever grace is, most writers assume that divine grace is grounded in the very being of God. Although the human mind cannot conceive of the essence of the divine being, theologians have for centuries discussed the attributes of God using language associated with human qualities, howbeit with some sense of similitude, analogy, and proportionality. Using metaphoric language (ontological language being impossible), the First Epistle of John equates the being of God with a divine attribute, "God is love,"[12] indicating that love is the primary attribute and essential to the nature of God. Therefore, grace is grounded in and emanates from the love of God.

Love is a relational term.[13] For God as love to be evident or manifest to humankind, there must be a divine-human relationship—God must be somehow present with humankind. That presence can be in the will or in the actions of God. However, God (as a spiritual being) does not have a spatial presence. As Thomas Aquinas pointed out, spiritual-divine beings manifest their presence through their actions, which is to say their power being exerted upon an object.[14] Therefore God's presence is evident through divine activity—the divine will is exercised with humankind in mind, or divine action is manifest in the lives of human beings.

To associate God's presence so closely with divine exertion of power is to run the risk of being misunderstood. Unfortunately, the term "power" tends to be associated with mighty forces in boisterous activities. However, real power can be quiet and tender. Soft violins can be more powerful than clashing cymbals. Power tempered by compassion can be comforting. In this sense, God's power can perhaps best be understood as God's *influence,* which can be manifest in a number of ways, ranging metaphorically from the still, small voice to the clap of thunder, and actively from comfort to destruction.

In these terms, the presence of God is always associated in some way with the active power or influence of the divine being, which springs from the essential attribute of divine love. And God's grace is associated at many levels with this active presence or power of God in the divine-human relationship. One might then define grace as "the active presence or power of God." Most of Wesley's uses of the term grace seem to assume this definition, whether he is talking about the nature of grace, the work of grace, or the results of grace.

The Work of God's Active Presence-Power-Influence in the *Via Salutis*

Wesley frequently refers to the *work* of God's grace in three soteriological contexts: preventing grace, justifying grace, and sanctifying grace. This distinction is not unusual; Hooker's structure and terminology are very similar.

God's Active Presence (Enlightenment)
Through the Prevenient Work of the Holy Spirit

Wesley understands grace first of all in terms of God's favor and mercy. This divine disposition toward humanity is a consequence of God's primary attribute of love; it is exhibited in the perfection of creation. Created in the image of God, humankind originally had the capability of holiness and happiness—that is, to love God and neighbor completely and to experience the joy and peace that comes through those loving relationships. However, through free choice, Adam chose to ignore the command of God. As a consequence of this disobedience, fallen humanity has lost both the ability to discern the good and the capability to choose it. Unable to know the good, distorted human reason is therefore incapable of informing the will, which cannot then choose the good.[15] In this condition, humankind stands in need of divine assistance to be saved from the inherited propensity to sin ("original sin") that has become part of human nature.

God's favorable inclination toward fallen humanity, however, became manifest again in the incarnation and atonement. God became flesh in the person of Jesus in order to redeem humankind from this sinful condition. This divine act of grace is the point where relational disposition and inclination become proactively self-giving and powerful. The event of Jesus Christ is the focal point of the drama of salvation and provides the source of saving grace for humankind. Although Wesley does not espouse any particular view of the atonement exclusively,[16] he is very particular to point out that the dynamic of God's redemptive act through Jesus Christ depends upon both Christ's active and passive righteousness (Christ's life and passion), not simply the latter (his death and resurrection).[17]

But humankind, as we have seen, is incapable of initiating any action that would result in salvation from sin. To espouse the possibility of such capability would be to claim a meritorious righteousness for humankind that would challenge the definitive views of Augustine on the total need for grace and would appear to espouse Pelagianism or "works righteousness." But Wesley is not willing to allow this dilemma to force him into a Calvinistic or Lutheran view of predestination, in which God's arbitrary will determines who is to be saved and who is not. Wesley is more inclined toward an Arminian view that allows for human free will to have a role in the drama.[18] But how can the human exercise of free will at any stage of the process of salvation, especially the beginning, be seen as anything other than a "good work" in the Pelagian sense—a human act, done in order to earn salvation?

In order to avoid the theological dilemma presented by a belief in both the sovereignty of God and the free will of humankind, Wesley chooses to espouse the doctrine of prevenient grace, which he usually calls "preventing grace"—the grace of God that "comes before" (from Latin, *prevenire*) any human action. Through prevenient grace, God provides universally to fallen humanity the possibility of knowing the good and thereby the potential of restoring the capability of doing the good. By holding that the gift of this knowledge that enables the will to choose properly is the result of God's grace, not human initiative, Wesley feels that he has avoided the pitfall of predestination on the one hand and the charge of works righteousness on the other.

The result of God's favorable disposition toward humankind becoming an active presence and power through prevenient grace is therefore knowledge or enlightenment. The recognition and acceptance of this divine gift is the necessary first step in Wesley's understanding of the spiritual pilgrimage in the way of salvation. It is the first evidence of divine grace in a person's experience; it is the first point of responsible choice by the will. This enlightenment (knowledge of the good) that comes through prevenient grace Wesley associates analogously with conscience, which he felt was commonly understood to be present in all humankind. He disclaims an exact parallel between conscience and prevenient grace in order to avoid any misconception that prevenient grace was part of created human nature instead of a divine gift offered to sinful humanity. But he claims the analogy in order to press its universal application to humankind.

Wesley also uses imagery of the senses to make his point about the enlightening nature of God's prevenient grace. Spiritual blindness is the condition of humankind tainted by original sin: "Natural man [is] born blind and continues so [and] is scarce sensible of his want." As long as humans remain in that state, they "are not sensible of their spiritual wants." But Wesley goes on to compare the condition of believers: "As soon as God opens the eyes of their understanding, they see the state they were in before; they are then deeply convinced, that 'every man living,' themselves especially, [is] by nature, 'altogether vanity'; that is, folly and ignorance, sin and wickedness."[19] In another sermon, Wesley uses the same imagery to point to its more positive consequences of this divine enlightenment: "May God open the eyes of our understanding; that . . . we may discern what is the good and acceptable will of God."[20] In such a way, the gracious enlightening presence of God's Spirit brings knowledge of the good.

The expected result of this enlightenment, or knowledge of the good, through prevenient grace is the recognition that one is not good but is sinful. Wesley occasionally says that persons must be "sensible" of their sinful condition in order to desire forgiveness.[21] A person must be convinced of this sinful state in order to recognize the need for change (conversion). This conviction that comes through God's enlightening presence Wesley sometimes calls the result of "convincing grace." These two terms, prevenient grace and convincing grace, both relate to the enlightening presence of God (grace) offered to all humankind—one speaking to its universal precedence, the other to its intended first result.

God's Active Presence (Liberation)
Through the Pardoning Work of Christ in Justification

Conviction of sin leads to an attitude-action of repentance and a desire on the part of the enlightened sinner for forgiveness (pardon) from God. Divine pardon is the saving gift of God's incarnate atoning activity in human existence, as we have noted. God's liberating presence or power as forgiveness Wesley calls "justifying grace." Through this divine intervention, humankind is justified, pardoned, freed from the guilt of sin, and his or her relationship with God is "made right." In Wesley's terms, the justified person is accounted as righteous (in a legal or forensic sense) by the work of Christ. Christ's righteousness is imputed to the believer. Such a change is "relative"—the person is not actually changed, but his or her relationship to God is changed. One is at the same time justified and still a sinner *(simul justis et peccator)*.

Pardon, or justification, can only be appropriated by humankind through faith *(sola fide)*.[22] But to have faith is not simply an independent human action; one does not "have faith" as a purely human initiative. Even the ability to exercise faith is the result of God's liberating presence or grace. Otherwise, to "have faith" would be to initiate a good work toward salvation. And of course, traditional Protestant theology tries to avoid even the appearance of relying upon good works for salvation. The faith-works dichotomy, especially prior to justification, permeates the typical Protestant mind-set.

Therefore, Wesley found himself in immediate controversy with his Calvinist adversaries when, in his mature theology, he pressed his view that good works were "in some sense necessary" for salvation, even before justification. At every opportunity, the searching penitent should engage in "fruits meet for repentance," such as prayer, Bible reading, attendance upon the Sacrament.[23] Critics immediately cried Pelagianism. But Wesley felt that any singular overemphasis on *sola fide* could result in antinomianism (anti-legalism), which he thought destructive of disciplined Christian living. Once again, through his view of grace, he tried to avoid opposite dangers, in this case of solafidianism and Pelagianism. He pressed his view that good works are only possible by the grace of God, just as faith is only possible by the grace of God. Both faith and good works can therefore be expected of the penitent sinner (as well as the redeemed Christian) since both are made possible by God's empowering presence or grace. He cuts through the faith-works Gordian knot with his pervasive doctrine of grace.

God's Active Presence (Empowerment)
Through the Influence of the Holy Spirit in Sanctification

Although Wesley sees God's active presence in pardoning the penitent sinner in justification as a relative change, he also recognizes that this divine action through the work of Christ results in a real change in the life and heart of the believer through the work of the Holy Spirit. Wesley thus distinguishes theologically between justification (what God does for us—pardon) and sanctification (what God does in us—holiness). However, the beginning of God's sanctifying grace (empowering presence and influence) through the Holy Spirit is evident in the justified person becoming a new creature (regenerate, born again). Thus, while Wesley understood pardon and regeneration to be theologically in separate categories, he recognized that new birth was most likely an immediate consequence of forgiveness and therefore chronologically part of a single event. This recognition appropriately reflects the fact that all manifestations of God's grace can be understood within the unitive term of active divine presence or power.

The work of God's gracious presence, through the Holy Spirit renewing the human heart, mind, and soul in the image of God in regeneration, continues throughout the process of sanctification, whereby the believer grows in holiness, or love of God and neighbor. Now a real change occurs in the believer's heart and life and, freed from the power of sin, he or she is able actually to become more holy. This work of God's presence-power in the life of humankind is not just a legal or forensic adjustment, as in justification, but rather begins a process that has therapeutic consequences.[24] Christ's righteousness is implanted in or imparted to the believer, who then grows in love. In talking about this righteousness, Wesley does not generally use the Thomist terms of infused or inherent (which are less active). But his view can be seen as very close to Thomas' understanding of *habitus,* so long as one understands that this righteousness does not reside in the human heart and life apart from God's active presence-power.[25]

The role of the Holy Spirit as the agent of sanctifying grace accentuates the understanding of grace as the active presence of God. The "influence" (literally "breathing in") of the Holy Spirit (*ruach*, "breath" or "wind") is an apt phrase to delineate Wesley's understanding of sanctifying grace. He takes the imagery even farther in his sermon "The New Birth":

[As soon as a person is born of God, he or she can begin to live in Christ.] God is continually breathing, as it were, upon his soul, and his soul is breathing unto God. Grace is descending into his heart; and prayer and praise ascending to heaven. And by this intercourse between God and man, this fellowship with the Father and the Son, as by a kind of spiritual respiration, the life of God in the soul is sustained, and the child of God grows up, till he comes to the "full measure of the stature of Christ."[26]

In fact, although the Spirit is not always named explicitly, as in this passage, the third person of the Trinity is in many ways the most apt focus of Wesley's understanding of grace. There are times when he equates grace and the Holy Spirit, such as in the sermon "The Witness of Our Own Spirit": " 'The grace of God' . . . means that power of God the Holy Ghost, which 'worketh in us both to will and to do of his good pleasure.' "[27] He also points to the work of the Spirit when he refers to true religion as "the consequence of God's dwelling and reigning in the soul."[28] In any case, God's loving presence enables us to love. Or, as Wesley pointed out further in his *Instructions for Children*, grace can be understood as the power of the Holy Spirit enabling us to believe, love, and serve God.[29]

Wesley's theology of salvation (soteriology) is trinitarian, synergistic, dynamic, and perhaps above all a thoroughgoing theology of grace—God's presence-power-influence is the active initiating and empowering element at every stage. While his view is certainly christocentric in typically Protestant fashion, Wesley's position is also very trinitarian, as salvation is from God, in Christ, through the Holy Spirit. If anything, Wesley's theology has a stronger pneumatological emphasis than many other mainline Protestant positions. The distinctive nature of that emphasis becomes evident in Wesley's understanding that the believer can know that he or she is a child of God.

God's Active Presence (Enlightenment)
Through the Holy Spirit in Assurance of Salvation

From an early age, Wesley felt that a person should certainly be able to sense God's redemptive love in his or her life and know that he or she was a child of God.[30] How could you be forgiven and not know it? How could you be a child of God and not sense it? Much of the motivation for Wesley's own lifelong spiritual and theological quest came from his own search for this assurance of salvation.[31]

Wesley was jolted out of his traditional reliance upon his own "sincerity" as an indicator of assurance when he met Peter Böhler in 1738. This Moravian convinced him that a person was not a Christian until true faith was confirmed by an assurance of salvation that was accompanied by absence of fear, doubt, and sin and the presence of love, peace, and joy. For several years, Wesley struggled with this expectation until he realized that his own theological tradition provided the framework for a more suitable answer. In the process of sorting out the distinction between justification and sanctification, Wesley also came to realize that pardon could coexist with sin, that faith could stand beside doubt, and that both fear and joy were continuing parts of the Christian experience. Assurance of faith, or assurance of salvation, did not depend upon a constant absence or presence of any particular sin or virtue.

Wesley is somewhat unusual within the Anglican tradition of his day in his emphasis on the possibility of having an assurance of salvation. Indeed, when he followed the Moravian view that a person was not a Christian without this assurance, he was treated as a fanatic. Even when he discarded the view that such an experience was necessary, he continued to feel that assurance of salvation was the normal expectation of the Christian.

This assurance, however, was not a guarantee of final salvation or eternal blessedness. Wesley speaks of assurance of justification and assurance of sanctification, but not assurance of heaven. Assurance of faith was an indicator of one's relationship with God in the present moment. And God gave this information through the Holy Spirit. To use Wesley's terminology, "The Spirit of God bears witness with your spirit, that you are a child of God."[32] That is to say, God's active presence through the Holy Spirit enlightens the believer as to his or her present state of salvation.

The Perception of God's Active
Presence-Power-Influence by the Spiritual Senses

For Wesley, there are at least three ways by which a person can know or sense the active presence-power-influence of God in his or her life: through direct revelation, spiritual senses, or feeling. The first way is the direct testimony of the Holy Spirit to the believer's spirit that he or she is a child of God. This direct witness of the Spirit with the person's spirit implies a human capacity to perceive direct revelation. Wesley explains the phenomenon further: "The soul as intimately and evidently perceives when it loves, delights, and rejoices in God, as when it loves and delights in anything on earth. And it can no more doubt whether it loves, delights, and rejoices or no, than whether it exists or no." Wesley follows this statement with a syllogism: "He that now loves God, that delights and rejoices in him with an humble joy, an holy delight, and an obedient love, is a child of God. But I thus love, delight, and rejoice in God. Therefore, I am a child of God."[33] By this reasoning, one can receive assurance through the direct witness of the Spirit with his or her spirit or soul.

Another way Wesley described the consequences of the work of the Spirit in regeneration looks much more like the British empiricism that was prevalent in his day. This perception of the means of spiritual knowledge represents a fascinating conjunction of pneumatology and epistemology in terms that echo empirical philosophy. Wesley talks of the possibility of knowing the things of God, as well as our spiritual status, by means of "spiritual senses." Two sources in English thought provide a basis for this perspective. First, the pervasive philosophy of John Locke in the eighteenth century considered knowledge to be acquired through inductive reasoning based on sense perception. Second, the Book of Homilies speaks of spiritual senses whereby we can, in Scriptures, "see the whole Christ with the eye of faith," whereas if we lack faith, our bodily eyes cannot see him.[34] It is no surprise, then, that Wesley adopts this philosophical language and theological imagery to help explain his concept of attaining knowledge of God and the things of God as well as of assurance by means of the spiritual senses.

The spiritual senses are primarily sight and hearing, the eyes and ears. The spiritual senses play an important function in several areas. As we have noted, the enlightening work of the Holy Spirit is important in bringing the knowledge of good and evil through prevenient

99

grace. The Holy Spirit also "opens the eyes" of the person of faith upon regeneration, providing information to the believer that the unbeliever cannot know because of a continuing disablement of such sense perception.[35] Wesley explains this phenomenon rather extensively in his sermon "The New Birth," in which he uses the analogy of the newborn child. Before natural birth, the child has eyes and ears, but cannot see or hear (so Wesley understood). After birth, the eyes and ears are opened, and the child can see and hear. So also, when God opens the eyes of believers upon their "new birth," they are enabled "to see God and the things of God." Among other things, the believer "is now sensible of God":

> The Spirit or breath of God is immediately inspired, breathed into the new-born soul; and the same breath which comes from, returns to, God: As it is continually received by faith, so it is continually rendered back by love, by prayer, and praise, and thanksgiving; love, and praise, and prayer being the breath of every soul which is truly born of God. . . . "The eyes of his understanding" are now "open," and he "seeth Him that is invisible." . . . His ears are now opened, and the voice of God no longer calls in vain. . . . All his spiritual senses being now awakened, he has a clear intercourse with the invisible world.[36]

Part of Wesley's description of the new birth includes the "unlocking" of the spiritual senses by the Holy Spirit to allow for the communication of assurance: "[The believer's] ears being opened, he is now capable of hearing the inward voice of God, saying, 'Be of good cheer; thy sins are forgiven thee'; 'go and sin no more.' "[37]

Wesley sometimes uses a third way of talking about perceiving truth from God, utilizing the language of "feeling." In some instances, he talks about "feeling" in the same sense as "knowing."[38] One especially explicit use of this language comes in a moment of critical self-examination concerning his lack of assurance of salvation, about seven months after his Aldersgate experience. At this point, he had a strong sense that he was no longer a child of God and explains his reasoning:

> I have not any love of God. I do not love either the Father or the Son. Do you ask, How do I know whether I love God? I answer by another question, How do you know whether you love me? Why, as you know whether you are hot or cold. You *feel* this moment that you do or do not love me. And I *feel* this moment I do not love God, which therefore

I *know,* because I *feel* it. There is no word more proper, more clear, or more strong.[39]

In the same sense that one can know the lack of assurance through a negative feeling, so also a person can know the presence of God through feeling, as Wesley exhorted a friend: "O believe, and feel Him near!"[40] And describing the Christian who is enlivened by the Spirit in the new birth, Wesley again alludes to the Book of Homilies when he says:

> He "feels in his heart" (to use the language of our Church) "the mighty working of the Spirit of God." Not in a gross, carnal sense, as the men of the world stupidly and wilfully misunderstand the expression, though they have been told again and again, we mean thereby neither more nor less than this: he feels, is inwardly sensible of, the graces which the Spirit of God works in his heart. He feels, he is conscious of, a "peace which passeth all understanding." He many times feels such a joy in God as is "unspeakable, and full of glory." He feels "the love of God shed abroad in his heart by the Holy Ghost which is given unto him." And all his spiritual senses are then "exercised to discern" spiritual "good and evil." By the use of these he is daily increasing in the knowledge of God, of Jesus Christ whom he hath sent, and of all the things pertaining to his inward kingdom. And now he may be properly said *to live:* God having quickened him by his Spirit, he is alive to God through Jesus Christ.[41]

Wesley's reference to "graces" in this passage is not unusual. He frequently uses the term in the plural to refer to the beneficial consequences of God's active presence and power upon the life of the believer. These graces, sometimes called virtues, are "the fruit of the Spirit." The list of "this glorious constellation of graces" is familiar and usually includes "love, joy, peace, longsuffering, gentleness, goodness, fidelity, meekness, temperance."[42] Wesley occasionally links the terms "gifts and graces" as synonyms for "gifts of God's grace."[43] In all of these references to graces, there is, as the term implies, an essential relationship to the active presence of God as the continuing source of these virtues.

The Means of Grace

Traditional discussions of the means of grace generally focus on the role of the sacraments within the life of the church. Wesley's understanding of the concept of grace and the means of experiencing God's active presence opens up a broader scope to the idea of the "means."

Wesley defines the means of grace as "outward ordinances" (sometimes called "outward signs, words, or actions ordained by God") "whereby the inward grace of God is ordinarily conveyed to man."[44] Much of Wesley's early writing equates the "means of grace" with the "ordinances of God." Neither term, however, is synonymous with the sacraments. When Wesley specifies these ordinances, he never lists baptism. His usual list does include the Lord's Supper, along with fasting, prayer, going to church, reading the scriptures, and Christian conference.[45] These are the "ordinary channels" by which God conveys his grace to the souls of humankind.[46] That is to say, these are the usual means by which God's active presence and power comes into human lives. Although the Holy Spirit plays a crucial role in the means of grace, the trinitarian grounding of Wesley's understanding of grace is also apparent. He points out that effectiveness of all the "instituted" means of grace depends upon the presence and power of the Holy Spirit—there is no merit whatsoever in our just doing these things independently. But he also specifies that Christ alone is the only meritorious cause of any good that comes from our exercising the presence of God.[47]

By 1745, Wesley had begun to distinguish between these ordinances of God, or "particular" means of grace, and other actions that he designated "general" means of grace: "universal obedience; keeping all the commandments; self-denial, and taking up our cross."[48] The list of general means eventually broadened out into a larger constellation of activities he designated "prudential" means of grace,[49] which he sees as complementing the "instituted" (particular) means of grace, or ordinances of God. The prudential means of grace, as noted in the "Large" *Minutes* (1763) of the Methodist conference, include specific activities in four categories, which can be summarized as follows:

1) As common Christians, to follow rules and arts of holy living.
2) As Methodists, to attend society, class, and band meetings.
3) As Preachers, to meet weekly with the society and bands, with the leaders; to visit the sick and the well; and to instruct masters and parents.

4) As Assistants (superintending preachers), to regulate the bands, visit the societies, and write reports regularly.[50]

These activities are expanded in some detail in the *Minutes*. But in differentiating them from the "instituted" means of grace, he admits that they operate at a different level of expectation. In fact, he explained that they could be used without always bearing fruit, which is not the case with the last few items on the continuing list: "watching, denying ourselves, taking up our cross, exercise of the presence of God. . . . Never can you use these means, but a blessing will ensue."[51]

These prudential means of grace seem to be a somewhat conglomerate list that does not bear the mark of careful codification. As a young man, Wesley may have gotten this idea from either John Scott or John Norris, the Cambridge Platonist, both of whose works he read in early 1731.[52] Later that year, he explained to a friend that he understood prudential means of grace to be "whatever helps me to conquer vicious and [to] advance in virtuous affection."[53] The role of such helps continually changed, seen in the shifting lists of rules and directions for the societies. In a later apologia for the movement, Wesley noted that their continually shifting the list of "these little prudential helps" was not a weakness but a "peculiar advantage which we enjoy."

> By this means we declare them all to be merely prudential, not essential, not of divine institution. We prevent, so far as in us lies, their growing formal or dead. We are always open to instruction, willing to be wiser every day than we were before, and to change whatever we can change for the better.[54]

The important thing to notice is that Wesley also considered these "helps" to be means of grace. And the last item in the list of the prudential means is very telling of his overall understanding of grace: the exercise of the presence of God.

Wesley thus expanded the horizons of his people's view of grace as God's active presence and the various means by which that grace can be experienced. A further example of his expansive view can be seen in his sermon "On Visiting the Sick." After suggesting that we commonly limit the term "means of grace" to the "ordinances of God," which he points out are usually termed "works of piety," he asks, "Are they the only means of grace? Are there no other means than these, whereby God is pleased frequently, yea, ordinarily, to convey his grace to them that either love or fear him? Surely there are works of mercy, as well as works of piety, which are real means of grace."[55]

In this particular work of mercy, Wesley presses his people to visit the sick in person: don't send money, don't send a doctor, don't send food—go yourself, peer into their eyes, and look into their souls. Wesley knew that the sick were often the poor, and such visits would not be pleasant. But he encouraged skittish followers such as Miss March to "creep in among these in spite of dirt and an hundred disgusting circumstances, and thus put off the gentlewoman." He admitted that he himself would rather spend time with "genteel and elegant people," but he could not do so and imitate the life of Christ.[56] He also pointed out that although in such visits there may be a "thousand circumstances [that will] shock the delicacy of our nature," she will receive a blessing that "will more than balance the cross."[57] The nature and source of that blessing is God's grace. Such visits are a means of grace—an activity through which God's active presence and power is known and felt. As Wesley told Miss March, "Go and see the poor and sick in their own poor little hovels. . . . Jesus went before you, and will go with you."[58]

Conclusion

Wesley's theology is full of grace. Even at the points where he speaks explicitly of "working out our own salvation," he enunciates the basic idea that our "working" must be seen as enabled by grace.[59] The synergism that seems implicit in his view is really the story of God's presence enlightening a person to the need for God's presence, which then liberates the person from sin and empowers a loving response to God's presence. The human response of "faith working through love," exhibiting works of mercy and piety (which themselves are a means of grace), is made possible by God's empowering presence.

For Wesley, God's grace is to be understood as relational, active, and powerful—it is God's active presence and power with and within us. God's grace on humankind is enlightening, liberating, and empowering through its prevenient, justifying, and sanctifying effects. This presence can be known, both by the "witness of the Spirit" and through the "spiritual senses." And the long list of virtues (which

Wesley sometimes calls "graces"), which are gifts of God's grace, such as love, peace, joy, humility, also provide evidence of the transforming presence and power of God in human life.

This view of grace, though never explicitly drawn out by Wesley, is fully in keeping with virtually every use of the term by him. In more traditional theological language, these uses demonstrate that he understands grace to be a divine disposition toward humankind (unmerited favor and mercy) that is actively self-giving in love (incarnation and atonement) and manifest by God's active presence and power (or influence, through the Holy Spirit) in human life. Grace is God's love present with humankind, recognizing the disposition, purpose, manner, and power of that loving divine presence. Or put more simply, grace is "God with us." Although this terminology brings to mind Isaiah's prophecy of the coming "Emmanuel," associated by Christians with Jesus,[60] the phrase must be seen in its trinitarian context: God with us at creation, God become flesh with us in Jesus Christ, God continuing to be with us through the Holy Spirit, to enlighten, liberate, and empower us.

Wesley's writings are full of references to "the presence and power of God," his journal frequently records that "the power of God was present with us," and his conclusions often state, "God was with us of a truth." He is speaking of the reality of God's grace, the active presence and power of God manifest in human lives. A complex theological idea resolves into a simple rhetorical phrase that evinces a powerful divine reality, recognized by Wesley on his deathbed when he said, "The best of all is, God is with us."

Notes

1. Even his own publication of *A Complete English Dictionary* (London: 1753) omits "grace."
2. See esp. Randy L. Maddox, *Responsible Grace: John Wesley's Practical Theology* (Nashville: Kingswood Books, 1994); Kenneth J. Collins, *The Scripture Way of Salvation: The Heart of John Wesley's Theology* (Nashville: Abingdon Press, 1997); and Theodore Runyon, *The New Creation: John Wesley's Theology Today* (Nashville: Abingdon Press, 1998).
3. Albert Outler was fond of referring to Wesley's "mediating" position as a "third alternative," whereas in fact it more often than not reflected Wesley's understanding of the basic Anglican mediative position.
4. John Wesley, *Journal and Diaries II,* ed. W. Reginald Ward and Richard P. Heitzenrater, in *The Bicentennial Edition of the Works of John Wesley* (Nashville: Abingdon Press, 1984–), 19:96 (Sept. 13, 1739); hereinafter cited as *Works*. He did, of course, acknowledge that he differed in significant ways from those clergy who differed (without knowing or admitting it) from church doctrine, namely those who did *not* distinguish sanctification from justification or saw sanctification as *prior* (rather than subsequent) to justification, those who claimed

that *our* holiness (rather than Christ's) is the cause of our justification, those who felt that *good works* (rather than faith alone) were a condition of justification, and those who viewed sanctification as an *outward* (rather than inward) thing.

5. To one critic, Wesley responded, "I still maintain 'the Bible, with the Liturgy and Homilies of our Church, and do not espouse any other principles but what are consonant to the Book of Common-Prayer.' You keenly answer, 'Granted, Mr. Methodist—but whether or no you *would not* espouse other principles, if you durst, is evident from some *innovations* you have already introduced' " (Letter " To the Editor of Lloyd's Evening Post" [Dec. 20, 1760], *Journal and Diaries IV*, in *Works* 21:292).

6. Esp. articles X, Of Free-Will, and XVII, Of Predestination.

7. Article XXV, Of the Sacraments.

8. Article XIII, Of Works Before Justification.

9. Richard Hooker, *Of the Laws of Ecclesiastical Polity* (London: Dent, 1964), 2:500 (Appendix to Part V). In the same section, Hooker uses slightly different terminology to explain these three kinds of grace: God's "undeserved love and favour, or his offered means of outward instruction and doctrine; or thirdly, that grace which worketh inwardly in men's hearts" (2:498).

10. Ibid., 2:504.

11. Wesley is not unusual in using the term within these two different sorts of categories. Hooker, as we have seen, uses grace in both of these senses. Aquinas ties the meanings more closely together when he speaks of grace as not only a divine disposition and power-action but also a quality that exists in the human soul (grace and "infused virtues" being different aspects of one identical essence); Thomas Aquinas, *Nature and Grace*, trans. and ed. A. M. Fairweather (Philadelphia: Westminster, 1954), 161. Hooker felt that Thomas went too far in considering grace an inherent quality or formal habit that causes human-kind's virtuous actions to be meritorious, even though Thomas himself was trying to protect the doctrine of sanctification from the charge of Pelagianism (*Ecclesiastical Polity*, 2:505).

12. First John 4:8, 16. V. 8: "He that loveth not knoweth not God; for God is love." V. 16: "God is love; and he that dwelleth in love dwelleth in God, and God in him" (KJV).

13. Wesley presents God "as intimately concerned with us and actively involved with even the minutiae of our lives. Thus, his view of God is mostly relational" (Daniel J. Luby, *The Perceptibility of Grace in the Theology of John Wesley: A Roman Catholic Consideration* [Rome: S. Thomae, 1994], 74).

14. The medieval question of how many angels can sit on the head of a pin is actually, in Thomist terms, a question of how many angels can act upon, or exert a power upon, the head of a pin. And since they do not take up space, the answer is, an infinite number.

15. Wesley follows more in the line of Aquinas and Hooker (more Aristotelian) than Augustine and Luther (more Platonic) in terms of epistemological and anthropological views that apply to the state of "natural man."

16. In different settings, Wesley makes use of various traditional views of the atonement: satisfaction (Anselm), ransom (Augustine), and moral example (Abelard). See Colin Williams, *John Wesley's Theology Today* (Nashville/New York: Abingdon Press, 1960), 77-89; see also Collins, *Scripture Way of Salvation*, 80-86.

17. Sermon 20, "The Lord Our Righteousness," 1.4, 2.9, in *Works*, 1:453, 457.

18. This Arminian view of the co-operant nature of grace might also be seen as reflecting a pre-Augustinian or non-Western (Eastern) view that takes this synergism for granted. See Maddox, *Responsible Grace*, 147-52.

19. Sermon 44, "Original Sin," 2.2, in *Works*, 2:176 -77.

20. Sermon 80, "On Friendship with the World," 4, in *Works*, 3:129. See also Sermon 12, " The Witness of Our Own Spirit," 18: " The joy of a Christian does not arise from any *blindness of conscience*, from his not being able to discern good from evil. So far from it, that he was an utter stranger to this joy, till the eyes of his understanding were opened [Eph 1:18], that he knew it not, until he had spiritual senses, fitted to discern spiritual good and evil" (*Works*, 1:311).

21. Such a sensible recognition is necessary for true repentance of sin, both before and after justification. See Sermon 13, "On Sin in Believers," 3.7, in *Works*, 1:323.

22. Wesley's definition of faith is twofold: (1) using terminology found in the Book of Homilies: "a sure trust and confidence in God that, through the merits of Christ, [a person's] sins are forgiven and he reconciled to the favor of God" (e.g., Sermon 18, "Marks of the New Birth," 1.3, in *Works*, 1:418); (2) using terminology of the book of Hebrews, "a divine evidence and conviction of things unseen" (e.g., Sermon 106, "On Faith," 1, in *Works*, 3:492).

23. Sermon 43, "The Scripture Way of Salvation," 2.2, in *Works*, 2:162. These works represent "works of piety," distinguished from "works of mercy" that are usually viewed as the focus of the concept, good works. He does, however, see both types as being possible only by God's grace and thus both as being channels or "means of grace" (see below for more). See Sermon 16, "The Means of Grace," in *Works*, 1:381.

24. Again, Wesley has been seen as combining the forensic view of early Western (Roman) Christianity with the therapeutic view of early Eastern (Greek) Christianity (see Maddox, *Responsible Grace*, 84-86). But this combination is neither new nor unique with Wesley—it is a natural part of his combined Anglican and holy living stance.

25. See Geoffrey Wainwright, *Methodists in Dialogue* (Nashville: Kingswood Books, 1995), 157. It is difficult to generalize Wesley's usage, here and elsewhere, because it depends so much on the context. In a pamphlet recounting a discourse between a predestinarian and his friend, Wesley is willing to have the friend defend "inherent righteousness" against the predestinarian's singular position of imputed righteousness.

26. Sermon 45, 2.4, in *Works*, 2:193.

27. Sermon 12, 15, in *Works*, 1:309. See also his references "the grace or power of the Holy Ghost," which seem to equate the two (" The Means of Grace," 2.6, in 1:383; " The Spirit of Bondage and of Adoption," 3.1, in 1:260.

28. *Journal and Diaries II* (Nov. 24, 1739), in *Works*, 19:123.

29. See also Sermon 25, "Sermon on the Mount V," 3.9, in *Works*, 1:560, and one of his favorite seals, which is inscribed "Believe, Love, Obey"; *Wesley and the People Called Methodists* (Nashville: Abingdon Press, 1995), xiii.

30. "Surely these graces are not of so little force as that we can't perceive whether we have 'em or not: . . . certainly we must be sensible of it" (Letter to Susanna Wesley [June 18, 1725], in *Works*, 25:169-70).

31. See my article "Great Expectations," which goes into this question in some detail up to 1739. *Mirror and Memory* (Nashville: Abingdon Press, 1989), 106-49.

32. This is actually scriptural language (Rom 8:16 —" The Spirit itself beareth witness with our spirit, that we are the children of God"). Wesley quotes or alludes to this verse nearly three dozen times in his sermons alone and used it for the text of two sermons on the witness of the Spirit (*Works*, 4:673).

33. Sermon 10, "Witness of the Spirit," 1.11, in *Works*, 1:275-76.

34. "An Information for Them which Take Offense at Certaine Places of Holy Scripture," in *Certaine Sermons or Homilies* (London: Bill, 1623), 145.

35. Wesley's imagery is usually of "opening" the eyes and ears, thus enabling latent ("sleeping") powers of spiritual sight and hearing, in keeping with the Thomist-Hooker line of theological anthropology and the "disordered" view of human nature after the fall. Although Wesley does point out that having spiritual senses that are not awake is in effect the same as having none at all (Sermon 45, "The New Birth," 2.4, in *Works*, 2:192), he does occasionally refer to having no spiritual senses and needing "new senses," which implies a different, more Augustinian anthropology of natural man, whose nature must be totally re-created by grace. See Sermon 3, "Awake, Thou That Sleepest" (Charles Wesley's sermon), 1.1, in *Works*, 1:142; Sermon 119, "Walking by Sight and Walking by Faith," 2, in *Works*, 4:49; Sermon 132, "On Faith," 18, in *Works*, 4:200; Sermon 130, "On Living without God," 14, in *Works*, 4:174. For Wesley's theological epistemology, see Rex D. Matthews, " 'Religion and Reason Joined': A Study in the Theology of John Wesley," Ph.D. dissertation (Harvard, 1986), 247-312.

36. Sermon 19, "The Great Privilege of Those that are Born of God" (1748), I.8-10; in *Works*, 1:434-35; see also II.1: "One who is born of God . . . continually receives into his soul the breath of life from God, the gracious influence of his Spirit, and continually renders it back; . . . by faith perceives the continual actings of God upon his spirit, and by a kind of

spiritual re-action returns the grace he receives, in unceasing love, and praise, and prayer" (*Works*, 1:435-36); and Sermon 45, "The New Birth," II.4, in *Works*, 2:192-93.

37. Sermon 45, "The New Birth," 2.4, in *Works*, 2:192-93.

38. See Matthews, "Religion and Reason Joined," 336-40.

39. *Journal and Diaries II* (Jan. 4, 1739), *Works*, 19:30, Wesley's italics.

40. Letter to Miss Damaris Perronet, in *The Letters of John Wesley*, ed. John Telford (London: Epworth, 1931), 5:234; hereinafter cited as *Letters* (Telford).

41. Sermon 45, "The New Birth," 2.4, in *Works*, 2:193.

42. See Gal 5:22-23, as translated in Wesley's *Explanatory Notes upon the New Testament* (London: 1755). Sermon 76, "On Perfection," 1.6, in *Works*, 3:75.

43. The usual combination is "gifts and grace," as in the questions for examining Methodist preachers, where he asks, "Do they have gifts (as well as grace) for the work?" *Minutes of the Methodist Conferences* (London: Mason, 1862), 1:31 (1746), 564-65 ("Large" Minutes).

44. *Journal and Diaries II* (Nov. 10, 1739), in *Works*, 19:121; and Sermon 16, "The Means of Grace," 2.1, where their purpose is described as "to be the *ordinary* channels whereby [God] might convey to men, preventing, justifying, or sanctifying grace" (*Works*, 1:381). Wesley reveals another concern when, in the *Appeal to Men of Reason and Religion*, he indicates that one of the "fixed rules" (i.e., General Rules) of the Methodist societies was "that every member attend the ordinances of God; i.e., *do not divide from the Church*" (*Works*, 11:83).

45. E.g., see lists in his *Journal* (Apr. 21, 1741, in *Works*, 19:146), the *General Rules* and *Directions given to the Band Societies* (in *Works*, 9:73, 79). See also Acts 2:42. Ole Borgen notes that Wesley lists at least two of these ordinances in 68 places in his works. The frequency of each within these lists is as follows: prayer, 61; Lord's Supper, 59; reading or hearing the Word, 54; fasting, 29; Christian conference, 28 (his calculations seem to have subsumed "going to church" under one or more of these other categories). (*John Wesley on the Sacraments* [Nashville/New York: Abingdon Press, 1972], 106).

46. In Sermon 16, "The Means of Grace" (2.1), Wesley is more specific: the ordinances are God's ordinary channels of conveying to humankind "preventing, justifying, or sanctifying grace" (*Works*, 1:382).

47. Sermon 16, "The Means of Grace," 2.2, 4, in *Works*, 1:381-83. In that sense, Christ could be said to be the only means of grace.

48. *Minutes*, 1:10-11 (1745), cf. 562-63.

49. *A Plain Account of Christian Perfection*, in *The Works of John Wesley*, ed. Thomas Jackson (Grand Rapids: Zondervan, 1959), 11:402.

50. See *Minutes*, 1:548-57.

51. *Minutes*, 1:554-57. What he had previously noted as "general" means have now become a subcategory under the "prudential" means of grace.

52. Wesley's diary records that he read Scott's *Christian Life* in March and April 1731, and began Norris's *Treatise concerning Christian Prudence* on June 10. Wesley's first use of the distinction between "instituted" and "prudential" means was in a letter to his mother the following day, June 11. Norris's distinction between means "such as are appointed and commended by God" and "such as are recommended by human prudence" is his own self-acknowledged expansion of Scott's description of means as arising either "by institution" or "naturally." See Norris (London: Manship, 1710), 258; and Scott (London: Kettilby, 1694), 33. Wesley published an abridgement of this work in 1734 (often republished). In his later listings of "instituted" and "prudential" means, Wesley follows Norris's first category fairly closely, but is very flexible in the second.

53. Letter to Mrs. Pendarves (July 19, 1731), in *Works*, 25:294; see also letter to his brother Samuel (Sept. 1731), ibid., 321-22. In June 1731, he had noted to his mother that the Oxford Methodists had been criticized for being "too strict in religion," which seemed mainly to entail "laying too much stress on the instituted means of grace" and "the multiplying prudential means upon ourselves so far . . . as to obstruct the end we aimed at by them." Letter to Susanna Wesley (June 11, 1731, ibid., 283). The desired goals at that point were their "advance in heavenly affections in general" or their "progress in some particular virtue."

54. *A Plain Account of the People Called Methodists*, in *Works*, 9:262-63.

55. Sermon 98, "On Visiting the Sick" (1786), 1, in *Works*, 3:385. See also Sermon 92, "On Zeal," 2.5, in *Works*, 3:313.

56. Letter to Miss March (Feb. 7, 1776), *Letters* (Telford), 6:207.

57. Letter to Miss March (Feb. 26, 1776), *Letters* (Telford), 6:209.

58. Letter to Miss March (June 9, 1775), *Letters* (Telford), 6:153.

59. "Inasmuch as God works in you, you are now able to work out your own salvation. . . . Secondly, God worketh in you; therefore you *must* work" (Sermon 85, "On Working Out Our Own Salvation," 3.5, 7, in *Works*, 3:207-8).

60. Isa 7:14; Matt 1:23. Thomas A. Langford has pointed out that "Jesus Christ is the definitive but not the exclusive expression of grace" ("Grace as Giver," unpublished manuscript).

AFTER WESLEY:
The Middle Period (1791–1849)

JAMES C. LOGAN

With pageantry and fanfare United Methodism celebrated the bicentennial of its founding in 1984. In the midst of the celebrative programs and pronouncements more sober reflections could be discerned. The General Conference meeting that year received, in the form of resolutions, calls from various quarters of the church to address the nagging problem of the church's confused sense of identity. One commentator observed, "United Methodism ended its second century with all the clarity of a wiperless windshield in the middle of a storm."[1]

Two resolutions in particular requested the formation of study commissions to deal with the theological and missional identity of the church. In their 1988 reports the work of these study commissions sounded strikingly similar notes. The commissions anchored the theological and missional identity of the church firmly in the Wesleyan view of the threefoldness of divine grace: "God's grace goes before us (prevenience), God's grace comes among us uniquely in the person of Jesus Christ (justification), and God's grace abides with us restoring our lives to an unrelenting love for God and neighbor (sanctification)."[2]

Rarely in the history of the people who claim John Wesley as their spiritual forebear and guide can be found as consistent and probing a statement of the Wesleyan mission of grace as was the mission commission's report, *Grace Upon Grace*. The missional vision as given

111

to the church unfolded in a characteristically Wesleyan logical fashion as (a) lives changed by grace, (b) a church formed by grace, and (c) a world transformed by grace.[3] One of the best-kept secrets in the church is that Thomas Langford was the principal author of the statement!

Approximately two hundred years earlier, 1786 –87 to be exact, the eighty-three-year-old Wesley undertook a final arduous and extended visitation of the Methodist societies and chapels in England, Ireland, and the Channel Islands. After fifty years of the revival the old man wanted to see how his children were faring. After surveying what he had seen and heard, he was not altogether pleased with the picture. In the little Oxfordshire village of Witney he penned his assessment.[4]

Focusing on Isaiah 5:4 ("What could have been done more to my vineyard, that I have not done in it? wherefore, when I looked that it should bring forth grapes, brought it forth wild grapes?"), Wesley addressed his people with what could be called his valedictory. Repeatedly he raised the question, "What could have been done in this vineyard which God hath not done in it?" Regarding doctrine? Regarding spiritual helps? Regarding discipline? Regarding outward protection?

In autobiographical style, Wesley reminded his people that he had passionately proclaimed and taught the scriptural message of justification, new birth, and sanctification—the gospel of grace as divine favor which pardons and divine power which transforms human character. Surely his people knew that "God has joined these together, and it is not for man to put them asunder . . . being as tenacious of inward holiness as any mystic, and of outward as any Pharisee."[5] He had supplied them with the spiritual helps of a system of itinerant preachers and a structure of local societies and class meetings.

As for discipline the old preacher reminded them that it was he who had codified for and given to the classes the disciplines whereby they could continue their journey of growing in grace. Surely they knew the marks of grace upon their lives individually and collectively: " 'doing no harm,' 'doing good,' 'attending upon all the ordinances of God.' "[6] In spite of opposition by persons in places high and low his preachers and local followers had abundant reason to praise God. "Through many dangers, toils, and snares" God had protected them and brought forth "a new thing in the earth."[7]

Wesley had discovered that his people had grown cool in their ardor of grace. Where once their hearts had burned within them with the grace of regeneration, now what modern sociologists call a "routinization of the Spirit" (Max Weber) had settled upon some while fanatical enthusiasm and heated imagination had seized others. The consequence was that they were now manifesting "all direful fruits, not of the Holy Spirit, but of the bottomless pit."[8] And in his mind he knew precisely the reason such had happened. That "grand poison of souls" had taken its toll—"the increase in goods," "the love of the world," "taking pleasure in the praise of men," "laying up treasures on earth." The crisis in the societies and chapels was nothing less than a crisis of grace. Where once they had known in the depths of their beings a conversion "by grace and grace alone," many had been seduced by a conversion to prosperity. On the other hand, for some their conversion by grace had become a license for flights of speculation and fanciful visions without the discipline of the society and class meeting. The gospel of responsible grace—grace going before and working in and through sinners so that they grow into the mind which was in Christ Jesus—was threatened on right and left.

The Wesleyans After Wesley

Contrary to Wesley's hopes and prayers, the period immediately following his death in 1791 was not as he had envisaged. Already the American Methodists, with his blessing in this case, had become a separate denomination. The same was to happen with the Wesleyan Connection in Britain. He had labored as best he could to ensure an organizational transition by providing for the "Legal Hundred," whereby the connection of preachers and societies would have a cohesive system of administration. Earlier he had sought to secure a doctrinal consensus on matters such as free universal grace, human agency empowered by prevenient grace, and salvation through Christ's justifying and sanctifying grace by drafting the *Model Deed*, which prescribed that preaching in the chapels must conform with the doctrines set forth in his *Sermons* and *Notes*. His plaintive cry of 1787, "What could have been done more in my vineyard?" could well have been his postmortem response.

Following his death, Wesley's successors faced challenges from within and from without the connection. Issues of internal order and discipline consumed much of their time. The wider societal context presented them with another agenda, a dual agenda, of defending themselves against the charges of dangerous fanatical sectarianism while at the same time offering a rationale for the separate existence apart from the Anglican Church.

The 1791 Conference reported a membership of 72,476, which continued to grow until 1820 when for the first time a membership decline was noted with some alarm. From outward appearances the organizational structure of conference and itinerancy which Wesley had prescribed had served them well even with the reported drop in membership. Wesleyan Methodists claimed in 1820 a membership of over 200,000. The organizational structure appeared to be relatively stable, though several "cracks" had occurred in the form of schisms or dismissals. No challenge surfaced regarding doctrine. Apparently Wesley had succeeded in securing the doctrinal distinctiveness of the Methodists. This was no doubt due as much to Charles' hymns as John's sermons. Methodists continued to sing with vigor, "And can it be that I should gain an interest in the Saviour's blood." For years the only theological controversies in the connection and in Conference hardly touched the Wesleyan "way of salvation."

Wesley had had his moments when he feared that difficulties might arise in the future. In the same year that he had undertaken his long journey around the circuits of societies and chapels, he expressed his fear, "I am afraid, lest they should only exist as a dead sect, having the form of religion without the power." [9] With the Model Deed of 1763, designed to be used in settling the property associated with the meetinghouses, the doctrinal boundaries within which the Methodist preachers would be held accountable were set forth. "Provided always, that the said persons preach no other doctrine than is contained in Mr. Wesley's *Notes Upon the New Testament,* and four volumes of *Sermons.*"[10] While only minimal doctrinal requirements governed the entering of the class (the desire to flee from the wrath to come), within the classes and societies there were definite doctrinal standards to govern teaching and preaching. A short, popularized New Testament commentary and a collection of sermons may have seemed to be peculiar guides to doctrinal standards. The clause in the Model Deed seemed to have worked. The Methodists were known by their ex-pressed faith in a universal grace accessible to all, prevenient grace working in all and enabling all to repent and rely in faith upon Christ who was their justification and sanctification. Although zeal for evangelical outreach was already waning before Wesley's death, his successors did not question the rightness of his doctrine.

Great challenges nevertheless confronted Wesley's people. These challenges lay more in the arena of polity than of doctrine. How were the Methodists to secure their identity as a distinct body among the dissenting bodies outside Anglicanism? How were they to resolve the growing tensions between laity and preachers? In a time of general social unrest how could they project themselves as a "respectable" people supporting the common order rather than being viewed as a threat to it?

Within less than twenty years following his death Wesley's people began to experience in overt form these tensions becoming breaks and divisions. The dissension and separations that occurred in British Methodism in the nineteenth century, and to a considerable extent similarly in North American Methodism, were focused upon polity rather than doctrine. In 1797 the Methodist New Connexion under the leadership of Alexander Kilham was established. The dividing issue was not doctrine but polity—the further extension of lay representation and voice in the movement. The Kilhamite movement foreshadowed the Methodist Protestant protest in the United States in 1828–30. When in 1806 the Independent Methodists emerged out of a series of "cottage meetings," these "independent" or "Quaker" Methodists claimed the rights of local church autonomy. Again, the issue was polity with the "independents" advocating congregational rather than connectional polity. The most colorful chapter in the story of dissension among the Methodists concerns the Primitive Methodists, who were expelled from Conference in 1807 and had established themselves as a separate people by 1811. Arising from the working-class coal miners in Cheshire, these "primitives" harked back to precedents in Wesley's revival—earnest evangelism, field preaching, and enthusiastic singing in the streets (for which they were labeled "Ranters"). In 1807 the eccentric American revivalist, Lorenzo Dow, preached at a meeting on an unremarkable hilltop in Cheshire and encouraged the leaders of the Primitive Methodists, Hugh Bourne and William Clowes, to employ the camp meeting as a chief means of evangelism. The Methodist Conference in the same year ruled, "It is our judgment, that even supposing such meetings to be allowable in America, they are highly improper in England, and likely to be productive of considerable mischief, and we disclaim all connexion with them."[11] Again, the dividing issue was not doctrine but polity and practice.

An account of a Primitive Methodist preaching service attests to the Wesleyan theological character of the message:

> The Sermon—who shall describe it? it was a Sermon to be heard, not to be reported. What a mixture of humour, passionate appeal, thrilling exhortations and apposite illustrations it was. . . . Laughter and tears this preacher commanded at will, and when he closed with heart-searching appeals to the unconverted to fly to the Cross of pardon, one almost wondered that men and women did not spring to their feet and rush somewhere—anywhere, exclaiming with Bunyan's Pilgrim, "Life, Life, Eternal Life!" The service was over, and, with the remembrance of that sermon as a life-long legacy, we retraced our steps homeward, stronger for having sat at the feet of this rugged Elijah of the coalpit, a hewer of coals for six days down in the deep dark mine, and a very flame of fire on the seventh.[12]

The Primitive Methodists for a time captured something of the Wesleyan revival which the Methodism Conference had nearly lost—namely, a passion for the economically lower class. Later in their history they, too, would experience rising prosperity among their members with a concomitant loss of much of their initial evangelical spirit.

The same narrative line continued across the nineteenth century. The controversies and splits among the Methodists centered on matters of polity and practice, not doctrine. Probably the most noted doctrinal controversy within the first decade of the nineteenth century centered on Adam Clarke, the biblical scholar and commentator. The most direct statement of his position is expressed in his note on Luke 1:35: "I am the more firmly established in the opinion advanced on Matt. 1:20 that the rudiments of the human nature of Christ was a real creation in the womb of the Virgin, by the energy of the Spirit of God."[13] He, therewith, denied the "eternal Sonship of Jesus." What was at stake for Clarke was an unqualified affirmation of the divinity of Christ, or else the atonement was called into question. Clarke's problem was not with "Sonship" but with "eternality." "If Christ be the Son of God as to his divine nature, then he cannot be eternal; for son implies a father; and father implies, in reference to son, precedency in time, if not in nature too."[14] Clarke sought to defend a high Christology in which Jesus was of a divine, "eternal and unoriginate nature." Anything short of this affirmation fell into Arianism terminating in Socinianism, and from Socinianism into Deism. Considerable controversy, to say nothing of confusion, followed Clarke's venture in Christology. What is interesting to note is that Clarke's theological sensitivities were similar to Wesley's in that he sought a high Christology for the sake of the atonement. The controversy was aired in Conference, and Clarke agreed neither to speak nor publish on the issue again. Wesleyan soteriology of grace had not been questioned and remained intact.

On the level of Conference, the Wesleyan standards remained unquestioned. Did the message of free grace engender a gracious piety so pervasive that doctrinal controversy simply did not arise? Or did the preoccupation with polity controversies obscure divergences in doctrine among his people? Perhaps no single or simple answer can be given.

Although officially and in practice the Wesleyan doctrine of grace prevailed, one factor affecting the passion with which it was held and propagated must be noted. Wesley's people were rising on the ladder of social and economic respectability. A. D. Gilbert notes, taking a sample from a number of nonparochial registers from 1830 to 1837 of the Wesleyan Connection, only one-fourth of the membership consisted of those in the classification of laborers, colliers, miners, and other occupations. Seventy-five percent of the membership comprised merchants, manufacturers, shopkeepers, farmers, and artisans.[15] In the revival Wesley had sensed an integral relationship between the message of grace and its reception by the poor and marginalized. He wrote in a letter, "I love the poor; in many of them I find pure, genuine grace, unmixed with paint, folly, and affectation."[16] The poor were not only the recipients of grace, but they became instruments of grace, indeed "means of grace," to Wesley and his followers. The passion for grace and the passion for the poor were fused into one evangelical ministry. By 1830 the Methodists were on the move "upward," and the particular ministry with the poor was being replaced by other concerns, namely, respectability. The remark of Jabez Bunting, four times elected president of Conference and for six years secretary of Conference, is indicative: "Methodism hates democracy as much as it hates sin."[17] The Primitive Methodists for a period were captivated by the passion of grace for the poor particularly among the colliers of Cheshire, Durham, and Northumberland. Mostly the Wesleyan Methodists, however, exemplified a laissez-faire attitude toward the social and economic ferment of the times, particularly as this related to the Chartist cause and the rise of the labor movement and unionism.

Wesley's analysis of his societies in 1787 had been prophetic. The gaining of wealth seemed to go hand-in-glove with the cooling of the passions of grace.

The Theologians After Wesley

The absence of notable debate about doctrine in Conference and through the connection does not give the full picture. There were theological minds who devoted more reflective consideration to theological issues. Even within Wesley's own time, he was not the only reflective theologian. It is a mistake to think that Mr. Wesley carried the full theological load during the revival.

The saintly vicar of Madley, John Fletcher (1729–1785), is a prime illustration to the contrary. So close was the personal relationship between Wesley and Fletcher that Wesley asked him to be his successor designate. Fletcher was particularly valuable to Wesley and the revival when the Calvinistic controversy became heated in the 1770s. Fletcher rose to defend Wesley of the charge of "works righteousness" made by the Calvinists in reference to Wesley's remarks in the 1770 conference of preachers. Wesley and Fletcher were one in their insistence upon the universality of grace accessible to all persons and on the grace-empowered will to respond to the message of justifying and sanctifying grace. Fletcher's *Checks to Antinomianism*[18] was the most able and staunchest defense of Wesley's theology in Wesley's own lifetime.

Although they were of one mind on the basic configuration of the doctrine of threefold grace, tension arose at several other points in Fletcher's thought. In the "fifth check," Fletcher seems to indicate that Pentecost (Acts 2) is the scriptural paradigm for sanctification. At Pentecost, he says, the disciples are filled with the Holy Spirit or "receive the Holy Spirit." For Wesley the entire threefold reality of grace rested upon a christological foundation. Grace is singular because Christ is uniquely singular. Fletcher seemed to shift the reality of sanctifying grace from Wesley's christological base to a pneuma-tological base. Wesley sensed this shift and wrote to Fletcher:

> It seems our views of Christian Perfection are a little different, though not opposite. It is certain every babe in Christ has received the Holy Ghost, and the Spirit witnesses with his spirit that he is a child of God. But he has not obtained Christian perfection.[19]

Apparently the two decided that a united front in the revival was of greater consequence, and the issue was not publicized widely during Wesley's lifetime. Fletcher, however, is even more emphatic when on March 7, 1778, he writes to Mary Bosanquet, "I would distinguish more exactly between the believer baptized with the Pentecostal power of the Holy Ghost, and the believer who, like the Apostles after our Lord's ascension, is not yet filled with that power."[20]

More definitive and decisive in this intratheological discussion within the revival was the posthumous publication of Fletcher's *Portrait of St. Paul*.[21] Here Fletcher spells out more clearly his doctrine of dispensations which he mentions in the *Checks*. For Fletcher, history was divided into three dispensations according to the trinitarian distinctions of Father, Son, and Spirit. These dispensations have both a divine and human side. For example, the dispensation of the Spirit begins with the effusion of the Spirit at Pentecost and focuses forward to the return of Christ. From the human side, that is the human response, this is both the time and experience of full sanctification. Here it is obvious that Fletcher had shifted the grace of sanctification to a pneumatological base. Wesley, too, wrote of dispensations or covenants, but he was making the attempt to distinguish between the "covenant of works" and the "covenant of grace."

Wesley and Fletcher remained close allies, but for later times Fletcher's notion of dispensations and "a separate work of the Holy Spirit" in addition to regeneration would become a very sensitive issue for the Methodists. Fletcher's work became very important by the mid–nineteenth century when the holiness revivals were under way. On the American scene Fletcher's *Checks* figured prominently on the Conference Course of Studies for pastors and soon-to-be pastors in the Methodist Episcopal Church. In fact, on the Course of Studies bibliographies Fletcher and Richard Watson were featured as prominently as Wesley himself! In effect what Fletcher seems to have done was to divide the Wesleyan order of grace into two discernible experiences: regeneration and entire sanctification. One is what Christ does for the believer, and the other is what the Holy Spirit does in and through the believer. Of course, Wesley too had spoken of entire sanctification as instantaneous, but he did not separate the instantaneous sanctification from the continuing process of sanctification. Wesley's strong trinitarian convictions would not permit him to separate the work of Christ and the work of the Holy Spirit. The grace of justification and sanctification is the act of the triune God in Jesus Christ through the Holy Spirit. For Wesley the logic of the tri-unity of the Godhead is one with the logic of the tri-unity of the grace of Christ.

The distinction of being Methodism's first systematic theologian belongs to Richard Watson (1781–1833). In 1823 the first edition of his *Theological Institutes* appeared in London, and over the remaining years of the nineteenth century this work would have a dominant influence on Methodists on both sides of the Atlantic.[22] When one opens the *Institutes,* one is immediately impressed with the fact that here is a theological world different from Wesley's. Watson sought to be a faithful Wesleyan in practice and in thought. His practice, however, would give more evidence of his Wesleyanism than did his thought. He differed little with Wesley in his soteriology as contained in the second volume of the *Institutes.* Yet the spirit of the volumes and the extended theological prolegomenon of the first volume reveal that distance between the two is not simply a temporal distinction of thirty years but a profoundly different understanding of theological method.

Watson's program was to deduce from Scripture the full range of Christian theological belief. To this end he begins with a defense of the veracity of the scriptural word. For more than one-hundred-fifty pages he expounds the four categories of evidence for scriptural authority: "presumptive," "external," "internal," and "collateral." These "evidences" or "proofs" are argued without recourse to any reference to the dual role of the Holy Spirit in the inspiration of both the writing and receiving of the scriptural message. Nowhere do we find references to the confirmation of the scriptural word in human experience through the witness of the Spirit. Watson's attempt was to establish the authority of scriptural revelation on purely rational grounds. An examination of M'Clintock's "copious index" reveals not a single entry in the two volumes of the word "experience."

That which follows is a long discussion of the existence and attributes of the Godhead with a clearly defined and rationally defended preference for the philosophical argument of "First Cause." The divine attributes of unity, spirituality, eternity, omnipotence, omnipresence, omniscience, immutability, wisdom, goodness, and holiness are then explicated without a reference to the defining revelation of God in Jesus Christ. What has happened to the christocentric revelation which Wesley expounded? So committed was Watson to the propositional revelation of scripture and to its rational defense and exposition that he allowed the doctrine of God to stand without its controlling criterion of the life, death, and resurrection of Jesus Christ.

What are we to make of this? It would not be fair to claim that Watson was purely a rationalist attempting to offer intellectual proof of scriptural revelation. Watson held that reason is one of the human faculties distinguishing humans from other forms of life. Related to revelation, reason is "regulated" or "enlightened" by revelation. Nevertheless, in his prolegomenon Watson's overarching concern was to present an apologia for revelation to meet the questions of the intelligentsia of his times. Contrary to Wesley's "practical divinity" as an attempt to win the hearts of his hearers, Watson's approach was an apologetics to command the minds of his readers. In an assessment of the power of reason Wesley and Watson may not have been far from each other. In the method of their employment of reason one is an evangelist and the other an apologist.

Langford has recently argued convincingly that Wesley's theological method was a dialectical one seeking to keep in tension the message and its context.[23] In the case of Watson, context seems to have gained the upper hand over message. Where Wesley sought a dialectical partnership between experience and revelation, in Watson the intellectual context governed by rational evidence and proof became the "dominant partner."

As a Wesleyan, Watson offered an exposition of soteriology marked with the Wesleyan distinctiveness of justification-sanctification. Little difference between Wesley and Watson appeared in their understandings of the atonement and the working of divine grace. What is interesting to observe, however, is that Watson made little reference to the doctrine of prevenient grace. In fact, the doctrine of the Holy Spirit is the really underdeveloped doctrine in his corpus. One can infer that prevenience was an assumption. An unexplicated assumption in this case, however, can be dangerous for the future theological development of the movement.

On the North American scene the frontier revivals of the Second Great Awakening—fueled primarily by an abbreviated Wesleyan Arminianism—had by Watson's time obscured the matter of prevenient grace. Historical exigencies demanded a simple, direct, and readily understood message, and soon that message was cast into a threefold theology: free grace, free will, and conversion. The American Methodist theologians, Asa Shinn, Nathan Bangs, and Wilbur Fisk, struggled with the Calvinist-Hopkinsian modifications and made some modifications themselves. Although they certainly did not intend to jettison the doctrine of prevenient grace, the modification from "prevenient grace" to "gracious ability" was more than semantical. When grace becomes adjectival, the weight increasingly falls upon human agency. The ghost of Pelagianism has always haunted the Methodists, and by the end of the nineteenth century that ghost was incarnate in both conservative and liberal thought alike.

Whether it be Wesley's anguished cry for the future of his people, "What more could have been done," or the church's search today for its identity, the ultimate aim is not to preserve a people called Methodists. The ultimate objective is to produce people who live by grace and manifest such living in a life of love for God and neighbor. Wesleyan "practical divinity" serves that missional end—lives changed by grace, churches formed by grace, and a world transformed by grace.[24] In such a mission of grace the tradition lives on—not as an end in itself but as a "means of grace."

Notes

1. Leonard Sweet, "The Fundamentalisms of Oldline Protestantism," *Christian Century* (March 13, 1985), 266.
2. *Grace Upon Grace* (Nashville: Graded Press, 1990), 5.
3. *Grace Upon Grace*, 29-34.
4. "On God's Vineyard," *Sermons III*, ed. Albert C. Outler, in *The Bicentennial Edition of the Works of John Wesley* (Nashville: Abingdon Press, 1984–), 3:503-17, hereinafter cited as *Works*.
5. "On God's Vineyard," in *Works* 3:507.
6. "The Nature, Design, and General Rules of the United Societies," in *Works* 9:67.
7. "On God's Vineyard," in *Works* 3:514.
8. "On God's Vineyard," in *Works* 3:515.
9. "Thoughts Upon Methodism," in *Works* 9:527.
10. "Minutes of Several Conversations," *Works of the Rev. John Wesley, M.A.*, ed. Thomas Jackson, 3rd ed., 14 vols. (London: Wesleyan Methodist Book Room, 1872), 8:331.

11. H. B. Kendall, *The Origin and History of the Primitive Methodist Church* (London, n.d.), 1:77.

12. *Primitive Methodist Magazine* (1896), 830-31.

13. Adam Clarke, *The Holy Bible, Containing the Old and New Testaments; the Text Printed from the Most Correct Copies of the Present Authorized Translation, Including the Marginal Readings and Parallel Texts with a Commentary and Critical Notes* (New York: N. Bangs and J. Emory, 1825–26), Luke 1:35.

14. Ibid.

15. A. D. Gilbert, *Religion and Society in Industrial England* (London: Longman, 1976), 63.

16. "Introduction," in *Works* 1:17.

17. Maldwyn Edwards, *After Wesley: A Study of the Social and Political Influence of Methodism in the Middle Period (1791–1849)* (London: Epworth Press, 1935), 48-49.

18. John Fletcher, *Checks to Antinomianism* (New York: J. Collard, 1827).

19. Letter to John Fletcher (March 22, 1775), in *The Letters of John Wesley, A. M.*, ed. John Telford, 8 vols. (London: Epworth Press, 1931), 6:146.

20. Letter of John Fletcher to Mary Bosanquet (March 7, 1778), in Tyerman, *Wesley's Designated Successor* (London: Hodder and Stoughton, 1882), 411.

21. John Fletcher, *Portrait of St. Paul,* reprinted in the *Works of the Rev. John Fletcher* (reprint, Salem, Ohio: Schmul Publishers, 1974), 166-69. Donald Dayton's volume, *Theological Roots of Pentecostalism* (Grand Rapids, Mich.: Francis Asbury Press of Zondervan Publishing House, 1987), has been a great help in following the Fletcher materials.

22. Richard Watson, *Theological Institutes* (New York: G. Lane and P. P. Sandford, 1843).

23. Thomas A. Langford, "John Wesley and Theological Method," in Randy L. Maddox, ed., *Rethinking Wesley's Theology for Contemporary Methodism* (Nashville: Kingswood Books, 1998), 35-47.

24. *Grace Upon Grace,* 29-34.

GRACE IN AMERICAN METHODISM:
The Testimony of Methodist Women

JEAN MILLER SCHMIDT

This essay explores the collective contribution of Methodist women to a theology of grace in American Methodism. Although clearly a majority in terms of presence (consistently two-thirds of members across the more than two-hundred-year history of the peoples called Methodist in America), Methodist women have had to struggle for institutional power and authority well into our own century. The principal sources for knowing what they believed about grace are their spiritual journals and letters (sometimes edited and published after their deaths as "pious memoirs,"[1] with a short biography by the editor), obituary notices, and other autobiographical and narrative materials. Until very recently only the exceptional woman preached sermons or wrote theological works. Nonetheless there is a surprising body of evidence demonstrating not only the centrality of grace, but also its meaning in the faith, spirituality, and lives of American Methodist women. Their writings might be seen as choice pieces of "practical divinity," intended, as Tom Langford suggested the resources in John Wesley's *Christian Library* were, to "nurture Christian living."[2]

The Sufficiency of Grace

I found his grace more than sufficient. I think the Lord does not bestow premature or unnecessary grace. All we can expect is grace equal to our day. (Mrs. Mary Mason, 1822)[3]

125

In their writings Methodist women referred frequently to the scriptural promises in 2 Corinthians 12:9: "My grace is sufficient for you, for power is made perfect in weakness," and Deuteronomy 33:25: "As your days, so is your strength." This "grace sufficient" theme seems to have been central to their theology and spirituality, particularly in relation to the Wesleyan doctrine of sanctification or Christian perfection, but also as they attempted to make sense of the struggles of their daily lives. Over an impressive span of geographical distance and for at least a century (c. 1770s to 1880s), I argue in this essay, women in this faith tradition arrived at a remarkable consensus that grace was sufficient: (1) to keep them in the way of salvation, (2) for holy living (and holy dying), and (3) to enable them to respond to God's call in terms of their own vocation.[4]

Grace was sufficient to keep them in the way of salvation. They understood what Albert Outler would later describe as the "heart of [John] Wesley's gospel": that "lively sense of God's grace at work . . . —sufficient grace in all, irresistible grace in none."[5] For them sanctification was not primarily a matter of virtue, but rather moment-by-moment dependence on divine grace.

Methodist women fundamentally affirmed the sufficiency of grace for all things, for living as well as for dying. They knew from experience that life is precarious, and that sometimes living is harder than dying. In the midst of their sufferings, griefs, illnesses, anxieties, and cares they relied on the assurance that God's grace would be sufficient for their day.

The feelings of inadequacy and unworthiness felt by many women (often ingrained by gender stereotypes) made it difficult for them to know how to respond to God's call. Growth in grace frequently meant trusting its sufficiency to enable them to do what God required of them, even if this meant transgressing the socially and ecclesiastically prescribed boundaries of appropriate female behavior.

In this essay I will illustrate how the Wesleyan theme of God's justifying and sanctifying—sufficient—grace was known and testified to by Methodist women, understood by them as a matter of relationship, and responded to in their vocational choices. I will conclude by assessing the significance of their narratives for a theology of grace in American Methodism.

Methodist Women and the Wesleyan Way of Salvation

You ask how I obtained this great salvation? I answer, just as I obtained the pardon of my sin—*by simple faith.* . . . I knew the faithfulness of my

God, and ventured on the promise . . . "My grace is sufficient for thee."
O the preciousness of these words! I shall praise God in eternity that
they are written in his book. (Hester Ann Roe [Rogers], 1778)[6]

This quotation is from a letter written by a twenty-two-year-old English
woman and Methodist class leader to her cousin, telling him how she
experienced Christian perfection. Like other writings of Methodist
women it illustrates how well they understood the Wesleyan "theology
of grace," so aptly summarized by Tom Langford: "Grace is God's active
and continuous presence. Definitively expressed in Jesus Christ, grace
covers the entirety of life: It creates, redeems, sustains, sanctifies, and
glorifies."[7] For Wesley grace was always relational; it could never be
possessed apart from God's continuing love and sustaining power.

Women who were actively involved in the Methodist movement
had the further nourishment and instruction of all the typical Methodist means of grace: the Lord's Supper, corporate worship, public
and private reading and study of Scripture, sermons that offered
"plain truth for plain people," a theology inscribed on the heart and
memory through singing (and devotional use) of hymns, and the
communal support of class and band meetings, prayer meetings, and
love feasts where the salvation narratives of the Methodist people were
shared to the edification of all.[8] In addition they had the very personal
support and guidance of other Methodist women, through letters and
visits that were part of female networks within the churches.

Many Methodist women followed the Wesleys' injunction to keep
a diary of their spiritual progress. As they poured out their hearts in
candid communication with their God in these journals they often
experienced God's forgiving and transforming grace. At the same
time this autobiographical writing was also an important means of
self-construction. As they read other women's published diaries and
letters they often found in them—in contrast to society's message of
women's inferiority—permission and encouragement to discover the
woman God was calling them to be.

Hester Ann Rogers as Pattern of Piety and Spiritual Guide

I felt a thousand fears suggested, that if I lived, I might lose what I now
enjoyed of the love of God; and perhaps be one day a dishonour to his

cause. But I said, Lord, thy grace is ever sufficient; thou art as able to keep me a thousand years as one day! (Hester Ann Roe [Rogers], 1776)[9]

The spiritual autobiography and letters of Hester Ann Roe (who married James Rogers, one of John Wesley's most trusted Methodist preachers, in 1784) were widely read by nineteenth-century Methodist women. In her lifetime and, after her death, through her writings, Hester Ann Rogers became a spiritual guide to many women and men. Like her friend and mentor John Wesley, Rogers drew on what she had learned from her own spiritual struggles to help others in their journeys of faith.

In the fall of 1774, the eighteen-year-old daughter of an Anglican rector made an unusual bargain with her mother: she would become a servant in her own house if her mother would permit her to attend Methodist meetings. Within weeks of negotiating this arrangement Hester Ann Roe had an evangelical conversion experience and soon became a member of the Methodist society. (Her spiritual autobiography demonstrates the importance of evangelical religion for young, single women as a source of identity and fulfillment apart from their families.)

Less than two years later, however, this young woman faced another turning point in her life. She was not only very ill, but also troubled by what she felt as the burden of her own sinfulness. When a visiting cousin begged her to take medicine, she told him she would rather die than live. Rebuking her for setting her own will above God's, he asked her a crucial question, "Are you willing to live [another] forty years, if the Lord please?" She had no immediate answer for him, but fell on her knees in prayer and asked God's help. At the young age of twenty she asked God to let her live as long—but only as long—as her life would glorify God and be useful to others. "Only perfect me in love," she said, "and let me live to thee, and spare me as long or as short a period as thou seest fit."[10] Almost immediately Hester Ann Roe began to recover from her illness, and not long after she also realized her desire to be perfected in love. Soon she was advising others seeking sanctification to rely on the promise, "My grace is sufficient for thee."

In 1804 *An Account of the Experience of Hester Ann Rogers* was published in its first American edition, together with her spiritual letters and funeral sermon preached by Thomas Coke. Methodist Book Concern records and accounts of Methodist circuit-riding preachers indicate that it quickly became a best-seller. Methodist women bought it for themselves, handed it down to daughters, nieces, and other female family members, and gave it to friends. By sharing women's spiritual autobiographies like that of Hester Ann Rogers, Methodist women helped one another understand the way of salvation according to the Wesleys, especially the connection between Christian perfection and trust in the sufficiency of God's grace.[11]

A few examples will illustrate the impact of these female models on other women's religious lives. From 1818 to 1828 *The Methodist Magazine* published the memoirs and obituaries of eighty-four American Methodist women. Some appeared in a regular feature entitled "The Grace of God Manifested"; others were simpler obituary notices. Together they give access to a greater diversity of Methodist women's experiences. When Mrs. Matilda Porter from Georgia died in her twenty-ninth year, her memoir recalled that she had resolved to seek salvation after reading "the life of Hester Ann Rogers." On her deathbed Mrs. Hannah Howe, wife of an itinerant preacher in New England and New York State, gave one of her sisters "the experience of H.A. Rogers."[12]

In 1836 Anna Maria Pittman, at the age of thirty-three, sailed with a group from Boston, around Cape Horn to Hawaii, and finally to the Oregon mission to become a teacher of the Flathead Indians. (She would later become the wife of the mission's leader, the Reverend Jason Lee.) The entire trip took ten months. Shortly before the group's departure from Boston, Pittman wrote her parents that it had been harder to say good-bye to them than she had let on. "Had I indulged in grief," she explained, "I would have been unhappy, and made those so about me. But I find the grace of God is sufficient." She added, "I received the life of H.A. Rogers, and much obliged to you. May I copy her example."[13]

Phoebe Palmer was probably unmatched among American Methodist women in her contribution to both the mid-nineteenth-century holiness revival and Methodist holiness teaching. For many years she and her sister Sarah Lankford led a gathering at their home known as the Tuesday Meeting for the Promotion of Holiness. Sarah Lankford had experienced the blessing of holiness in 1835, after reading *An Account of the Experience of Hester Ann Rogers.* Phoebe Palmer's sanctification experience came about a year later and she too had been helped by reading Hester Ann Rogers. In fact Rogers may well have been an important influence on a central aspect of Palmer's holiness theology, her "altar terminology." In a 1776 letter, for example, Rogers professed feeling "very unworthy," yet convinced that God accepted her "offering up [her]self and [her] services on that . . . altar which sanctifieth the gift." Phoebe Palmer told readers of *The Way of Holiness* (1843) that instead of its being "presumptuous to believe" in the reality of sanctification, it would grieve God's spirit were she to doubt "the all-sufficiency of his grace" to sustain her in the "full enjoyment" of this blessing.[14]

The July 1841 issue of the *Guide to Christian Perfection* contained the testimony of Sarah Lankford's holiness experience, including her account of how the *Life* of Hester Ann Rogers had guided her to the experience. Other women wrote that they had also found "H.A. Rogers' Life" helpful in seeking sanctification. Still others encouraged readers that God's "grace would be sufficient" to enable them to consecrate themselves to God. As one "Sister in the Fulness of Christ" testified, "I have found his yoke easy, and his burden light; the grace of God has been sufficient to keep me" for thirteen years.[15]

Through the Tuesday meeting, her published writings, and through personal letters, Phoebe Palmer herself became a spiritual guide for many Methodist women. She wrote often in the 1840s to both acquaintances and close friends. Palmer, who understood well the struggle between domestic and spiritual responsibilities, had been instrumental in encouraging her friend Mary James to consider writing (religious autobiography, poetry, hymns, and especially "Christian correspondence") as a religious vocation.

On a visit Palmer found the young mother engaged in making clothes for her children. When she learned that James made all her children's clothes and her own as well, Palmer was clear in her reproof: "The work required of you, writing for Jesus, is of vast importance. This no one can do for you, but making garments others can do in your place." In a long letter to James (published in 1846 in the *Guide to Holiness*), Palmer sympathized with her friend, whose new baby was keeping her preoccupied, and urged her to "exhibit the power of grace to sustain in circumstances where thousands of Christian mothers are placed, and where, alas, too many are prone to let go their hold on the all-sufficiency of grace."[16]

Christian Perfection Not a State but a Relationship

I asked the Lord to take me to that better world, that I might sin no more, but I was reminded that I was a probationer, and that there were many duties and trials before me, but I felt assured that His grace would be sufficient for the day. (Elizabeth [Lyon] Roe, 1824)[17]

Although the message of early Methodist circuit-riding preachers in America apparently gave primary attention to conversion rather than to sanctification, Methodist women seem never to have lost sight of the Wesleyan emphasis on Christian perfection. Perhaps it was easier for them than for most men to grasp that holy living was, as David Watson suggested, "a relationship to be sustained rather than a state to be attained."[18] Here I want to address three aspects of Methodist women's quest for Christian perfection as the goal of the Christian life, available to and necessary for all: (1) God's grace manifested in those who are "poor and weak" in the world, (2) God's grace sufficient for holy living and holy dying, and (3) Christian perfection not a matter of virtue, but of moment-by-moment dependence on God's grace.

Part of the appeal of early American Methodism was its radical spiritual egalitarianism. In the late-eighteenth and early nineteenth-century society of Bishop Francis Asbury, poverty and weakness were words often used to describe, respectively, African Americans and women. Yet this worldly logic was confounded by God's power, for those who were poor and weak in the world were recognized within the Methodist family as rich and strong in the spirit. Historian Donald G. Mathews has pointed out that such liminal people powerfully conveyed the love and salvation of God to the rest of the Methodist assembly, bringing that sense of communal bonding, individual esteem, and human equality that Victor Turner called "communitas."[19] Even a cursory examination of Bishop Asbury's letters to women suggests the extent to which he found spiritual power in those whom the world regarded as "weak." In 1796, for example, Asbury wrote to Mrs. Martha Haskins of Philadelphia, asking her with Sister Dickins (wife of John Dickins, Methodist Book Agent and preacher) to begin a weekly woman's prayer meeting: "Oh my sister you have a suffering, dying life but the grace of God is sufficient for you. . . . Women are weak, but remember Eve, and Sarah, Miriam, Deborah, Hannah,

Shebah's Queen, Elizabeth, Anna, Phebe and such like, bring the gifts to enrich the temple of God."[20] Asbury encouraged the entire Baltimore society, women and men, blacks and whites, to meet together once a week (in addition to classes segregated by sex and race), that the whole society might be renewed.

Fifty-four of the death memoirs of American Methodist women published in *The Methodist Magazine* (referred to earlier), mentioned the woman's age at death. Twenty-six, or roughly half of these women, died in their twenties, six died between the ages of twelve and nineteen, and eight died in their thirties. That is, forty of these fifty-four women died before they reached the age of forty. Women at this time lived with the constant threat of death, whether the possibility of their own death in childbirth, or the frequent loss of a child, or even a spouse. Some historians have suggested that this proximity to death made women more open to the consolations of religion. It was often the women who modeled for the community of faith a supreme benefit of religion, holy dying, or the ability to face death unafraid.

Wesleyan theology taught that grace was sufficient, but not irresistible, and that forgiveness and regeneration were no guarantee of final perseverance. Methodist women's journals and letters frequently spoke of their "fear of falling," of losing God's love, or of dishonoring God's cause. They were comforted by the assurance that God's grace was "sufficient to keep them," and by moment-by-moment dependence on that gracious relationship. They were careful to distinguish mere feeling from the witness of God's spirit in assurance of justification or sanctification. Frances Merritt, wife of Methodist preacher and presiding elder John Merritt, advised a young pastor's wife in Colorado in the 1880s who was seeking sanctification not to "look for feeling," but to "walk by faith." Look to Christ, she said, ask forgiveness and try again, and "cling to the promise, 'My grace is sufficient for thee.' "[21]

"Who Is Sufficient for These Things?": Responsible Grace and Women's Vocational Choices

I arose, and spake to the people, and had great liberty. . . . Whatever may be said against a female speaking, or praying in public, I care not;

for when I feel confident, that the Lord calls me to speak, I dare not refuse. (Fanny Butterfield Newell, 1818)[22]

Methodist women frequently if not typically experienced God's grace as power within themselves and their communities. For many women, religious submission to God led to a loss of inhibiting self-consciousness and a new sense of inner authority. Through the experiences of conversion (justification and new birth) and sanctification, it was not unusual for them to find not only God, but also a worthy role in this world. As they struggled with their call, they affirmed that only God's grace was sufficient for them to overcome a "man-fearing spirit."

Fanny Butterfield, who became the wife of Methodist circuit-riding preacher Ebenezer Newell, and Jarena Lee, a free black woman born in New Jersey and widowed after a few years of marriage to a minister, were two of the earliest known American Methodist women to experience a call to preach, in 1809 and 1811, respectively. From the published spiritual memoirs of these two women, we know something about how they experienced and responded to their call.[23] In dreams each woman saw herself preaching to large crowds. Since their churches did not condone a woman's preaching, they felt their call as a terrible cross for a poor female to bear. Yet, as each expressed it, when they shrank from taking up the cross, they were pierced through with many sorrows. Both women felt inadequate, asking "who is sufficient for these things." Mrs. Zilpha Elaw, another early African American female preacher, answered directly, "our sufficiency is of God."[24]

Fanny Newell frequently traveled around her husband's circuit exhorting the people after his sermon. In a near-death experience a few days after the birth of her first child, she met Christ and was told to "go back," and "declare the works of the Lord to the children of men." She subsequently served with her husband for a full year in frontier outposts on the border of Maine and Canada, filling what was clearly a public evangelistic role.

When Jarena Lee asked the Reverend Richard Allen for permission to preach in 1811, he responded that the rules of Methodism "did not allow for women preachers."[25] Eight years later, after he had become the first Bishop of the African Methodist Episcopal Church (a newly organized independent black denomination), Richard Allen recognized Jarena Lee's call to preach and gave her his permission to become an itinerant evangelist. In the 1820s to 1840s, she traveled thousands of miles (many of them on foot), from upper New York State to Maryland and as far west as Ohio, preaching to large congregations, both black and white.

Born a slave in Maryland, Amanda Berry Smith was a washerwoman who became a well-known holiness evangelist in the 1870s and published her *Autobiography* in 1893. Throughout her account she took comfort in that familiar biblical promise: "My grace is sufficient for you. If you trust Me you shall never be confounded."[26]

Mrs. Willie Harding McGavock from Tennessee was instrumental in organizing a Woman's Foreign Missionary Society in the Methodist Episcopal Church, South, in 1878. In 1891 Willie McGavock seemed to be dying. After a powerful spiritual experience, she reported being called back to life. Although confined to her bed for eleven weeks and in "an invalid's chair" for an entire year, she continued to help forward the cause of missions. As she explained to a friend, "I had found it far easier to die than to live; but if my Father has more work . . . for me, he will give me grace sufficient. I am gradually recovering."[27]

In 1869 Maggie Newton Van Cott was granted a preacher's license in the Methodist Episcopal Church. Like many women before her, she had experienced her call to preach in a dream. (She dreamed that someone told her, "you must preach," and having ascended the pulpit and preached to a "dear old gentleman," she was amazed to be told it was John Wesley!) When people misunderstood and misrepresented her as a woman preacher, she once prayed to die and be removed from the situation. However, she heard a consoling voice whispering in her soul, "My grace is sufficient."[28]

Beginning in the 1860s Methodist women moved into much more public positions of leadership in both church and society through the women's home and foreign missionary societies, the Woman's Christian Temperance Union, the struggle for ordination and full clergy rights (not successfully concluded for The Methodist Church until 1956), and the deaconess movement as a new public ministry for women. Methodist women in these years did not write as much about grace sufficient, although their public activism was clearly motivated by a deep Methodist piety. The fact is that Methodist women no longer engaged as much in private spiritual reflection. Frances E. Willard, intrepid leader of the WCTU for nearly two decades, is a good illustration of this. Willard kept a journal from her sixteenth through thirty-first years, and again in her fifty-fourth and fifty-seventh years. In the intervening years, as Carolyn De Swarte Gifford explains, Willard "realized that it was time to act," and became an "internationally renowned leader of temperance and women's rights reforms." No longer "confined to the private medium of her journal," her writing— now including speeches, pamphlets, articles, and books—had become "a public act."[29]

As Frances Willard led WCTU women into new spheres of public activity, she and they affirmed that it was God's power that enabled them to do what they did. Missionary women became famous for their organizational skills, but they were clear that the purposes of all that organizing were deeply spiritual. Jennie Fowler Willing, one of the most energetic of these missionary women, believed in "heart purity," and thought the missionary sisterhood was united by "shared fire." Anna Oliver was one of the women who (unsuccessfully) sought ordination in the Methodist Episcopal Church in 1880. Oliver not only took her stand on her firm sense of call, but her reorganized church in Brooklyn was founded on holiness principles. Following their motto, "Not I, but Christ," Methodist deaconesses relinquished all other pursuits for the sake of the "mothering" work of ministering to the poor, visiting the sick, praying with the dying, caring for the orphan, seeking the wandering, comforting the sorrowing, and saving the sinning.[30]

Methodist women's responses to God's call and their experiences of God's restoring, renewing, and sanctifying—sufficient—grace must be interpreted in relation to the diversity of their lives and particularity of their struggles. Today, women in this faith tradition do not commonly speak of "grace sufficient," but they still resonate with its reality. They are more apt to talk about responding to God's grace, but they still experience and trust in its dynamic and liberating power.

Albert Outler used to refer to John Wesley as a "folk theologian." He explained that Wesley was "by talent and intent" neither a speculative nor a systematic theologian, but an "effective evangelist guided by a discriminating theological understanding."[31] The collective contribution of Methodist women may perhaps be understood in a similar light: at their best they functioned as folk theologians, their writings as pieces of "practical divinity." This essay has attempted to demonstrate how well they knew and how faithfully they lived the Wesleyan theology of responsible grace. Most of all it seems to have been their special joy and mission to give testimony to the sufficiency of God's empowering grace to form Christ-like character.

Notes

1. Joanna Bowen Gillespie's term to describe this genre of religious writings of evangelical women. See her article " 'The Clear Leadings of Providence': Pious Memoirs and the Problems of Self-Realization for Women in the Early Nineteenth Century," *Journal of the Early Republic* 5 (Summer 1985), 197-221.

2. Thomas A. Langford, *Practical Divinity: Theology in the Wesleyan Tradition* (Nashville: Abingdon Press, 1983), 17.

3. Elizabeth Mason North, *Consecrated Talents: or, The Life of Mrs. Mary W. Mason* (New York: Carlton & Lanahan, 1870; Garland Reprint, 1987), 93-94.

4. See also Jean Miller Schmidt, *Grace Sufficient: A History of Women in American Methodism* (Nashville: Abingdon Press, 1999).

5. Albert C. Outler, Introduction to *Sermons I*, in *The Bicentennial Edition of the Works of John Wesley* (Nashville: Abingdon Press, 1984–), 1:98. Wesley believed God's grace could be resisted; it was co-operant. As Randy L. Maddox explains, Wesley "understood grace to be responsible—it empowers our response, but does not coerce that response." See his *Responsible Grace: John Wesley's Practical Theology* (Nashville: Kingswood Books, 1994), 86.

6. *Account of the Experience of Mrs. Hester Ann Rogers* (New York: John C. Totten, for the Methodist Episcopal Church, 1804). I used a slightly later edition: (Baltimore: J. Kingston, 1811), 104-5.

7. Langford, *Practical Divinity*, 20.

8. See Randy L. Maddox's helpful discussion of the means of grace as "wait[ing] for God's grace *responsibly*," in *Responsible Grace*, 200-216.

9. *Account*, 38.

10. Ibid., 38. Also *The Life of Faith Exemplified; or Extracts from the Journal of Mrs. Hester Ann Rogers* (New York: Carlton & Porter, 1861), 23.

11. The memoirs of both English and American women were part of what Jo Gillespie called "a functional pious memoir canon" circulated among evangelical readers in America (Gillespie, "Clear Leadings," 197).

12. *The Methodist Magazine* 10:2 (Feb. 1827): 85; 1:1 (Jan. 1818): 25.

13. Theressa Gay, *Life and Letters of Mrs. Jason Lee* (Portland, Oreg.: Metropolitan Press Publishers, 1936), 119. That Anna Maria's youngest sister was named Hester Ann Rogers Pittman is further evidence of the high regard in which Rogers was held as an exemplar of female piety.

14. Rogers, *Spiritual Letters* (attached to *Account*), 188; Phoebe Palmer, *The Way of Holiness, with Notes by the Way* . . . (New York: Piercy and Reed, 1843); reprint ed., *The Devotional Writings of Phoebe Palmer*, Higher Christian Life Series (New York: Garland Publishing, 1985), 126.

15. *Guide to Christian Perfection* (Boston) 3:1 (July 1841): 8-16; 2:12 (June 1841): 274; 3:9 (Mar. 1842): 219-22.

16. *The Life of Mrs. Mary D. James, by her Son* (Joseph H. James), Intro. James M. Buckley (New York: Palmer & Hughes, 1886), 235; *Guide to Holiness* 9 (1846): 135-37.

17. Mrs. Elizabeth A. [Lyon] Roe, *Recollections of Frontier Life* (Rockford, Ill.: Gazette Publishing House, 1885; Arno Press Reprint, 1980), 614. This idea of "probationary" as subject to a period of testing and trial was basic to early Methodism, whether to church membership or to acceptance into ordained ministry.

18. David Lowes Watson, "Methodist Spirituality," in *Protestant Spiritual Traditions,* ed. Frank C. Senn (New York: Paulist Press, 1986), 225.

19. Donald G. Mathews, "Francis Asbury in Conference," unpublished paper.

20. *Journal and Letters of Francis Asbury,* vol. 3: *The Letters,* ed. J. Manning Potts, et al. (Nashville: Abingdon Press, 1958), 140-41.

21. Frances Potter Peck, *Memoir of Frances Merritt,* with an Introduction by Bishop Henry White Warren (Cincinnati: Cranston & Curts, 1892), 130-31.

22. *Diary of Fanny Newell; with a Sketch of Her Life, and an Introduction by a Member of the New England Conference of the Methodist Episcopal Church,* 4th ed. (Boston: Charles H. Peirce, 1848), 207-8.

23. In addition to the *Diary* of Fanny Newell, see "Religious Experience and Journal of Mrs. Jarena Lee" in *Spiritual Narratives,* ed. and intro. Sue E. Houchins, Schomburg Library of Nineteenth Century Black Women Writers (New York: Oxford University Press, 1988).

24. Zilpha Elaw, *Memoirs of the Life, Religious Experience, Ministerial Travels, and Labours of Mrs. Zilpha Elaw, An American Female of Colour; Together with Some Account of the Great Revivals in America,* in William L. Andrews, ed., *Sisters of the Spirit: Three Black Women's Autobiographies of the Nineteenth Century,* 49-160 (Bloomington: Indiana University Press, 1986), 49.

25. *The Life and Religious Experience of Jarena Lee* (1836) in Andrews, ed., *Sisters,* 36.

26. See *Autobiography: The Story of the Lord's Dealings with Mrs. Amanda Smith, the Colored Evangelist,* with an Introduction by Bishop Thoburn, of India (Chicago: Meyer & Brother, 1893), 147-49.

27. Mrs. F[rank] A. [Sarah Frances Stringfield] Butler, *Mrs. D. H. M'Gavock: Life-Sketch and Thoughts* (Nashville: Publishing House of the Methodist Episcopal Church, South, 1896), 124-35.

28. John O. Foster, *Life and Labors of Mrs. Maggie Newton Van Cott, the First Lady Licensed to Preach in the Methodist Episcopal Church in the United States* (Cincinnati: Hitchcock and Walden, 1872), 152-53, 168.

29. *Writing Out My Heart: Selections from the Journal of Frances E. Willard, 1855–96,* ed. Carolyn De Swarte Gifford (Urbana: University of Illinois Press, 1995).

30. From the description of the duties of the deaconess in the plan approved by the Methodist Episcopal Church in 1888.

31. Albert Outler, ed., *John Wesley* (New York: Oxford University Press, 1964), 119.

PART III:
THEOLOGICAL ESSAYS

GRACE INCARNATE:
Jesus Christ

JONATHAN R. WILSON

At the center of Christian theology stands God's grace. And at the center of God's grace stands Jesus Christ. John Wesley knew this well; so also did Charles Wesley. A majority of John's sermons concern Jesus Christ as the one who climactically establishes and reveals God's grace.[1] Many of Charles' hymns likewise concern the grace of God revealed in Jesus Christ.

At the center of the Wesleyan tradition, then, we find a theology of grace centered in Jesus Christ. However, because the grace of God in Christ was taught by the Wesleys through sermons and hymns, their theology is always more than simply the grace of God in Jesus Christ: it is also the grace of God in Jesus Christ *for us*. In Thomas Langford's phrase, theology in the Wesleyan tradition is always "practical divinity."[2]

Therefore, my task in this chapter is to give an account of grace incarnate in Jesus Christ that also shows how that grace shapes our life together. In order to do that I will draw on the image that Paul uses in Romans, Jesus Christ as the "Second Adam." My purpose in this chapter is not to exegete Paul's use of this image. Rather, I will take this image from Paul and seek to give a narrative account of how the image of Christ as the Second Adam illuminates the meaning of grace incarnate in Jesus Christ for the salvation of humanity. In other words, I do not think that my account is the one that Paul would give if he were able to tell us more about what he meant. But I do think that my account fits Paul's thinking and the larger story of Jesus Christ that we get from the Old and New Testaments.

In taking this approach I am not trying to present a comprehensive "Christology."[3] Even a lengthy book on Jesus Christ can never exhaust his meaning for us. In this chapter I will simply take one of the many images that the New Testament applies to Jesus Christ and show how it brings together many strands of the biblical story and teaches us grace incarnate.

To understand Christ as the Second Adam, I will begin with an account of the First Adam. This account will help us understand what God intended the first Adam to be. It will also tell us what the first Adam lost in the fall into sin. Then we will be in a position to consider what Christ as the Second Adam restored to lost humanity. After we have considered this, we will turn to Christ as the "Last Adam," the beginning of a new human race restored in the image of God. Finally, we will consider how our conformity to the image of Christ by the work of the Holy Spirit is God's grace working to redeem humanity.

First Adam: The Image of God

We can only understand the image of Christ as Second Adam if we understand the First Adam as the image of God. The account of the First Adam as made in the image of God is found in Genesis 1:26-27:

> Then God said, "Let us make humankind [Heb. *adam*] in our image, according to our likeness; and let them have dominion over the fish of the sea, and over the birds of the air, and over the cattle, and over all the wild animals of the earth, and over every creeping thing that creeps upon the earth."

> So God created humankind in his image,
> in the image of God he created them;
> male and female he created them.

Although I have been using "Adam" to this point, and although the Hebrew text uses the word *adam,* from this point forward I will use the term "First Human" rather than "First Adam." I do this to remind us that both male and female are created in God's image. In Genesis 1 "Adam" is used to refer to both male and female humans. Only in Genesis 2 is it used more particularly to refer to the first male human.

In Genesis 1:26-27, then, we have a description of the first human—humankind—made in the image of God.[4] What "the image of God" means has been the subject of much discussion. In this chapter, I will take it to mean that humans are made for four relationships and four responsibilities that correspond to those four relationships.[5] This is certainly not the only way to describe the image of God in humanity, but as we will see it reflects the text and gives us the foundation for the story of Christ as the "Second Human."[6]

The first relationship for which humankind is made is a relationship with God. This is shown in the text by the fact that we are made in the image of *God*. It is confirmed by God's immediate address to the first human: "God blessed them, and God said to them, 'Be fruitful and multiply, and fill the earth and subdue it; and have dominion over the fish of the sea and over the birds of the air and over every living thing that moves upon the earth' " (Gen 1:28).

This passage not only tells us that humans are made for a relationship with God, it also tells us our responsibility in that relationship: God blesses us and we are to be obedient to God. The blessing of God is obvious from God's pronouncement. Our responsibility to obey is evident from the fact that God's address to us is an imperative. In our relationship to God, God blesses and commands, we receive blessing and obey.

The second relationship for which we are made is a relationship to one another. This is evident in the fact that humankind is created male and female. It is confirmed by God's command to "be fruitful and multiply." This command can only be obeyed if we are in relationship as male and female.

The responsibility that corresponds to this relationship is not yet obvious in the text of Genesis 1, but at the climax of Genesis 2, we are told that the man and woman are to become "one flesh." This phrase does not refer merely to the act of sexual intercourse; it also refers to the responsibility that we have as human beings for mutual love toward one another. This mutuality between husband and wife is a profound expression of the mutual love that all humans are to have for one another. It models for us the mutuality that we are to practice in appropriate ways in all our human relationships.

The third relationship for which we are created is a relationship to the rest of creation. Clearly, we humans are part of the created order, but as the image of God we are also given a special relationship to the rest of creation. This special relationship is captured by the responsibility that we are given for the rest of creation. We are to "fill the earth, subdue it, and have dominion."

In the midst of debates about the environmental crisis of our time, this responsibility deserves special attention. Some take this command to be a warrant for humans to do as we please with creation, or at the very least, to use creation for our own purposes. This understanding of our responsibility for creation is wrong for at least two reasons. First, it is wrong because it fails to take into account that God issues this command prior to our fall into sin. It makes an enormous difference that this command is given by God to an originally righteous humanity. Fallen, sinful humanity can very easily distort this command to "do what you want with creation." Second, it is wrong to take this command as a warrant for environmental degradation because we only have responsibility for the rest of creation as stewards serving under the one who made the earth and all that is in it—God.[7] Therefore, our responsibility for creation must always be related to the righteousness of God revealed in the rest of the Bible.

The fourth relationship for which we are made is a relationship to ourselves. It is only hinted at in Genesis 1 and 2, but it becomes clear in Genesis 3 that this relationship for which we are made is an important one. When we consider Genesis 3, we will see why Genesis 1 and 2 only hint at it. The hint comes in Genesis 2:25: "And the man and his wife were both naked, and were not ashamed." To be naked and unashamed is to be unaware of oneself. In other words, the man and the woman were not self-conscious; that is, they were not conscious of themselves.

Admittedly, it is not easy to grasp this condition, but it will become clearer as we consider what the first human loses in the fall. Before we do that, however, I will briefly note the responsibility that accompanies this relationship to oneself. In relationship to myself, I am responsible to have integrity. Perhaps this may best be understood if it is put negatively: I am not to be divided against myself. Or put positively, I am to be a whole person before God, made in God's image.

The Fall of the First Human

As created in the image of God, the first human exemplifies what God intends for humankind. But we know that humankind today does not reflect that image as God intended it. Our relationships are broken and our responsibilities are unfulfilled. This failure is the result of the fall of the first human.[8]

The story of the fall is narrated in Genesis 2. Although there are many issues to debate in this passage, I will be concerned solely with the way this story affects the relationships and responsibilities that we were given as the image of God.

The first thing that we see in this story is the failure of the first human to fulfill our responsibility to God. In place of obedience, we find disobedience. God commanded that we not eat of the tree of the knowledge of good and evil, and we disobeyed. This disobedience leads immediately to the breaking of our relationship to God: "They heard the sound of the LORD God walking in the garden at the time of the evening breeze, and the man and his wife hid themselves from the presence of the LORD God among the trees of the garden" (Gen 3:8). In passing, we should note here that we also see the beginnings of God's grace in that God did not leave them alone in their sin, but called out to them.

The second thing that we see in this story is the breaking of the relationship and responsibility that the man and the woman have for each other. When God asks what happened, the man immediately places the blame on the woman and, further exemplifying the break with God, indirectly places the blame on God (Gen 3:12). The brokenness of this relationship is further described in the words of God, that the woman's desire will be for her husband and he will rule over her. This relationship between man and woman and by extension among all humankind is not God's original intention for creation; it is a result of the fall of the first human.

The third thing that we see in this story is that the relationship between the first human and the rest of creation is broken (Gen 3:16-19). As humankind seeks to multiply and fill the earth, the woman shall have pain in childbearing. As humankind seeks to rule over the earth, the earth will resist. Labor, intended by God to be a fulfillment of our humanity, now becomes, under the fall, a curse.

The fourth thing that we see in this story is the brokenness of the relationship of the first human, each to the other. In their sin they come suddenly to the realization that they are naked. They become self-conscious and ashamed. Here now we can understand their original condition—before the fall. In right relationship to God, they are not conscious of themselves: they are naked and unashamed. Thus, they could not even be conscious that they were not self-conscious. Now, after the fall they become aware of themselves. To be ashamed is to be aware of a self that is not what God intended us to be. To be ashamed is to be divided in oneself and to be aware of that division.

In the midst of this story of God's gracious gifts to the first human made in God's image, we have some hints of God's continuing graciousness. As I noted, God comes searching for the first human even in fallenness. As well, we can see God's unwillingness to abandon the first human to fallenness in God's promise of enmity between the serpent's "seed" and the woman's "seed" (Gen 3:15). This story continues through the Old Testament in Israel's history, but for the sake of brevity I will move immediately to its climactic revelation in the story of the Second Human.

Jesus Christ: The Second Human

The story of the first human is the story of increasing sin. Made in the image of God, graciously given relationships and responsibilities, the first human fell from grace into sin. But in the same passage where Paul claims Jesus Christ as the Second Human, Paul also asserts that "where sin increased, grace abounded all the more" (Rom 5:20). This abundant grace comes to us in Jesus Christ. To understand its abundance, I will return to the story of humankind made in the image of God so that we may see how Jesus Christ restores that image.

In the first place, we see Jesus Christ restoring our relationship to God. Jesus' claim for his relationship to the Father, "The Father and I are one" (John 10:30), is certainly a claim about his full divinity, but we should also read it as a claim about the relationship of his humanity to the Father. In the gospels, we see Jesus in unbroken relationship to the Father; he does what the Father tells him. His "cry of dereliction" on the cross (Matt 27:46) underscores his own unbroken relationship to the Father and his restoration of the image of God, because it is a cry that comes from his identification with sinful humankind.

In the Gospels we also see that Jesus fulfills the responsibility that corresponds to his relationship with God: he is perfectly obedient to the Father (John 5:19; 8:28). In his letter to the Philippians, Paul underscores this point in his hymn to Christ: "He humbled himself / and became obedient to the point of death— / even death on a cross" (2:8). This unbroken relationship to the Father and perfect obedience to him is the foundation for Jesus' restoration of the image of God.

In the second place, we see in Jesus Christ the restoration of the relationship that we are to have with one another. We see this clearly and undeniably in Jesus Christ's love for all humankind. In his ministry he welcomes all who will come to him: outcasts, marginalized, those who are natural enemies (such as a Zealot and a tax collector). He reveals himself as Messiah to a Samaritan woman (John 4) and commends the faith of a Gentile (Luke 7:9).

Since the relationship between man and woman is at the center of our relationships as human beings, Jesus' relationship to women deserves special attention. In a society that regarded women as constitutionally incapable of intellectual understanding, Jesus welcomed women into his band of disciples (Luke 8:1-3) and commended Mary's interest in his teaching (Luke 10:42). In a society that viewed women as a cause of immorality, Jesus allowed himself to be anointed by "sinful woman" (Luke 7:36-50) and even commended her act. In a society where women were a cause of impurity, instead of shrieking and condemning the bleeding woman who touched him, Jesus' power healed her; he commended her faith and bid her "Go in peace" (Luke 8:48). Women were with him at the cross and were the first witnesses of his resurrection.

In his relationship with others and his love for all, Jesus continues the work of restoring the image of God in humankind. We see this climactically in the cross of Christ. This is the supreme act of love: to die for others. And the others for whom Christ died are those who were his enemies, all who are descendants of the first human. In this sacrifice of love, Jesus Christ as the Second Human makes possible a new humanity, his descendants remade in the image of God.

In the Gospels we also see Jesus' restoration of the relationship that we are to have with the rest of creation in the miracles that he performs. We are accustomed to thinking of the miracles as demonstrations of the divinity of Jesus Christ. This way of thinking is not wrong, but it is incomplete. If humankind was intended by God to "rule over" creation, then we are intended by God to command creation. But we must be careful here: our rule over creation is to be in accordance with God's desires, not our own sinful desires.

In Jesus Christ we see this perfect rule over creation. When Jesus gives sight to the blind, restores hearing to the deaf, makes the lame walk, calms a storm, feeds the hungry, and restores life to the dead, he is revealing God's intention for creation. At the same time, he is also restoring the rightful relationship between humankind and the rest of creation. Later in this chapter we will consider the question that naturally arises, "Are we meant to do these same things as God's image is restored in us?"

Finally, in Jesus' life we see the restoration of our relationship to ourselves. Jesus had nothing to hide; he did nothing in secret. His only self-consciousness was an awareness of his relationship to God and his mission. In this self-consciousness, there is no shame. This "shameless" self-consciousness will become important when we later consider our conformity to the image of God restored by Jesus Christ.

The Second Adam and the Last Adam

In Romans 5, Paul identifies Jesus as the Second Adam; in 1 Corinthians 15, he identifies Jesus as the Last Adam (v. 45) and connects this identification with Jesus as the Second Adam (v. 47). In the former passage, Jesus' identity as the Second Human is tied by Paul to the experience of death. In the latter passage, Jesus' identity as the Last Human is tied by Paul to his resurrection.

I would need another essay to begin to explore the connections between the Second Human, his righteousness, and his death. Here I must be content to note the direction that such an exploration would take. As the Second Human, Jesus was perfectly righteous by living "rightly" the relationships for which the first human was made. In this righteousness he restores the image of God.

Moreover, in a world ruled by Sin, death is the consequence of such righteousness. We might think of death as what God required of Jesus Christ, but we would be wrong. Rather, death is the consequence of the first human living out of alignment with God's intentions. For the Second Human, Jesus Christ, who lived in alignment with God's intentions, death comes as a consequence of living rightly in a world that lives wrongly. We could not abide the righteousness of Jesus Christ and so we killed him.

The death of Jesus Christ is the ultimate expression of his identity as the Second Human living in accordance with God's intention for humankind. In the face of death, he does not turn from a right relationship of obedience to God. He does not abandon righteousness. Likewise, confronting our bloodlust and our condemnation, he does not turn from a right relationship to humankind, but loves us even—especially—in death. In his death, he does not turn away from creation but experiences that which is faced by all creation as it groans under the weight of Sin and longs for redemption. Finally, he goes to his death on the cross, condemned as a traitor and blasphemer, knowing who he is and to what he has been called. He knows himself fully and does not turn from who he is in order to avoid crucifixion.

But if his life is truly aligned with God's intentions, then the life that he lives cannot be destroyed by death. The resurrection vindicates Jesus Christ as the Second Human and reveals God's approval of his restoration of the image of God in humankind. His resurrection is not something "added on" to his life after death, it is the very expression of the life that he lived. Death cannot rule over the One who lives in perfect alignment with God's intention.

In his resurrection, then, Jesus Christ is also the "Last Adam." The designation "Last" indicates that his work is done. God's intentions for humankind have been fulfilled in Jesus Christ. But the grace of God does not end there. It is extended from Christ to a new race of humankind who are identified with him as he has identified with them. For those who are "in Christ," his righteousness brings them into right relationship with God, with one another, with creation, and with themselves.

Conformed to the Image of Christ

For the Wesleyan tradition, the grace of God in Jesus Christ is always also the grace of God for humankind; grace *in* Christ is also grace *for* us. This grace for us finds its completion in the work of the Holy Spirit, who brings new birth and right relationships. This work of the Holy Spirit conforms us to the image of Christ and in doing so also restores the image of God in us.

The work of the Holy Spirit begins with new birth. Since the sin of the first human we have all been born into a race destined for death and for separation from God, one another, creation, and ourselves.

In the language of the New Testament, we are destined for hell. This is the consequence of "life" lived out of alignment with God's intention. Now, through the conformity of Jesus Christ to the image of God and the transformative work of the Holy Spirit, a new race of humanity is being formed in the image of God. But we can only join this new race of humanity if we are "born again." In other words, since our first birth is birth into a race that has lost the image of God, that image can only be restored if we experience a "second birth."[9]

Through the work of the Holy Spirit, which begins with new birth, we are conformed to the image of Christ and made "righteous" (Rom 5:17). That is, we are enabled to live rightly in our relationships to God, one another, creation, and ourselves. Another way we express this is to say that we are "justified" (Rom 5:16), we are aligned with God's intentions. Still another way that we describe this grace of God in Christ is to say that we are given "eternal life" (Rom 5:21). If death could not defeat the life that Jesus lived, it cannot defeat the life that we live in Christ.

This new birth, which brings us into Christ's righteousness, restores the image of God so that we live in right relationships as God intended. The first relationship that is restored is our relationship to God. We are made obedient (1 John 3:21-24). What we could not do, born in the lost image of the first human, we are enabled to do when we are born in the image of the Second Human.

The second relationship that is restored as we are conformed to Christ is our relationship to one another. As Christ loved us so we are to love one another and lay down our lives for others, even our enemies (Matt 5:43-48). This love and this sacrifice are not meaningless, powerless gestures of a psychologically sick humanity; they are expressions of trust in the power of a life lived in right relationship to God's intentions. For this reason, "Blessed are those who are persecuted for righteousness' sake, for theirs is the kingdom of heaven" (Matt 5:10).

We are also restored to a right relationship to creation through conformity to the image of Jesus Christ. Here is a problem that I must address. I have argued that Jesus' right relationship to creation is revealed through his "miracles." But today miracles like the ones Jesus performed are not a typical experience for most Christians. Space does not permit a full response to this situation, but I will make two observations. First, Christians outside the secularized West more often report miracles like the ones Jesus performed. Second, in the secularized West we may simply be blind to our "rule" over creation. We see our ability to heal and feed others as something accomplished through human effort, apart from God's grace. Moreover, our "rule" is often an expression of our sinful rebellion, our greed for creation, and our tyranny over it, rather than of our right relationship to creation.[10] Only through Christ may we be rightly aligned with the rest of creation so that we do not fear it, but receive it as God's good gift over which we rule in righteousness.

Finally, through conformity to the image of Christ we are restored to a right relationship to ourselves. Since we are made righteous in Christ, we have nothing to hide, nothing of which to be ashamed. The "self" of which I am ashamed has died and a new "self" has been born in Christ (Rom 6:1-4). Therefore, we are to put off our old selves, made in the image of sinful humankind, and put on our new selves, made in the image and likeness of Christ. This conformity to the image of Christ is the work of the Spirit (Eph 4:20-24).

Finally, we must note that our conformity to the "Second Human" in our lives by the work of the Holy Spirit leads to our conformity to the "Last Human": "Just as we have borne the image of the man of dust, we will also bear the image of the man of heaven" (1 Cor 15:49). Paul follows this assertion with a description of our resurrection into an imperishable, immortal life. We who are conformed to Christ in this Age will live with him in the Age to come.

Conclusion

Approaching the grace of God incarnate in Jesus Christ as I have in this chapter has not led us into the traditional christological debates about Jesus' full humanity and divinity. But the story that I have narrated, of the first human and of Christ as Second Human and Last Human, has enabled us to see God's grace revealed in Jesus Christ for us. Many may want to further describe this revelation in traditional christological categories. Such descriptions are certainly appropriate to the story that I have told, because what we have seen is the story of Jesus Christ as fully human, fully divine. We know God's grace in Jesus Christ only if he is fully God *with* us and God *for* us, and only if he is fully the Second Human *with* us and the Last Human *for* us. This is, finally, the grace of God incarnate in Jesus Christ for our salvation and for the salvation of the world.

Notes

1. For a full-length study of John Wesley's Christology, see John Deschner, *Wesley's Christology: An Interpretation* (Grand Rapids: Francis Asbury Press, 1988; orig. ed., Dallas: Southern Methodist University Press, 1960).

2. Thomas A. Langford, *Practical Divinity: Theology in the Wesleyan Tradition*, rev. ed. (Nashville: Abingdon Press, 1998), vol. 1. Langford introduces his chapter on John Wesley with these words: "Theology, for John Wesley, was intended to transform life. Always in the service of presenting the gospel, theology was to underwrite the proclamation of the grace of God given in Jesus Christ for the redemption of all people. . . . Definitively expressed in Jesus Christ, grace covers the entirety of life" (p. 20).

3. My approach may be considered an example of "Adam Christology." The scholarly discussion of this approach is voluminous and filled with controversy. One helpful presentation is James D. G. Dunn, *The Theology of Paul the Apostle* (Grand Rapids: Eerdmans, 1998), 199-204, 241-42. See also his *Christology in the Making: A New Testament Inquiry into the Origins of the Doctrine of the Incarnation* (Philadelphia: Westminster Press, 1980), 98-128. My purpose here is not to answer all the questions about Adam Christology, but to provide another example of its appropriateness.

4. John Wesley's comments on the image of God are conveniently excerpted in Robert W. Burtner and Robert E. Chiles, eds., *John Wesley's Theology: A Collection from His Works* (Nashville: Abingdon, 1982), 109-12.

5. See the similar account of the image of God in humankind given by H. Ray Dunning, *Reflecting the Divine Image: Christian Ethics in Wesleyan Perspective* (Downers Grove, Ill.: InterVarsity Press, 1998), 77-95, 109-19.

6. There are many errors we can make in our talk about the "image of God." I am not here trying to describe the essence of human nature or give criteria for discerning who is and is not "made in the image of God." Rather, I am using this "image" to tell the story of God's grace in Jesus Christ. For some helpful warnings about our use of the "image of God," see Mary McClintock Fulkerson, "Contesting the Gendered Subject: A Feminist Account of the *Imago Dei*," Rebecca S. Chopp and Sheila Greeve Davaney, eds., *Horizons in Feminist Theology: Identity, Tradition, and Norms* (Minneapolis: Fortress Press, 1997).

7. For more on this complex issue, see Jonathan R. Wilson, "Evangelicals and the Environment: A Theological Concern," *Christian Scholar's Review* (forthcoming).

8. A lot of theological energy has been devoted to the best way to describe the effects of the fall upon the image of God in humankind. Is the image destroyed, erased, distorted, or marred? Each of these terms ascribes a different depth to the effects of the fall. I will not try to adjudicate this debate here. For now I will simply follow the story where it takes us.

9. Here the reader may rightly hear echoes of John Wesley's "Aldersgate experience," however we may interpret that event.

10. In this situation we might also see our ecological crisis as the consequence of our sinful desire to rule over creation.

RETHINKING COMMON GRACE:
Toward a Theology of Co-relation

ROBERT K. JOHNSTON

In a class on the Holy Spirit which I took from Professor Langford in the 1970s, he spoke of the relationship between the human spirit and the Holy Spirit, not in terms of the "correlation" of Paul Tillich's methodology, but in terms of the "co-relation" of John Wesley's. Tom Langford understood humankind's transcendent thrust to be rooted in the "before-handedness of God" (Evelyn Underhill) and to be at times serendipitously transformed by the continuing presence of the Spirit in our lives. This essay is written in appreciation and honor of my friend and mentor. It seeks to extend his co-relational perspective.

Common grace—the wider work of the Holy Spirit throughout and within all creatures and creation—is problematic for many contemporaries, both within and outside the church. Within the church, once creation is described in the past tense, the experience of God as the life-giving Spirit in all things is too often ignored in favor of the Spirit of faith. Theological textbooks focus on the Holy Spirit as the Spirit of redemption and sanctification. The rise of Pentecostalism and the charismatic movement has only reinforced the church's understanding of the Spirit's role primarily in terms of the Christian life. (The Spirit is, after all, described in the Third Article of the Creed.) Little is said with regard to the Spirit's role in nature's continuance or culture's outworking, except perhaps to assert God's presence.[1]

Within the larger society, the Holy Spirit's broader activity is similarly given short shrift. There is, for example, a negative theism that has characterized much of the religiosity of modernity (one thinks of the divine absence in many of the novels of John Updike) and a this-worldly spirituality that is typical of much of postmodernity (the gentle eco-feminism of the novels of Barbara Kingsolver comes to mind). The propositional and pious approaches of Christian theology are alike rejected. There is a nearness to the Spirit, but it remains out of reach. Comments Martin Marty, ours is an "epoch of homelessness," where Presence and Providence are largely absent.[2]

What has happened to that "awareness of God in, with and beneath the experience of life, which gives us assurance of God's fellowship, friendship and love"?[3] Such an experience of the Spirit was referred to in the early church. They spoke of special grace, that singular historical appearance of the grace of God in Christ Jesus. But those like Augustine also recognized a common grace into which we are all born, Christians and non-Christians alike. There is Grace present in the peach tree that blooms and in the rise and fall of political societies. The Spirit of life, said Augustine, "helps the good choices of created spirits, judges the evil ones, and orders all of them, giving powers to some and not to others."[4]

Nature and Grace

Augustine's profligate life prior to his conversion might hold some of the initial answer as to why the doctrine of common grace has been so easily ignored or too narrowly defined within the subsequent life of the church. The blessings of common grace were not celebrated by Augustine lest he fall back into idolatry or the sins of the flesh. (Augustine was even cautious with regard to enjoying his food.) His theology of revelation remained suspicious of nature and human experience. Christianity was rooted in the Word, more than in the Spirit. In the Reformation era, the desire to proclaim "justification by grace through faith" again made the church suspicious of anything that might be interpreted as "natural theology." The experience of the Spirit was described largely in terms of the Word incarnate. And in the time of the Enlightenment, John Wesley needed to take human thought and action with increased seriousness, but at the same time the secular spirit of the times needed to be challenged and human sinfulness reasserted.

And yet, occasional Christians through the ages have continued to give voice to the larger life of the Spirit. They have experienced the extent of God's grace to be as broad as common human history and as far-ranging as creation itself. They have not denied the Spirit's christological concentration, but have also refused to be limited to it. Elizabeth Barrett Browning captures well the paradox of common grace:

> Natural things
> And spiritual,—who separates those two
> In art, in morals, or the social drift,
> Tears up the bond of nature and brings death,
> Paints futile pictures, writes unreal verse,
> Leads vulgar days, deals ignorantly with men,
> Is wrong, in short at all points. . . .
> . . .
> Earth's crammed with heaven,
> And every common bush afire with God;
> But only he who sees, takes off his shoes—
> The rest sit round it and pluck blackberries. . . .
> . . .
> Not one day, in the artist's ecstasy,
> But every day, feast, fast, or working-day,
> The spiritual significance burns through
> The hieroglyphic of material shows,
> Henceforward he would pain the globe with wings,
> And reverence fish and fowl, the bull, the tree,
> And even his very body as a man.[5]

One thinks as well of the Danish movie *Babette's Feast,* based on the story by Isak Dinesen. Babette, a famous chef from Paris, comes to a bleak, religiously severe, nineteenth-century village where without complaint she serves the small, pietistic congregation the codfish and ale-bread soup they consider appropriate for Christians. There is little of pleasure here. But when given the chance, Babette prepares with her own money an extravagant anniversary dinner in honor of the founder. The elderly members of the community, who have been bickering continually, show up for the dinner intent on not enjoying the food, believing any bodily pleasure to be sin. Nevertheless, the feast proves both sensual and spiritual. A slow transformation in the community occurs as grudges soften and conflicts resolve. A distinguished, but despondent, general who is visiting his aunt attends the feast and, overcome with gratitude, comments on the surprising, sacramental grace he has just experienced. In his shortsightedness he has falsely imagined that divine grace is finite, but, he says,

> Grace is infinite. We need only await it with confidence and receive it in gratitude. Mercy imposes no conditions. . . . [In this meal] mercy and truth are met together. And righteousness and bliss shall kiss one another.[6]

One can scarcely imagine a speech like this coming from Augustine's mouth. Dinesen's general speaks even more expansively:

> My friends, we have been told that grace is to be found in the universe. But in our human foolishness and short-sightedness we imagine divine grace to be finite. . . . The moment comes when our eyes are opened, and we see and realize that grace is infinite. . . . Grace, brothers, makes no conditions and singles out none of us in particular; grace takes us all to its bosom and proclaims general amnesty.[7]

Grace's Cosmic Reach: Two Traditional Approaches

Grace has a cosmic range; it refers to the activity of the Holy Spirit, "the Lord and giver of life" (the Nicene Creed). The Spirit is active in the world and in history, bringing to completion the creational as well as the redemptive purposes of God. Although this has been more readily recognized in the common experience of Christians as suggested by the two foregoing illustrations, it has not been so easily integrated into the formal theology of the church. In the Protestant tradition, two descriptions of grace's wider expression do stand out—those of John Calvin and John Wesley—but even these are not without their limitations, falling short of the Spirit's expanse.

John Calvin's Common Grace

For Calvin, the seeming contradiction of humankind's total depravity on the one hand and the common-sense recognition that non-Christians have accomplished much that is good in civilization on the other led him to develop his doctrine of *common* grace.[8] How is it that those outside the church seem to receive God's gifts? How is it that they accomplish much that is true, good, and beautiful? How is it that civilizations continue to advance? Why is it that some people seem uniquely gifted? It is, he recognized, the Spirit who quickens all. Yet how is this to be reconciled with the fact that only some are predestined for salvation?

Unaided reason and unredeemed nature can do no good, Without the Spirit, there is darkness. Moreover, according to Calvin, the doctrine of free will in humankind risks robbing the sovereign God of his honor. Instead, it must be asserted that human society is utterly dependent on the Spirit's unmerited favor. This divine grace is to be distinguished from saving Grace, but it is not to be denied. There is a God-given earthly knowledge, just as there is heavenly knowledge. It is everywhere diffused, though unequally distributed, and it sustains all things. The Spirit's role in creation is the source of government and all religious aspiration, the liberal and manual arts, philosophy and science. Wrote Calvin:

> Whenever we come upon these matters in secular writers, let that admirable light of truth shining in them teach us that the mind of man, though fallen and perverted from its wholeness, is nevertheless clothed and ornamented with God's excellent gifts. If we regard the Spirit of God as the sole fountain of truth, we shall neither reject the truth itself, nor despise it wherever it shall appear, unless we wish to dishonor the Spirit of God. . . . But shall we count anything praiseworthy or noble without recognizing at the same time that it comes from God? . . . Let us, accordingly, learn by their example how many gifts the Lord left to human nature even after it was despoiled of its true good.[9]

Calvin's doctrine of common grace thus moves deductively from his understanding of God's sovereignty and humankind's sinfulness to the necessity of positing the Spirit's empowerment in order to explain all "natural" goodness.

There is an evident caution and a certain abstraction to Calvin's argument. (Even when experience is mentioned, it is of past civilizations and leaders.) This becomes particularly evident as the discussion of common grace is extended by such later Calvinist theologians as Jonathan Edwards, Herman Bavinck, Herman Kuiper, and John Murray. For Calvin and his followers, two aspects have stood out. First, given Calvin's stress on human depravity, common grace has been seen in terms of *restraint*. Calvin speaks, for example, of humankind being able to know the second tablet of the Law, for it preserves civil society.[10] Or in the more colorful words of Jonathan Edwards, "There are in the souls of wicked men those hellish principles reigning, that would presently kindle and flame out into hell-fire, if it were not for God's restraints."[11] And second, given special grace, common grace is deemed *insufficient*. Bavinck states it well:

> By his common grace he restrains sin. . . . Yet common grace is not enough. It compels but it does not change; it restrains but does not conquer. . . . To save the world required nothing less than the fullness of his grace and the omnipotence of his love.[12]

There is, for all practical purposes, two different graces—the one to sustain, the other to save.

It is true that Calvin and his followers recognized that the richness of nature and culture are to be credited to God's common grace, as well. And it is even recognized that this is because God delights in his handiwork, which in turn resounds to the glory of God. But prior to this recognition and qualifying of it are the twin needs to understand common grace as (1) restraining sin and (2) being distinct from salvation. Common grace might be cosmic, but its expression remains cautious.

John Wesley's Prevenient Grace

At the Methodist Conference of 1745, John Wesley recognized that he and his followers had come "to the very edge of Calvinism":

> (1.) In ascribing all good to the free grace of God. (2.) In denying all natural free will, and all power antecedent to grace. And (3.) In excluding all merit from man; even for what he has or does by the grace of God.[13]

Yet for John Wesley, other motivations were at work than for John Calvin as he framed his universal doctrine of grace. In particular, Wesley was interested in exploring the interaction between divine grace and human agency. While affirming original sin, Wesley realized with other Enlightenment thinkers the possibility of human understanding and activity. He also rejected the Calvinist doctrine of predestination, that the offer of saving grace was restricted to the elect.

Rather than speak of a common grace, which is nonsalvific and focused more on sin's restraint, Wesley developed a more unitary and positive understanding of grace centered in the one work of the Holy Spirit. His term for that aspect of divine grace which precedes and extends beyond our salvation was *prevenient* grace. By this he did not mean chiefly what modern English usage suggests (i.e., "restraining," "preventing"), but the eighteenth-century sense of "coming before" or "preparing." In his sermon "The Scripture Way of Salvation," Wesley spoke of "preventing grace" as

> all that "light" wherewith the Son of God "enlighteneth everyone that cometh into the world," showing every man "to do justly, to love mercy, and to walk humbly with his God"; all the convictions which his Spirit from time to time works in every child of man.[14]

There is for Wesley no thought of human autonomy or natural goodness; certainly, no Pelagianism. It is God who "breathes into us every good desire, and brings every good desire to good effect."[15] There is no independent, salutary human action; only humankind's reaction to the indwelling Spirit. But at the same time, Wesley recognized that there is present in all people a gracious drawing after God, which if we yield to it, increases more and more and produces real goodness.

In his helpful study of Wesley's theology, *Responsible Grace,* Randy Maddox notes that while Western theologians, including Calvin, identified God's grace primarily in terms of a forensic *pardon,* Wesley was more influenced by the Eastern theologians who construed grace primarily in terms of an enabling *power.* While recognizing grace as unmerited pardon, Wesley also understood it as "that power of God the Holy Ghost which 'worketh in us both to will and to do of his good pleasure.' "[16] Such restoring grace was universally available, though also resistible. It was that which lay behind and empowered our partially restored human freedom and which "came before" our sense of the need for God's offer of salvation. Here was a common grace which was one of a piece—that is, on the same continuum but not identical—with saving grace. For Wesley, there was only one grace, and it was to be understood as a "grace upon grace."[17]

In his sermon "On Working Out Our Own Salvation," Wesley argued for the universal presence of grace in the context of sinful humanity:

> For allowing that all the souls of men are dead in sin by *nature,* this excuses none, seeing there is no man that is in a state of mere nature; there is no man, unless he has quenched the Spirit, that is wholly void of the grace of God. But this is not natural; it is more properly termed "preventing grace." . . . Everyone has some measure of that light, some faint glimmering ray, which sooner or later, more or less, enlightens every man that cometh into the world. . . . So that no man sins because he has not grace, but because he does not use the grace which he hath.[18]

Some Wesleyan interpreters have mistakenly understood prevenient grace as an ability to initiate righteous action, a gift given to the human spirit. But Thomas Langford is no doubt correct when he writes, "Prevenient grace must always be recognized as God's activity, it is not a gift of power given over to persons, as their possession; it is not a gift from God, it is the gift of God; it is the continuous presence of God, encountering persons, sensitizing persons, and inviting persons."[19]

While Calvin saw *common* grace in more negative terms, as God's activity in "preventing," or restraining, sin and evil and thus creating the possibility for a subsequent and largely independent saving grace, Wesley understood prevenient grace more positively, as preparing the way for grace upon grace. Yet for both, the focus is always directly related to God's calling in Jesus Christ. For Calvin this is a distinct gracious activity toward the elect; for Wesley, it is a continuous and deepening activity offered by the Spirit, but which can be resisted by humanity. With both, however, re-creation takes precedence over creation in their discussions. The fear of an independent human rationality or freedom keeps common grace from being more fully explored by them.[20]

Reconsidering Common Grace

What would a doctrine of common grace look like if it were motivated more by questions of creation than re-creation? Is a more full-orbed doctrine possible while maintaining a commitment to the uniqueness of Christ's saving grace? Has the history of Christian theology looked at the biblical discussion too narrowly? Could we be helped by turning to those portions of Scripture which find their center in creation theology rather than in *Heilsgeschichte* (saving history)? In answering these questions, it is necessary to begin where Calvin and Wesley concentrated their attention, with the New Testament passages which have a larger salvific intention. But we must not end there. The Old Testament's understanding of the overarching presence and activity of the Spirit which animates creation and empowers humankind needs also to be heard.

Common grace is understood by many in the church to be limited, at least practically, to God's activity in both convicting individuals and preserving society. It clarifies our situation as sinners and protects us from the chaos we otherwise would create. Although there is truth in such assertions, they are also incomplete. For example, whether in popular parlance or in the theology of the church, conscience is often seen only in negative terms, as giving someone a sense of guilt or an awareness of sin, of causing that person to feel uncomfortable. The positive role of conscience in encouraging the good is ignored. The *locos classicus* for a Christian understanding of conscience as convicting us of sin is Paul's argument in Romans 1 and 2 (cf. Rom 1:20, 2:1, "Therefore you have no excuse . . .").

For theologians, as well, our conscience is typically linked to the Word, "the true light, which enlightens everyone" (John 1:9). As Wesley says, "And it is his [the Son of God's] Spirit who giveth thee an inward check, who causeth thee to feel uneasy, when thou walkest in any instance contrary to the light which he hath given thee."[21] This reticence in giving to conscience a more positive function that is not explicitly christological stems from the perceived danger of a theological retreat into a "works righteousness," by which people make a claim upon God rather than vice versa. It stems from confusing the Spirit's initiative in sensitizing our conscience with independent human activity.

But according to Scripture, conscience, even after the Fall, is always guided by the light of God's revelation. It is not an independent human faculty. Romans declares:

When Gentiles, who do not possess the law, do instinctively what the law requires, these, though not having the law, are a law to themselves. They show that what the law requires is written on their hearts, to which their own conscience also bears witness; and their conflicting thoughts will accuse or perhaps excuse them. (Rom 2:14, 15)

Reflecting on this passage in his commentary on the book of Romans, Calvin suggested that *God* imprints on the hearts of non-Christians "a discrimination and judgment by which they distinguish between what is just and unjust, between what is honest and dishonest."[22] Wesley says something similar in his sermon "On Conscience": "For though in one sense it may be termed 'natural,' because it is found in all men, yet properly speaking it is not *natural;* but a supernatural gift of God, above all his natural endowments."[23] Wesley makes the observation that the word "conscience" "literally signifies 'knowing with another.' "[24] Conscience is based in grace; it is "written on their hearts" by the Other (cf. Paul saying, "I am not lying; my conscience confirms it *by the Holy Spirit,*" Rom 9:1, emphasis added).

But if conscience is based in common grace, not natural law—if it is always "knowing with another"—then its positive function should more easily be affirmed, even by Calvinists and Wesleyans. If it is through conscience that we judge our own thoughts and actions as to whether they deserve praise or blame, merit or censure, then conscience has the possibility of motivating us toward the good, as well as keeping us from the evil.

I am writing this article as news is surfacing about a Swiss bank security guard who saw old ledgers about to be shredded and rescued them from destruction. These ledgers contained the names of Jews whose money was wrongly confiscated following World War II. Having recently seen the Steven Spielberg film *Schindler's List,* the guard believed he must also do what he could to right the injustice of the Holocaust. His action exposed the bank's cover-up and led to a settlement of more than a billion dollars for Jews worldwide, even as it cost him his job and forced him to take political asylum in the United States to avoid patriotic backlash.

Stories such as this illustrate the positive role conscience may play. It not only instills fear in us; it also provides motivation to follow the truth, to do the good, and to appreciate the beautiful. We need to look once again at Paul's subargument in Romans 2. Within his larger apologia concerning sin and salvation, Paul also describes the possibility of real obedience (2:7, 14-15, 29), which is the specific result of the Spirit's common grace, and which itself results in real praise from

God (2:29).[25] Rather than conscience being limited to its *"convicting"* function, conscience should be viewed more broadly also in terms of the Spirit's *"convincing."* It is our conscience that causes us to help one another, to return money that is found, to even put our own life in jeopardy in order to right an injustice.

Just as theologians have narrowed the role of grace with regard to our consciences to that of convicting us of sin, failing to recognize the Spirit's dialectical role in both *convincing* and *convicting* our human spirits, so theologians have undialectically understood common grace's global thrust to be simply concerned with *preserving* the world from destruction, failing to recognize adequately the Spirit's role in *providing* all that is good. The pattern for God's preserving grace is established early in Scripture. Humankind sins in the garden and is punished with death; however, the sentence is postponed and the first couple is instead sent out to live "east of Eden" (Gen 3:24). When Cain kills his brother, he is made to wander, but is nonetheless given a "mark" by God so no one would kill him (Gen 4:15). When the Lord saw the wickedness of humankind and sent a flood, it was followed by a rainbow (Gen 9:16). God's preserving, common grace is evident from the beginning of history. As Emil Brunner has written, "Wherever both the omnipotent creator and sin are taken equally seriously, there must needs arise a third concept, that of God's gracious preservation."[26] And Scripture demonstrates this to be the case. Preserving grace does not deny the human spirit by overriding sin; but it does neutralize its worst consequences (cf. Ezek 18:23, 32; Rom 2:4; 9:22; 2 Pet 3:9).

Common grace's preserving function is illustrated through Paul's discussion of the state in Romans 13. There, rulers are understood as appointed by God "to execute wrath on the wrongdoer" (Rom 13:4). We are to pay authorities our taxes and offer them our respect, for political leaders hold back the effects of evil and sin, lest the world degenerate into chaos and destruction. While similarly recognizing the preserving function of civil rulers (they "punish those who do wrong"), 1 Peter 2:14 provides a wider perspective. The gracious enabling of political authority also enables them to "praise those who do right."

God's preserving-providing grace also has its locus outside the confines of the political arena. Marriage and work are additional expressions of human culture, which are discussed biblically as being rooted in God's empowering grace. Although Paul advises that if one cannot practice self-control, he or she should marry ("For it is better to marry than to be aflame with passion," 1 Cor 7:9), a biblical understanding of marriage (and the experience of countless couples including my wife and me!) suggests more than this negative justification. It was Adam who was graciously provided with Eve as his partner. And the writer commenting on this, concluded, "Therefore a man leaves his father and his mother and clings to his wife, and they become one flesh" (Gen 2:24). Marriage has a sanctity grounded in common grace, which couples through the ages have recognized (cf. Eph 5:21, 22, 33).

As for work, the writer of the book of Ecclesiastes had no illusions about finding out through his own efforts life's meaning or mystery. His work will not "save" him. But the writer Qoheleth (the "Preacher") also did not shrink from recommending that we find enjoyment in our work. After all, our toil is a gift "from the hand of God" (Eccl 2:24). Work can prove vain when motivated by self-conceit (cf. Eccl 1:12–2:23; 4:4; 6:7). But Qoheleth can also recognize:

> Likewise all to whom God gives wealth and possessions and whom he enables to enjoy them, and to accept their lot and find enjoyment in their toil—this is the gift of God. (Eccl 5:19)

"He's Got the Whole World in His Hand"

The common grace of the Spirit not only convicts, it convinces; it not only preserves, it provides. As the spiritual proclaims, "He's got the whole world in his hand." Such an affirmation might serve as a definition of "common grace." John Wesley recognized that to separate anything from God was a form of "practical atheism." In his sermon "Upon our Lord's Sermon on the Mount, III," Wesley proclaimed,

> But the great lesson . . . is that God is in all things, and that we are to see the Creator in the glass of every creature; that we should use and look upon nothing as separate from God, which indeed is a kind of practical atheism; but with a true magnificence of thought survey heaven and earth and all that is therein as contained by God in the hollow of his hand, who by his intimate presence holds them all in

164

being, who pervades and actuates the whole created frame, and is in a true sense the soul of the universe.[27]

For Calvin, too, every experience of the Spirit's creation is an experience of the Spirit itself.[28] As Job cries, "The spirit of God has made me, / and the breath of the Almighty gives me life" (Job 33:4; cf. Job 34:13-15; Jas 4:15). So too the Psalmist, "When you send forth your spirit, they are created; / and you renew the face of the ground" (Ps 104:30; cf. Ps 136:25).

One would imagine that the theme of God's universal, life-giving presence would have been developed, therefore, into a robust, life-affirming theology of common grace. It is, after all, the consistent witness throughout Scripture. Jesus reminds us that the Father's hand is on the sparrow, just as he numbers the hairs of our head (Matt 10:29, 30). Truly the "LORD is good to all" (Ps 145:9; cf. Matt 5:45). But rather than proclaiming this positive message to Christian and non-Christian alike, the church has chosen more often to restrict its understanding of the Spirit's blessings chiefly to Christians and to view common grace as primarily clarifying our common sinfulness and protecting humankind from itself.

To give yet another example, when interpreting Paul's doctrine, theologians have turned repeatedly to Paul's accusations of our common sinfulness as found in his letter to the Romans, but have given scant mention to Paul's more positive apologetic presented in Acts. In his argument in Romans 1, Paul makes the clear presence of God's "eternal power and divine nature, invisible though they are," the basis of God's wrath. Although we know God through his universal Spirit, we do not honor him (Rom 1:18-23). We therefore stand condemned (Rom 2:1). Alternatively, in Paul's sermons in Acts, God's presence in the sun and rain is presented as an invitation to believe (Acts 14:15-17). As he reminds the Athenians, "For 'In him we live and move and have our being'; as even some of your own poets have said, 'For we too are his offspring'" (Acts 17:28). We need not become univocal in our approach to the Spirit's actions outside and beyond the church's life. Scripture is not.

Common grace can open out into a partial, but real expression of faith, just as it can help identify our sin. Here is the force of the book of Ecclesiastes. Although wisdom, riches, and pleasure make no difference with regard to one's ultimate fate and often only showcase life's vanity, when recognized as the gifts from God that they are, they also are not to be ignored. We cannot "save" ourselves; but life is not to be disparaged. Death is the great leveler (2:14-16); greed, the real motivator (4:4). Life proves amoral all too often (8:9-14), and God's ultimate will remains mysterious (3:11, 6:12). *And yet*, for Qoheleth, life is not simply vain. As a gift from God life must be judged good. Sometimes Qoheleth commends common grace by saying it is "good" (5:18-20) or "there is nothing better" (2:24-26; 3:12, 22; 8:15). Other times, he actively calls his reader to enjoy life as a gift from God (9:7-10; 11:7-10). Qoheleth can both decry and celebrate human life's possibilities, almost in the same breath (cf. 4:2 and 9:4).

As Elizabeth Huwiler points out, interpreters of the book of Ecclesiastes have had "difficulty giving equal emphasis to the book's negative evaluations and to its positive call." They have failed to hear the Spirit's dialectical call. Observable life is finally incoherent (and thus, Christians would add, further revelation in Jesus Christ is necessary). Here is the negative function of prevenient grace. And yet, the joys of common grace are also to be valued. The anguish of Qoheleth's investigation of life is knowing how to hold onto these two truths in tandem.[29] At times, Qoheleth's experience causes him to hate life (2:17; 4:2). But he goes on to commend life, for it is God's gift (3:13):

> There is nothing better for mortals than to eat and drink, and find enjoyment in their toil. This also, I saw, is from the hand of God; for apart from him who can eat or who can have enjoyment? For to the one who pleases him God gives wisdom and knowledge and joy.
>
> (Eccl 2:24-26)

The grace of God is gratuitous. As Jesus said to Nicodemus, "The wind [or Spirit] blows where it chooses, and you hear the sound of it, but you do not know where it comes from or where it goes" (John 3:8). Qoheleth recognized that though some gather and reap, God will give it to another. His frustration is thus real and his recognition of human sinfulness pervasive. Yet common grace is present. God gives us the days of one's life, the ability to eat and find enjoyment, our wealth and work, even our very spirit, or breath. We can rejoice in him. As James would later counsel, "Every generous act of giving, with every perfect gift, is from above, coming down from the Father of lights, with whom there is no variation or shadow due to change" (Jas 1:17).

Jürgen Moltmann, in his book *The Spirit of Life,* speaks of the Spirit's "immanent transcendence."[30] It is this that the doctrine of common grace celebrates. Rather than limiting the wider work of the Spirit to convicting and preserving, however, we need to discover, as well, the Spirit's positive role in convincing and providing. While the legacy of the Reformation has been to underplay the Spirit's work in the world as a whole in favor of an emphasis on the Spirit's role in creation, the church, and the individual believer, such a dichotomy is both unbiblical and unnecessary.[31] Grace is after all grace. Common grace will not save; but neither should it be reduced to the negative complement of salvation. The Spirit is "the Lord and giver of life"—all life.

Notes

1. Jürgen Moltmann comments: "This redemptive Spirit is cut off both from bodily life and from the life of nature. It makes people turn away from 'this world' and hope for a better world beyond. They then seek and experience in the Spirit of Christ a power that is different from the divine energy of life" (Moltmann, *The Spirit of Life* [Minneapolis: Fortress Press, 1992], 8).

2. Cf. Martin E. Marty, "Christianity and Literature: Covertly Public, Overtly Private," *Christianity and Literature* 47, no. 3 (Spring 1998): 261-83.

3. Moltmann, *Spirit of Life,* 17.

4. Augustine, *The City of God,* abridged version, Vernon Bourke, ed. (Garden City, N.Y.: Doubleday, Image Books, 1958), v. 9, 107.

5. Elizabeth Barrett Browning, "Aurora Leigh," quoted in Elizabeth Dreyer, *Manifestations of Grace* (Wilmington: Michael Glazier, 1990), 223-24.

6. *Babette's Feast,* Gabriel Axel, director (1987). Available through Orion Home Video, 1988.

7. Isak Dinesen, *Babette's Feast and Other Anecdotes of Destiny* (New York: Vintage, 1988), 40-41, quoted in Robert Jewett, *Saint Paul Returns to the Movies* (Grand Rapids: Wm. B. Eerdmans, 1998), 53.

8. John Calvin, *Institutes of the Christian Religion,* John T. McNeill, ed. (Philadelphia: Westminster, 1960), II.ii.12-17, 270-77.

9. Ibid., II.ii.15, 273-75.

10. Ibid., II.ii.24, 284.

11. Jonathan Edwards, *Works,* vol. 4 (New York: 1881), 315, quoted in John Murray, *Collected Writings,* vol. 2 (Carlisle, Pa.: Banner of Truth Trust, 1977), 98. Cf. Calvin, *Institutes,* II.iii.3.

12. Herman Bavinck, "Common Grace," Raymond C. Van Leeuwen, trans., *Calvin Theological Journal* 24, no. 1 (April 1989): 61.

13. Minutes, August 2, 1745, quoted in Thomas C. Oden, *John Wesley's Scriptural Christianity* (Grand Rapids: Zondervan, 1994), 253.

14. John Wesley, Sermon 43, "The Scripture Way of Salvation," 1.2, in *The Bicentennial Edition of the Works of John Wesley,* ed. Albert Outler (Nashville: Abingdon Press, 1984 –), 2:157, hereinafter cited as *Works.*

15. Wesley, Sermon 85, "On Working Out Our Own Salvation," 1.2, in *Works,* 3:203. Cf. Wesley, Sermon 51, "The Good Steward," 1.8, *Works,* 3:286: "Add, lastly, that on which all the rest depend, and without which they would all be curses, not blessings: namely, the *grace* of God, the power of his Holy Spirit, which alone worketh in us all that is acceptable in his sight."

Cf. also Sermon 11, "The Witness of the Spirit, II," 5.4, *Works*, 1:298: "There may be foretastes of joy, of peace, of love—and those not delusive, but really from God. . . . Yea, there may be a degree of long-suffering, of gentleness, of fidelity . . . (not a shadow thereof, but a real degree, by the preventing grace of God). . . . But it is by no means advisable to rest here; it is at the peril of our souls if we do."

16. Wesley, Sermon 12, "The Witness of Our Own Spirit," 15-16, in *Works*, 1:309-10, quoted in Randy L. Maddox, *Responsible Grace: John Wesley's Practical Theology* (Nashville: Kingswood Books, 1994), 85.

17. Wesley, Sermon 1, "Salvation by Faith," 3, *Works*, 1:118; cf. Sermon 43, "The Scripture Way of Salvation," 1.8, *Works*, 2:160.

18. Wesley, Sermon 85, "On Working Out Our Own Salvation," 3.4, *Works*, 3:207.

19. For a helpful description of four different interpretations by Wesley scholars of prevenient grace's relationship to saving grace, see Thomas A. Langford, "John Wesley's Doctrine of Justification by Faith," *Bulletin of the United Church of Canada Committee on Archives and History* 29 (1980): 55-61.

20. "As an Enlightenment man, [Wesley] saw an atheistic world as the object of the principal struggle, with the attack focused on scientific interpretations of human life. Wesley was fighting to escape the use of natural-science models to account for human character. In that battle he opposed the Deists . . . Isaac Newton . . . and David Hartley. . . . In opposition, he intended to hold nature and grace together. . . . In spite of his efforts, Wesley was unable to provide a completely adequate intellectual schema, but his sense was profoundly right." (Thomas A. Langford, *Practical Divinity: Theology in the Wesleyan Tradition* [Nashville: Abingdon Press, 1983], 29-30).

21. Wesley, Sermon 105, "On Conscience," 1.5, *Works*, 3:482.

22. John Calvin, *Commentary on Romans* (2:14, 15), quoted in L. Berkhof, *Systematic Theology*, 3rd ed. (Grand Rapids: Wm. B. Eerdmans, 1946), 441.

23. Sermon 105, "On Conscience," 1.5, *Works*, 3:482.

24. Ibid.,1.1, 481.

25. Klyne Snodgrass, "Justification by Grace—To the Doers: An Analysis of the Place of Romans 2 in the Theology of Paul," *NTS* 32 (1986): 80.

26. Emil Brunner, *Natural Theology* (London: Geoffrey Bless, 1946), p. 27.

27. Wesley, Sermon 23, "Upon our Lord's Sermon on the Mount, III," 1.11, *Works*, 1:516-17.

28. Cf. Moltmann, *Spirit of Life*, 31-38.

29. Elizabeth Huwiler, "Ecclesiastes," in Roland E. Murphy and Elizabeth Huwiler, *Proverbs, Ecclesiastes, Song of Songs*, vol. 12, New International Biblical Commentary, Old Testament (Peabody, Mass.: Hendrickson, 1999), n.p.; cf. Robert K. Johnston, "Confessions of a Workaholic: A Reappraisal of Qoheleth," *CBQ* 38 (January 1976): 14-28.

30. Moltmann, *Spirit of Life*, 31.

31. Donald McKim, "The Stirring of the Spirit Among Contemporary Theologians," *Perspectives* 13, no. 5 (May 1998): 19.

VISIBLE GRACE:
The Church as God's Embodied Presence

PHILIP D. KENNESON

In his book about the plight of American public schools, *The End of Education*, Neil Postman argues that most analyses of public education remain remarkably superficial. Although everyone from the President of the United States to the local school board argues over whether what is needed is more testing, national standards, or more computers, Postman suggests that what is needed is a different kind of conversation. Instead of arguing over the techniques or means of education, Postman insists that what is most needed is a discussion about the purpose or "end" of public education. As long as no consensus exists with regard to what schools are *for*, it is impossible to adjudicate different proposals for revitalizing them. In short, if people do not agree about *what* they are trying to do, then arguments about how to do it *better* are bound to be frustrating and fruitless. Or as Postman poignantly notes, "We can make the trains run on time, but if they do not go where we want them to go, why bother?"[1]

A similar case could be made concerning the plight of the church in the United States. The church is having a difficult time finding its way in the new cultural context that is emerging; as a result, numerous proposals have been offered about how to "do" church better. Some have suggested, for example, that the church needs to offer a more "contemporary" style of worship that will appeal to younger generations, while others have surmised that the church has an "image" problem, and so what is needed is a marketing plan designed to make the church more appealing in the eyes of religious consumers. How should we evaluate such proposals? Simply asking if they "work" begs a more fundamental question: work at doing *what*? If our task as the church involves more than getting people to attend a worship service on Sunday morning, then we will need a clearer view of what the purpose or "end" of the church is before we will be able to discern whether this or that proposal will help us do it better. In what follows, therefore, I offer a reminder about the purpose of the church in God's economy of salvation, a reminder that I hope may serve as a touchstone for discernments about how best to be who God has called us to be.[2]

Grace Upon Grace

The title of this essay suggests that the church may be understood as "visible grace." Before attending in the next section to the notion of visibility, I begin by articulating as clearly as possible what I mean by "grace." Since each essay in this volume speaks to this matter in some way, I highlight only those aspects of grace that are most pertinent to this chapter.

Grace as God's Free Presence

At the most fundamental level, God's grace is nothing other than God's very presence. When we long for and pray for God's grace, we are desiring and asking for nothing other than God's own presence. When we sense that we are daily sustained by God's grace, we are sensing nothing other than God's own presence. When we gather for the Eucharist to receive God's grace in the sacraments, we are receiving nothing other than God's own presence. God's grace is simply God's own presence, God's self-gift.

Such a notion does, of course, raise an obvious question. If in pouring out God's grace God becomes more present to us than God was before, does not this in some sense imply God's prior absence? This important and complex question has been addressed in various ways in the Christian tradition; for our purposes here, only a brief response is necessary. If we affirm with the Christian tradition that the continuing life of the cosmos is sustained by God's grace, then we must affirm that God is never completely absent. Yet some Christian thinkers have suggested that one way of imagining God's act of creation is to imagine God's creation of a sphere of life in which God's overwhelming and unambiguous presence is withdrawn in order to make human freedom possible.[3] In other words, if humankind was to be something other than simply an appendage of God, then the very act of creating someone truly *other* than God necessitated creating a space relatively free of God's presence. Only in such a space would human beings be human beings and not simply the reflex of God. The glory of genuine communion with God and one another would be impossible without the freedom of desire and will, yet such freedom would be impossible within the shadow of God's overwhelming presence. In short, to receive God's self-gift we must not already have it; to choose freely to receive it, we must also be free to reject it. Thus, God's act of creation begins not with an impressive display of raw power, but with a profound act of self-limitation or *kenosis*. In this way, God's gift of God's presence is made possible by the prior gift of God's absence, God's gift of freedom woven into the very fabric of creation. Hence, although God's presence is required to sustain the very existence of the cosmos, God deigns to be absent, to be hidden, to be veiled in ambiguity, lest God's overwhelming presence negate the conditions necessary for the kind of communion God desires and for which we have been created.

Grace as God's Reconciling Presence

When the "God of peace" offers God's self as a gift, the acceptance of this gift brings peace in the form of reconciliation, healing, wholeness, salvation—in a word, *shalom.* Even when God draws alongside of God's people in order to sound a word of judgment, that word is issued for the ultimate good of the people of God. Moreover, if grace is understood as God's presence, then Christians believe there is no more definitive embodiment of that grace than the person of Jesus Christ. The story we tell of Jesus Christ as Emmanuel, as "God with us," remains the definitive narrative for our understanding of the depths of God's grace and mercy. In the person of Jesus Christ, God has inextricably bound the very life of God to the life of creation. Christians affirm that this inexplicable mystery, which stands at the heart of Christian faith and practice, reveals the unfathomable

171

lengths to which God will go in order to be present to and for the creation.

Though Christians have often disagreed over the centuries concerning how best to conceptualize this mystery we call the Incarnation, most have affirmed Scripture's testimony that Jesus was enabled to do and be what he did and was by the power of the Spirit. From his conception to his ascension, Jesus is preeminently the bearer of the Spirit. However, the story of Jesus does not end with his ascension. The Spirit of God—which is also called "the Spirit of Jesus" (Acts 16:7; Phil 1:19)—is poured out upon the gathered community at Pentecost, signaling a decisive eschatological moment in the history of God's relation with humanity. As Peter remarks on the day of Pentecost, this outpouring of God's spirit upon all flesh is a sign that a new age has begun (Acts 2:17).

Thus, the reconciliation of God and the created order made possible by Jesus Christ is not completed at the cross and resurrection. Because God's ultimate desire is that this gift of reconciliation be offered to and accepted by the entire created cosmos, God creates and empowers the church—the body of Christ—to continue this "ministry of reconciliation."

> So if anyone is in Christ, there is a new creation: everything old has passed away; see, everything has become new! All this is from God, who reconciled us to himself through Christ, and has given us the ministry of reconciliation; that is, in Christ God was reconciling the world to himself, not counting their trespasses against them, and entrusting the message of reconciliation to us. So we are ambassadors for Christ, since God is making his appeal through us; we entreat you on behalf of Christ, be reconciled to God. (2 Cor 5:17-20)

Grace as God's Empowering Presence

If what has been said is true, then God's free and reconciling presence enables us to receive ourselves as a gift. That is, God's transforming presence makes possible a new kind of life, a life that can never be humanly engineered, but can only be received from the hand of God. This "new creation" is manifested not only on the personal level, but also on the corporate level. Just as each of us receives our truest selves from the hand of God, so too the church receives its truest life and identity from God's hand.

172

Though God's self-gift is always the first and most definitive moment of grace, it is not intended to be the final moment. God's abiding self-gift of the Spirit enables and empowers us to give ourselves as well, both to God and to our neighbors. To the extent that the Spirit-empowered gift of the church to the world embodies concretely the reconciliation begun in Christ, the church—as the body of Christ—can be rightly regarded as "visible grace."

The Church as Visible Grace

As these essays attest, God's grace is manifested in many different ways. One of the most scandalous ways in which God has promised to be present is in and through the church. For many people, including many Christians, this promised presence of God in and through the church is more scandalous than the presence of God in and through the human being Jesus Christ. Jesus was special, we say. Jesus was sinless. So although it remains difficult to imagine the presence of God in a human being, our insistence on the unique character of Christ at least helps to make such a claim tenable. What does not seem tenable to many people, however, is the claim that the church—the all-too-sinful church with which we are all well acquainted—might in any analogous sense be used by God to mediate God's presence to the world. How is this possible? What would it mean for the church to serve God and the world in this way?

I believe the church has been called to serve God and the world as a sign, sacrament, and herald of God's presence and God's reign. In each case, what the church offers the world is something it has first received only by God's prior gracious initiative. As a result, the church's identity and mission as a mediator of God's presence remains inextricably tied to its identity as a recipient of God's self-gift. The church has not, therefore, been called to privilege, but to mission. Moreover, the church must always remember that the gift of God's presence always remains the free gift of God. The church does not possess God's presence as if it were an object in which the church could traffic, nor is the church a conjurer that can make God do its bidding. Rather, the church continually receives the Spirit, this self-gift of God, in order that it might in turn manifest the presence of God to the world. As Jesus instructed his disciples, "Freely you have received, freely give" (Matt 10:8).

The remainder of this section briefly explores the vocation of the church as "visible grace" by examining the church's vocation as a sign, sacrament, and herald of God's presence in the world. As a reminder of God's continuing desire to be present to, in, and through the creation in visible and tangible ways, this section also draws upon three prominent images of the church: the people of God, the body of Christ, and the community of the Spirit.

The People of God as Sign of God's Presence

Israel was called to be the people of God in order to be a light to the nations (Isa 42:6-7; 49:6; 60:2-3). That is, God called out a people who would be set apart for a special task: being an embodied sign, a pointer, to the God who desires to be in intimate communion with all creation. Israel was not chosen for this task because of its own merit; rather, Israel seems to have been chosen precisely *because* it was of no account, so that such choosing would serve to reveal something about God (Deut 7:6-9). Indeed, Israel's identity as a people is inseparable from its call to be God's people; that is, Israel's very identity *as* a people is a gift of God, who calls Israel to live in the world as sign of God's presence, God's reign, God's salvation. As Gerhard Lohfink notes:

> Foundational to an important strand in the tradition of Old Testament theology is the idea that God has selected a single people out of all the nations of the world in order to make this people a sign of salvation. His interest in the other nations is in no way impeded by this. When the people of God shines as a sign among the nations (cf. Isa 2:1-4), the other nations will learn from God's people; they will come together in Israel in order to participate, in Israel and mediated through Israel, in God's glory. But all this can happen only when Israel really becomes recognizable as a sign of salvation, when God's salvation transforms his people recognizably, tangibly, even visibly.[4]

With Israel's call and experience as its reference point, the early communities of disciples came to understand themselves as "the people of God," as a "chosen race, a royal priesthood, a holy nation, God's own people," as a people who were once not a people but who had become a people by God's grace in order that together they might proclaim the acts of him who called them "out of darkness into his marvelous light" (1 Pet 2:9-10). Like Israel, the church's very existence as a community of faith is a gift in a double way. First of all, our existence as the church is a gift from God, who calls us together as a living, embodied witness to God's continued presence and work in the world. To the extent that our life together points beyond ourselves to the God we worship and serve, that life serves as a visible sign to the world of God's presence. Thus, the gift of our corporate life has been given to us not simply for our benefit, but also as a gift to the world, as a sign that God continues to be active in the world in visible, palpable ways.

As the people of God, we are called to be a light to the nations. We are called to live in such a way that our lives point to the God we worship and serve. We are called to be a visible manifestation of what God is doing in the world. The light we offer to the world is not our own light, but is light nonetheless, light that we have received and reflect back to the world in order that the world may be drawn toward that light.

How might the church in our day serve as such a sign? One way would be through embodying a different understanding of our "gifts." The Spirit brings into being a new "charismatic" community whose corporate life is ordered around mutual service. Such service is made possible by the gifts *(charismata)* of the Spirit, gifts that have been given to each member of the community for the building up of the entire community (Eph 4:11-13). Thus, in the midst of a society that constantly teaches us that our gifts and abilities are our own, and that teaches us that we are entitled and expected to use them for our personal aggrandizement, stands a people who have been called to embody before the world a life marked by the mutual enrichment enabled by their God-given spiritual gifts. A community that orders its life in this way is a visible sign of God's presence in the world. Such a community is visible grace.

The Body of Christ as Sacrament of God's Presence

One of the most powerful and unsettling images in all of Scripture is the church as "the body of Christ." Bodies, as we know, are visible, and in calling the church the "body of Christ," Scripture suggests that the church can be rightly understood as the visible, Spirit-animated presence of Christ. Thus, when Jesus confronts Saul on the road to Damascus, Jesus does not simply ask him why he is persecuting his disciples; rather, Jesus asks, "Saul, Saul, why do you persecute *me?*" (Acts 9:4). This close identification of the church with Christ makes many people understandably nervous, since it may wrongly serve as a pretext for legitimating whatever the church does or is (such as when the church becomes the *persecutor* rather than being the *persecuted*). In such a context, it may prove quite helpful to understand the church as sacrament of God's presence.

A sacrament is more than—though not less than—a sign. While a sign points to something beyond itself, a sacrament does so by partially embodying that "more" to which it points.[5] Just as the Spirit makes it possible for the bread and the wine of the Eucharist to be more—though not less—than bread and wine, so the Spirit makes it possible for the life of the gathered community to be more—though not less—than a gathering of human beings. That "more" made possible by the Spirit's self-gift is nothing less than a visible, palpable embodiment of God's reconciling work. Thus, the church is not merely a sign pointing to God's work of reconciliation, but by the grace of God the church is also a tangible embodiment of it, even if an imperfect one. This is why Scripture also identifies the church as the "first fruits," as a kind of foretaste, of what God desires for all of creation (2 Thess 2:13; Jas 1:18).

When the early church discerned that, in Christ, God had "broken down the dividing wall" between Jew and Gentile and thus created in Christ "one new humanity in place of the two" (Eph 2:14-15), the church rightly understood that its daily life must be conformed to this new reality. When Jewish and Gentile followers of Jesus sat down together to break bread, this table fellowship was not simply the *result* of the reconciliation brought about by Jesus Christ, but was in a stronger sense a sacramental embodiment of it. This visible, tangible practice of sharing food was itself capable of being a channel through which God's reconciling presence might be made visible to the world. What the church in every age and place must discern, therefore, is what it would mean in that time and place for the community to have its corporate life transformed by the Spirit into a sacrament of God's presence in the world.

The Community of the Spirit as Herald of God's Presence

As noted, the church may serve as the sacrament of Christ's presence in the world when it allows the Spirit's reconciling presence to make a visible, tangible difference in its corporate life. In doing so, the community of the Spirit may be used by God to announce or herald God's presence and reign in the world. Unfortunately, the church has too often believed that the message it announced could be separated from the life it embodied. But the church must never understand its vocation as involving the proclamation of a disembodied message, as if such were possible. Because all messages are embodied messages, the perennial challenge for the church is to remember that its embodied life—a new life made possible by the reconciling work of the Spirit—is itself part of the good news of reconciliation. As John Howard Yoder reminds us:

> The church is then not simply the bearer of the message of reconciliation, in the way a newspaper or a telephone company can bear any message with which it is entrusted. Nor is the church simply the result of a message, as an alumni association is the product of a school or the crowd in the theater is the product of the reputation of the film. That men and women are called together to a new social wholeness is itself the work of God.[6]

Although this embodied witness to God's self-gift is crucial to the church's vocation as herald of God's grace, its calling is not thereby exhausted. The church is also called to announce the presence of God's reconciling work in the world wherever that presence and work is manifested. Because God's Spirit is not confined to the church, neither is God's reconciling work. Yet such work is often not recognized *as* God's work because one must by grace be given eyes to see it as such. As a community of the Spirit, the church is entrusted with the task of naming God's work in the world as *God's* work so that the world may know of God's continuing presence. Often such naming brings with it an implicit judgment on the church should it refuse to cooperate with the Spirit's work in the world. Thus, to name the civil rights movement in the United States or the environmental movement throughout the world as in some sense the work of God's reconciling Spirit is at the same time to call the church to discern how best to cooperate with the Spirit's work. If "judgment begins with the household of God" (1 Pet 4:17), then the church's vocation in the world as a community of the Spirit can never be an occasion for triumphalism or arrogance. Rather, the church's vocation as sign, sacrament, and herald of God's presence—as people of God, body of Christ, and community of the Spirit—is always *from* grace, *in* grace, and *through* grace.

The Church's—and Grace's—Invisibility

In closing, a brief word is in order about the church's—and grace's—irreducible invisibility. As noted in the foregoing section, the character of the church as God's embodied presence in the world is crucial to its identity and mission. Yet critical though this character is, we would be remiss were we to speak only of the church's visibility. The church does not always appear to the world as God's embodied presence and this for several reasons. First, as noted, God's presence in the world is never unambiguous, but always remains hidden within the ambiguity of the created order. As a result, God's self-gift is always a double gift: first, the gift of God's presence, and second, the gift to see and receive this gift *as* gift. This double initiative on God's part is what I understand to be at stake in the notion of prevenient grace. Without this double initiative on God's part, God's grace remains invisible as God's grace, just as the church remains invisible as God's embodied presence.

Second, God's grace and God's presence remain irreducibly invisible to the extent that they remain irreducibly *more than* any finite embodiment of them. Thus, when the church at its best has spoken of the invisible church, it has spoken thus as a way of calling our attention to the communion of saints that extends over time and space and thus remains invisible to all but God. Hence, even when the church is most visible, the power of its visibility is as a sign, a sacrament, a herald of that which remains invisible, of that which is yet to be revealed in all its fullness. Or to speak eschatologically, every visible "now" draws its power from a more definitive and largely invisible "not yet."

Finally, and more disturbing, is the fact that God has given us the ability to render the church as God's embodied presence invisible, thereby rendering the church as God's embodied grace invisible as well. Thus, while the first two reasons are factors of our finite and created existence, this final reason stems from our sinfulness. In short, God's grace and God's people often remain invisible *as* God's grace and God's people whenever we refuse to open ourselves to God to be channels of that embodied presence to the world. Lest we risk eclipsing God's sovereignty, we must, of course, readily affirm that God remains capable of making God's self-gift visible despite our failures and even through them. Nevertheless, although we must never assume that *we* make God's presence visible, neither should we desire to fail at the task God has given to us in order that grace may abound.

As the people of God, the body of Christ, and the community of the Spirit, we have been called to offer a visible, palpable expression of God's presence in the world. By the grace of God, the church will at times remain faithful to its calling and offer to the world such an embodied expression. At other times, the church will fail to remain faithful, and God will choose either to be present despite us (and thereby judge our unfaithfulness), or to remain invisible. May God help us—by grace—to do all within our power to ensure that the church remains open to God's transforming presence, thus making it possible for the church to be what God has called it to be: visible grace.[7]

Notes

1. Neil Postman, *The End of Education: Redefining the Value of School* (New York: Random House, 1995), 61.
2. I have tried to address some of the problems that church marketing creates for the way we understand the church's identity and mission, in *Selling Out the Church: The Dangers of Church Marketing*, co-authored with James L. Street (Nashville: Abingdon Press, 1997).
3. For one articulation of this position, see Jürgen Moltmann, *God in Creation: A New Theology of Creation and the Spirit of God* (New York: Harper and Row, 1985), esp. 86-93.
4. Gerhard Lohfink, *Jesus and Community: The Social Dimension of Christian Faith* (Philadelphia: Fortress Press, 1984), 28.
5. This point is underscored by Avery Dulles, who writes: "A sign could be a mere pointer to something that is absent, but a sacrament is a 'full sign,' a sign of something really present. Hence the Council of Trent could rightly describe a sacrament as 'the visible form of an invisible grace.' Beyond this, a sacrament is an efficacious sign; the sign itself produces or intensifies that of which it is a sign. Thanks to the sign, the reality signified achieves an existential depth; it emerges into solid, tangible existence." See *Models of the Church*, expanded edition (New York: Image Books, 1987), 66.
6. John Howard Yoder, "A People in the World," in *The Royal Priesthood: Essays Ecclesiological and Ecumenical*, ed. Michael G. Cartwright (Grand Rapids: Wm. B. Eerdmans, 1994), 74.
7. My first formal attempt at articulating the importance of the church's visibility for its identity and mission was in my doctoral dissertation directed by Professor Thomas Langford: "The Reappearance of the Visible Church: An Analysis of the Production and Reproduction of Christian Identity" (Ph.D. Diss., Duke University, 1991). I remain indebted to Professor Langford for his guidance, insight, and wisdom.

PERSONS, PURPOSE, AND GRACE

PHILIP A. ROLNICK

What could possibly be the point of a created universe entirely plunged in the darkness of unconsciousness, unable to know or appreciate that it is there at all? . . . Mind and love are at the root of all being. The person is ultimately the key to why there is anything and not rather nothing.[1]

Once we ask why there is something and not nothing, we are actually asking about the purpose of existence. Something distinctively human emerges in asking this kind of question, since presumably, dogs, squirrels, and oak trees go about their business untroubled by such things. And one of the most interesting things about human beings is that in addition to having enough commonality to be identified as members of a species, we partake of something beyond generality and machinelike individuality—personality.[2] This essay will explore how the personal aspect of humanity is closely related to the most basic purpose of human life and how person and purpose are at root dependent upon grace.

The Theological Origin of the Concept

Until Christian theology began to wrestle with certain problems arising from the Incarnation and its trinitarian implications, the concept of person was virtually unknown. Nonetheless, few concepts can claim a *terminus a quo* of such nobility. The claim that Jesus of Nazareth is both divine and human, that he is the "Word *(logos)* made flesh," forced Christian theologians to consider how the Son, and then the Spirit, are related to the Father. If the three are equal in status (which appeared necessary in order to support the dominant soteriological understanding), then how could their plurality be affirmed while retaining the essential unity and monotheistic nature of God? Furthermore, the question arose, how are the divine and human natures of Christ related? The first notions of person appear in the solutions to these vexed questions, solutions that took' many generations to accomplish.[3]

After the Nicene Creed (325 CE) declares the Son to be *homoousios* (of one substance) with the Father, the Cappadocians, Basil (c. 330–379), Gregory of Nyssa (c. 330–395), and Gregory of Nazianzus (329–389) further clarify that God is one *ousia* (nature) equally and fully expressed in three *hypostaseis,* the Father, Son, and Spirit. Finally, in the Chalcedonian Definition (451 CE), Christ is said to have two natures, divine and human, unified in one *hypostasis.* The use, history, and evolution of these terms is a complicated tale; but for our purpose, "person" begins to emerge as the Greek term *hypostasis* and its Latin translation, *persona,* play a vital role in the historic solutions of trinitarian and christological controversies.[4] Indeed, these solutions are virtually unthinkable without some notion of the person.

Later Boethius (c. 480–c. 524) further defines the concept: *"Persona est naturae rationalis individua substantia"* (person is an individual substance of a rational nature). So the understanding of person comes to denote an underlying support for other qualities, one of which must include a rational nature.

In the thirteenth century, Thomas Aquinas further develops Boethius' earlier use of *incommunicabilis* in regard to person, that is, that which is personal is not fungible, it cannot be exchanged. In all interactions with other beings, the person retains its unique reality. Hence the concept of person evolves to a new understanding: a nontransferable, unique, self-possession. Aquinas further contends: "'Person' signifies what is most perfect in all nature."[5]

Now if God is not part of nature, how can God be said to be a person? Arguing analogically, Aquinas insists that "person" is properly applied to God as well, "but in a more excellent way." Thus God is not only the cause of the personal in humankind, God is personal in an infinite manner, without limitation.[6] What God is and what God has created humans to be are closely interrelated. Allowances for levels of being are always made when terms are used both of the infinite perfection of God and the always limited ways of human beings. However, the meaning of our most important terms, such as "person," is not weakened by this interrelation. Instead, meaning is clarified and intensified as humans purposely enter an intentional relationship with God, a relationship that opens, stimulates, and encourages human participation on ever higher levels through imitation of divine perfection. We recognize that what we have is limited but extremely valuable and may be strengthened and increased through closer relation to its source—to God. And the Incarnation of the Son, the *personal* demonstration of the way, truth, and life, ensures that such closer relation is possible.

What is the theological value of this long development? As Christians have attempted to understand themselves as *imago Dei*, made in the image of God (Gen 1:26-27), evolving understandings of divine personality have presented a transcendent goal to the human situation and possibility. What ought we to become? What could we be if we could conform our will to God's? What does it mean that God became human in the life of Jesus? As Thomas A. Langford puts it, "It is precisely in the Incarnation, in Jesus Christ, that the world is fully recognized as a personal world; it is with this One that the most genuinely personal encounter with God is to be found."[7] The Word of God does not arrive impersonally. In the Incarnation the Word, the communication of God, is accomplished *personally*, in the lived and dynamic reality of human friendship and historical community. In this divine-human meeting in Jesus we are given a window (revelation) into the divine nature of personhood, and simultaneously, the human person who is addressed by this twofold being is given a sense of direction for the personal and spiritual life.

Grace: The Origin, Structure, and Purpose of the Person

If in eternity the Son is the one who has received all that the Father gives, then everything that can be affirmed about the Father can be affirmed about the Son, except that the Son is Son and not Father. In this unique relation of Father to Son is the first and infinite act of grace, that is, the first gift. The "first" personal act of the First Person is the complete giving of personal being.[8] The "second" personal act is the free reception of the gift offered. Not being a slave, the Son could have refused any or all of the Father's gift. The original greatness of the Son is in the complete acceptance of the Father. Every gift has both gift-giver and gift-receiver. Hence, every act of grace involves someone's will to give and another's will to accept.

While the source of the Son's existence may be thought of as infinite gift, the Son joins with the Father in giving all that they are to the Spirit. Hence, the Son is not only receiver, but also communicator, actor, and giver. The further movement of the trinitarian God is displayed in the mighty act of the creation of the universe, an act that again exemplifies personal movement toward others in the expansion of life. This process of giving and receiving is what W. Norris Clarke has called the "breathing of existence." [9] In this pattern of grace, gift giving and gift receiving, receptivity is seen to be a *positive* quality of being. The overall pattern of one person giving the self and another receiving it is the pattern of love, and "God is love" (1 John 4:8, 16).

Listening, attending to the will and knowledge of another, is a verb. Listening attentively is an *action*. It is something that we do. The spiritual value of listening is manifest in the being of the Son as the one who originates through openness to the Father. In the Son, God displays an infinite capacity to listen. But listening does not preclude speech; in fact, listening precedes meaningful speech. The Son who has received all from the Father is likewise the Word; the Son has a great deal to say. Likewise, human beings who attend to another with their full being participate in acts of love that generate new and creative exchanges among people. As John Macmurray puts it:

> The power of speech is sometimes defined as the capacity to express ourselves. This misses an essential point; for the power of speech is as much the capacity to understand what is said to us as it is to say things to other people. The ability to speak is . . . the capacity to enter into reciprocal communication with others. [10]

Listening increases capacity. It is especially appropriate to finite beings who always have more to experience and learn. Listening is the spiritual methodology of growth and is the natural partner of our need to express what we have ourselves discovered. Listening with one's whole being to the self-communication of another is participation in grace.

The self that moves toward others is following the trinitarian trend of the universe. In the Creation God is giving the gift of life, and in the Incarnation God is giving the gift of the divine self. As Jesus puts it, "For those who want to save their life will lose it, and those who lose their life for my sake, and for the sake of the gospel, will save it" (Mark 8:35). Here again the same movement away from self and toward the other is displayed—the movement of love. The grace-filled act of giving oneself away is the paradoxical path to finding and fulfilling the self.

The origin of the human self, like the putative origin of the Son and Spirit, is completely dependent upon others. The further necessity of nurture, education, and instruction in order for humans to reach maturity should reinforce this notion of life as an original gift from others. Nonetheless, once the gift has been given, a certain self-possession and self-consciousness arise, a sort of qualified independence. In fact, the achievement of relative independence en route to ultimate interdependence is the hope of those who bestow life in the first place. No decent parent obstructs a child's capacity to be self-governing. On the contrary, the love and nurture that good parents provide is designed to foster persons who become self-governing and thus possess their own integrity. Personal integrity originates in grace and fully finds itself in the grace of giving itself away, but at some point, there must be something present in the self which is worth giving away.

Where medieval definitions of person tended to focus on substantiality (the self-possessing quality), more modern treatments have tended to focus on relationality. But understood within a grace-originated and grace-directed framework, "person" can be seen as a "self-possessing, self-communicative, and self-transcending" synthesis of substantiality and relationality.[11]

The In-Itself Aspect of the Person

The point of being a person may be to enter into relations with other persons, but something substantial must be present in order to accomplish relationship. As Clarke puts it, "A relation cannot relate nothing."[12] So what is the something of persons that enters into relations?

At root, personality is not a component of anything, and the value of personality disappears if it is seen as a means to an end or as a part of a whole.[13] Quite to the contrary, personality is a whole. It includes all the interiority of the person and all the creative activity which might arise from it. As Nicholas Berdyaev put it, "Personality is not only rational being, but also free being. Personality is my whole thinking, my whole willing, my whole feeling, my whole creative activity."[14]

In this holistic sense personality is the unified and unifying aspect of the human self. Bodies change outwardly in appearance and inwardly in cell structure. People change their minds about important issues. People undergo character development or perhaps degeneration. Yet somehow, in spite of any and all changes, personal identity remains throughout life. Any concept of individual history would be impossible without personality constancy through the vicissitudes of life experience. Any concept of ethical responsibility would vanish without a perduring identity of the self. Thus Berdyaev's definition: "Personality is changelessness in change."[15]

However, while personality must be fundamentally changeless, while it must be the unified and unifying element of the self, it must also have an *expansile* capacity in order to carry out its unifying function. Otherwise, every change of the many components entering into the self would change the self-identity. But if a new self is created with every change, then no self can take responsibility for the past or plan for its future.

The potential of personality is to deepen its own identity through ever greater unification of ever more substantive components. Thus as the mind and body acquire new knowledge, skills, and discipline, as more is understood and as more decisive action becomes possible, as character is formed and confirmed through teaching and habit, there is more substance for the expansile personality to unify. In this process the personality does not become something else; it becomes more intensively itself as it exercises its unifying force on the more substantive components of the self. Likewise, where mind and body are undisciplined and character degenerates, the personality is correspondingly diminished, as less of the good is present to unify while negative elements disrupt and may even disintegrate personal unity.

The capacity of changelessness in change is closely related to the *freedom* which characterizes personality. Although much of life is genetically or socially determined, the realm of the personal comes as what Berdyaev calls "interruption" to predictable processes of cause and effect. People do not always exercise their freedom, but when they do, dramatic revelation of the personal and closely related spiritual sometimes occurs. Thus Luke reports Jesus to exclaim over the pounding of nails, "Father, forgive them; for they do not know what they are doing" (Luke 23:34); and similarly, Stephen is recorded to say, "Lord, do not hold this sin against them" (Acts 7:60). Jesus and Stephen have no control over the external events that variously confront them; however, each remains free to respond with the constancy of their highest commitments. Although it was heroically difficult to respond in personal freedom under circumstances of facing a brutally painful death, their doing so dramatically highlights the integrity of the person.

Intellect, Will, and Action

Many things *happen* to us, and these happenings are processed in the interiority of persons, especially in the manner in which we react to what happens to us. However, we are not merely victims adrift in a relentlessly cruel world. Even in the case of the worst possible happenings, as in the crucifixion of Jesus and the stoning of Stephen, we remain in some sense free to interrupt the chain of events with the creatively personal. As Karol Wojtyla, Pope John Paul II, puts it, "It is because of the person's exclusive power over the will that *will is the person's power to be free.*"[16]

Both Wojtyla and Macmurray contend that the person is revealed in action. The basic distinction between to act and to happen is that action involves purpose, deliberation, and choice: "Human behavior is abnormal or irrational when it can only be understood as the effect of a cause, and not by reference to the intent of an agent."[17] Action is characterized by intellect and will and so reveals the person who acts. The mind must have some knowledge of what it seeks, and the will is the part of us that, informed by knowledge of the object outside itself, "wants." Many things may move the will (motives), but what the will wants, chooses, and executes in action constitutes intention. The capacity to want, deliberate among competing wants, choose, and execute in action constitutes much of the in-itself nature of the person.

Relationship: The Purpose of the Person

In a universe whose origin and destiny is grace, a key purpose of developing the in-itself aspect of the person is to make greater

187

contributions in relationship with others. Putting the point strongly, perhaps too strongly, Macmurray contends: "The Self exists only in dynamic relation with the Other. . . . The Self is constituted by its relation to the Other; . . . it has its being in its relationship; and . . . this relationship is necessarily personal."[18] Persons can only be known by entering into relationship. If we merely observe others, we can only know them as objects.

Relationship involves us in the riskiest yet most potentially joyful aspect of life. Love is inconceivable apart from relationship; it is self-involving with the other. When we say that God is love and that the purpose of our lives should be to love others as Christ has loved us (John 13:34), the relational purpose of the personal is displayed. However, the risk of moving toward another in love can be so frightening that we hold back; for rejected love, which amounts to the rejection of our person, can bring life's greatest pain. The one rejected in romance, the parent whose recalcitrant child has stopped the ear to further conversation, and the Teacher whose disciple leaves the table of a last supper to enter the permanency of night all know the risk of self-involving love. Nonetheless, in spite of the risks, the possibility of love offered and received is worth any and all costs.

The stagnated self, the one who no longer moves toward the other, is a dying self. In moving toward others, in love, the self transcends itself through the realization of its personal purpose, a purpose that can only be realized by shifting the center from the self to the other. Such a self has learned that this is a grace-oriented universe. By freely and intelligently responding to the world and to others in love, by recentering from the ego to the other, by openness to relationship, a mutual and cumulative enrichment takes place. Louis Dupré has observed: "It is the nature of the self to be always more than itself,"[19] and the self does so by knowing and loving others. Self-transcendence, accomplished in movement toward God and other people, and in seeking to understand the principles of the created universe, paradoxically redounds to the benefit of the self who transcends—but only so that this self can personally give yet more to others.

Personal, Principle, and Moral

Much complexity and occasional perplexity arise from finding ourselves in a material world with a spiritual purpose. In a commentary on John Oman, Langford observes: "The whole creation is so ordered as to develop, try, mature, and enrich man's self-determination and fulfillment of moral personhood."[20] Once we see ourselves as citizens of a creation, then the difficulties and dangers of human life are lit up with spiritual value. As English poet Gerard Manley Hopkins put it: "The world is charged with the grandeur of God." Something meaningful, a personal *gravitas,* is achieved when we successfully grapple with the difficulties of our situation. Creation then becomes the locus where the will of God and the will of humans may meet as the finite progressively explores the meanings and values of the Infinite latent within the potentials of the creation and illuminated in the Incarnation of Christ.

As the action of God, the creation results from the divine intellect and will. Largely due to the account of creation in Genesis 1, Jewish and Christian theology have always taken the cosmos not just as given, but as something good. The early Greek fathers of the church spoke of humanity's "amphibian" nature, capable of both material and spiritual existence.[21] Humanity thus partakes of both natural dispositions, which are shared with other animal and plant life, as well as a freely self-directed intellect and will that are capable of spiritual response. As a result, humans must confront both material and spiritual complexity, and consonant with the Judeo-Christian tradition's affirmation of creation, seek their unification. For Jews and Christians, moral and spiritual achievement cannot be undertaken apart from the world; rather, moral and spiritual achievement are won through engagement with the world. The human person and communities of persons must seek to unify the material, intellectual, and spiritual. Unlike dualistic outlooks, which claim that only the spirit matters, the Jewish and Christian affirmation of creation claims that it all matters. Hence, the material and spiritual are to be unified through the personal exercise of knowledge and will.

As David Burrell observes, "The transcendence of the first cause . . . disposes natural things to act according to natural laws, and intentional beings to act freely."[22] But humanity finds itself in a kind of middle position. As part of the biological realm, we are subjects of natural laws; as intentional beings we are, through the application of knowledge and will, free to study and thus in some measure transcend the natural realm. As "amphibian" beings we must discover our own unity in combining the world of natural necessities and the relations of personal, spiritual freedom.

The givenness of the material world acts as a brake upon the human tendency to be egocentric or arbitrary and as an encouragement to be realistic and fair. As a result, the seemingly impersonal laws of nature bear invaluable training for the personal life of individuals and communities. Without an underlying realm of universal law, we could never begin to enact the distinctions that nourish the personal life. Thus Macmurray insists, "The personal life necessitates the effort to distinguish between the true and the false, the good and the bad, the real and the unreal; and to act *in terms of* these distinctions."[23] Without an arena where true and false, good and bad, real and unreal could be tested under conditions of strict equality, the free exercise of the will would become meaningless and the personal life vitiated.

The strict equality that we find in the givenness of universal laws inevitably rewards *realistic* efforts and ignores or punishes all others. In engaging the world, learning has more to do with discovery than invention *ex nihilo*. As Michael Polanyi puts it, "The effort of knowing is thus guided by a sense of obligation towards the truth: by an effort to submit to reality."[24] Human beings fantasized about flying for millennia; but the actual achievement of flying took place when the Wright brothers, and others after them, discovered universally accessible principles of aerodynamics. Discovery of latent principle is achieved by creative conformity to the givenness of reality. Strict equality is manifest because Japanese, Germans, and any others can learn to fly by the route of the same or similar conformity—by submitting to reality. Thus Polanyi concludes, "Responsible action excludes randomness, even as it suppresses egocentric arbitrariness."[25] Furthermore, responsible action is linked to universal principles, for the belief in the universality of scientific principles

> sustains a constructive effort and narrows down this discretion to the point where the agent making the decision finds that he cannot do otherwise. *The freedom of the subjective person to do as he pleases is overruled by the freedom of the responsible person to do as he must.*[26]

Responsibility exercises and strengthens the personal.

The distinction between the merely subjective and the responsible is crucial for the operations of human persons. Paradoxically, greater personal transcendence is accomplished through an act of epistemological humility, that is, by submitting, we could even say *listening*, to the reality that would be discovered. That which is personal and transcendent becomes more fully manifest, more muscular, by successful engagement with impersonal principles (strict equality) found within nature. New "contact with reality" (Polanyi's term) only results from careful attention: listening to, observing, and contemplating what is other than self. By realistic reckoning with the external, we are made more realistic. Hence, even the impersonal, universal laws of the material world are given for the sake of the personal, a central insight of the Jewish and Christian understanding of creation. Human concepts of fairness, accuracy, truth, and justice are proximately grounded in the engagement of the material world. In engaging the principles of the world, the responsible exercise of the personal is linked to the universal, is objectively tested, and thus immeasurably strengthened.

Similar to Polanyi's notion of "submitting to reality," Karol Wojtyla writes, "The essential surrender of will to truth . . . seems finally to account for the person's transcendence in action, ultimately for his ascendancy to his won dynamism."[27] This "essential surrender" holds the secret of the relation between the personal and the impersonal and the moment wherein fully human life begins. To be a person of principle is to be one who has accomplished this surrender of will to truth. Great good ensues from this surrender—good which becomes increasingly present in the one who has surrendered; good for the work such a person does; and good for all the relations that person holds. By surrendering to truth, it is as though God has received a personal agent amid the work of creation. As Paul puts it, "We know that all things work together for good for those who love God, who are called according to his purpose" (Rom 8:28). The discovery of truth is one of the purposes of creation. Its pursuit is worth all the error and pain which result from our numerous failures. But for those who have been called and responded, for those who have accomplished the creative surrender, even failure becomes a learning experience on the path to greater accomplishment.

Because the grace trend of the universe directs the self away from the self in surrender to truth, one of the many ways to understand sin can be as the undue focus upon the self. An enlarged and overindulged subjectivity may not be a good dwelling place for the human intellect and will. Just as the personal is strengthened by principle, so too it is weakened by willful refusal to submit to reality. As Eberhard Jüngel writes, "Sin is nothing other than the compulsion toward oneself into which man places himself."[28]

Whereas personality manifests unity or integrity, sin disrupts and may even disintegrate personal unity through the perversion of purpose. Wojtyla observes:

> While self-determination means that man can govern himself and possess himself, disintegration on the contrary, signifies a more or less deep-seated inability to govern, or to possess, oneself.
>
> The ability to govern, or to possess, oneself so strictly connected with self-determination, establishes . . . the transcendent backbone of the human person. In some respects and in some cases disintegration may be considered as a collapse of this backbone, though even then it does not contradict or destroy the transcendence itself of the person in the action.[29]

Moral conduct is one of the earmarks of the person, and morality is inconceivable apart from the knowing and willing of truth that transcends the person choosing. Although sin is an injury to unity, perhaps even a grave injury, immorality is only possible if there is a personality, a responsible person.

Personal purpose is to be sought in the unification of nature, culture, and spirit by the pursuit of the true, the beautiful, and the good. Wojtyla calls these three "absolute points of reference" and "absolute exponents of value."[30] Where God is understood to possess these qualities infinitely, humans may *participate* in these transcendental qualities. The possibility of such participation amounts to the potentiality of the moral and spiritual life. Truth, beauty, and goodness are given to humankind as potentials of our "amphibian" lives. Personal performance, character, reveals the degree to which these qualities are successfully actualized. Action is thus the covenantal seal of human intention. In action our knowing and willing are joined in personal commitment. To the degree that our commitment intends and then actualizes the true, beautiful, and good we may have achieved something of the divine will. According to Aquinas, "The nearer things come to God, the more fully they exist."[31] By moving toward these three "absolute points of reference," individuals and communities become more real, which is another way of saying that they have enacted more of the will of God.

The actuality of the creation holds within it latent potential for human creativity, what we might call the grace of the possible. We could neither achieve a praiseworthy character nor be found morally culpable were it not for the *ought* latent in the natural, cultural, and spiritual potentials that confront us in our personal freedom. The minutes and hours of each day are thick with possibility, and hence, personal responsibility.

Purpose: A Sense of the Whole

Once laboratory rats learn to run a maze, structural differences in their behavior become apparent. As Polanyi reports:

> The animal ceases to explore the details of the walls and corners on its way and attends to these now merely as signposts. It seems to have lost its focal awareness of them and developed instead a subsidiary aware-ness of them which now forms part of the pursuit of its purpose.[32]

Gaining a sense of the whole comes from understanding purpose, and understanding purpose comes from unifying the parts. It is almost tautologous to say that the purpose of life is personal and that the personal is what unifies and gives a sense of whole to human life. Yet the unified and unifying aspect of human personality is more complex, for it does not merely understand principle and pattern from the material world, it takes whatever understanding and virtue it possesses into its most fulfilling activity—relationship with other persons.

The human person can function as a knowing subject, but not in a fully personal way. The fully personal requires an engaged reciprocity and replete mutuality. As Kant understood in the second statement of the categorical imperative, persons can do things for one another; they can be useful to one another. However, the value of the person must be recognized not for what it can do, but simply as an end in itself, for its personal being. The greatest moments of relationship seek nothing except relationship itself.

In moments of genuine relationship, as Martin Buber has portrayed in *I and Thou,* the other person ceases to be an object, and our intellectual

193

knowing is transformed into personal relating. Similarly, Clarke contends that "the final goal and perfection of the whole universe is, literally, the *communion between persons,* who in turn gather up the whole universe in their consciousness and love and thus lead it back to its Source."[33] Personal being is the fullest, most luminous being, and such personal being is only experienced in communion with other persons. Spiritual experience is a function of personal relations. As Buber explains spirit,

> Spirit is not in the I but between I and You. It is not like the blood that circulates in you but like the air in which you breathe. Man lives in the spirit when he is able to respond to his You. He is able to do that when he enters into this relation with his whole being. It is solely by virtue of his power to relate that man is able to live in the spirit.[34]

The power to relate and to do so with one's whole being is the power of the personal. As persons enter into relations with the full integrity of their personalities, the spirit may arise in the unique "betweenness" of each personal event.

Although personality is a whole, complete independence is both undesirable and impossible to human persons. Aside from the divine grace that originally makes life possible, and the actions of our human parents to give birth, nurture, and instruct us, the inevitably incomplete finite consciousness is beautifully compensated by conversation. Conversation does not merely fill a need; it potentially adds beauty and deep personal enjoyment. The sophomoric observation that human understanding is relative is partially true. However, the relativity is meaningful because persons and communities of persons can share their relative comprehension and so mutually and personally enrich one another by progressing toward Wojtyla's "absolute points of reference" (truth, beauty, and the good).

The maintenance of community relations requires justice, the most meager of the virtues, but also the most easily universalized and the sine qua non of the other virtues. Justice functions as a kind of lower limit to other virtues.[35] But while justice confronts us as something that we ought to do, friendship provides a higher pleasure, a spiritual pleasure of our personal freedom. Where justice is a minimum requirement of morality, "To create community is to make friendship the form of all personal relations."[36] A society can function where justice is practiced, but a community comes into being where friendship, *philia* love between persons, is practiced. Furthermore, in the countless conversations that enter into the fabric of a society and perhaps a community, "Our adherence to the truth can be seen to imply our adherence to a society which respects the truth, and which we trust to respect it."[37] Community, as a place where truth is respected and friendship is practiced, is the beautification and intensification of the personal. As in Macmurray's definition, morality and community are inextricable: "A morally right action is an action which intends community."[38]

To intend community may well be the ground of morality, but the current closeness of our global village presents a new challenge to all persons and communities. While addressing the person in community, Wojtyla insists upon a truly global community: "Indeed, it is the community of men, of all men, the community formed by their very humanness that is the basis of all other communities. Any community detached from this fundamental community must unavoidably lose its specifically human character."[39] In this particular moral challenge of our generation, the unifying aspect of personal life is again at issue. But this is an issue which Christian theology and ethics is especially fit to meet; for Christianity, even though it has often mistakenly taken the route of exclusivity, has profound resources to contribute to the realization of this kind of universal community.

Conclusion

Unless a Person is at the Source of all things and beings, unless the purpose of the universe is divine intention to share life with persons, then how might the personal ever have arisen in a world locked into the necessity of cause and effect? Personal being is itself a gift, perhaps the greatest gift that God gives. Personal being includes the possibility of love, and relations of mutual love are the ultimate telos or purpose that makes sense of all the bother, effort, risk, and struggle of having a universe. The gift of being made *imago Dei* and the further grace possibility of becoming *imago Christi* call humankind to live up to the nobility of the personal and relational in grace-directedness to others. A rich environmental experience confronts us in which error and evil are always possible, but no more so than the possibility of truth and the good. The challenge of integrating the material, cultural, and spiritual within the person is a privilege granted to humankind. Morality, which is uniquely a function of persons, arises from the implied *ought* given with the privilege. In the space and time granted to us, we ought not to behave as we please but as movement toward the good, true, and beautiful demand. But in a grace-oriented universe, personal achievement is never for the sake of the individual alone. Instead, greater personal achievement means greater potential for grace— for giving a more virtuous self to others. Thus even the ought of self-development turns out to be other-directed.

In the freshness of the finite, the movement of grace seeks new relational developments of love. As Hopkins poetically sensed, "There lives the dearest freshness deep down things."[40] In creating something new, something actual, God also creates new potential. The finite realm does not have to exist; its existence is contingent upon the divine choice to create it and foster it. The creation of the universe represents a divine choice and an intelligent plan. In knowledge and by choice the divine makes something where before there was nothing *(creatio ex nihilo)*. Hence the finite creation bears the birthmark of freedom. Within the framework of creation, universal laws may be progressively discovered as human beings first learn principles of universal justice and then may learn friendship and love. In this realm that originates in freedom and is meant to be inhabited by free beings, divine and human persons may meet in the realm of intellect and will. And this meeting may be the ultimate purpose of creation.

Notes

1. W. Norris Clarke, *The Universe as Journey: Conversations with W. Norris Clarke, S.J.*, ed. Gerald A. McCool (New York: Fordham University Press, 1988), 80-81.
2. Attempts to mark critical differences among the terms "personality," "person," "personal," and "personal identity" have been made without, in my judgment, much success. For example, John Macmurray avoids the term "personality" because it has come to mean "the quality or set of characteristics which distinguish one person from another . . . stressing the element of difference between persons instead of what they have in common." See John Macmurray, *Persons in Relation* (London: Faber and Faber, 1961), 25. Instead, Macmurray prefers the term "person." Now the problem here is that Macmurray, like almost every other writer who addresses this general issue, needs to differentiate between "individuals" (which are common to every species) and "persons." If what persons are doing when they enter into relations with one another is somehow different from what bees do when they relate, *mutatis mutandis*, to one another, then some specific value unique to the individual needs to be present in the parties who enter into relation. Otherwise, interaction would devolve to coupling of parts or components, and this devolution would defeat the point of

discussing this issue, whether under the title of "persons," "personality," or any other such term. As we shall discuss, Nicholas Berdyaev is especially helpful on this point when he insists that personality is never a part of a whole; instead, personality is best understood as a unified whole. Hence, this essay shall employ the various terms with less attention to belabored distinctions and more to grammatical fit.

3. For a detailed account of how the original Greek and then Latin terms evolved into the understanding of orthodox Christianity, see Bernard Lonergan, *The Way to Nicea: The Dialectical Development of Trinitarian Theology*, trans. Conn O'Donovan from the first part of *De Deo Trino* (London: Darton, Longman, and Todd, 1976); and Jaroslav Pelikan, *The Emergence of the Catholic Tradition (100–600)*, vol. 1 of *The Christian Tradition: A History of the Development of Doctrine* (Chicago: University of Chicago Press, 1971).

4. The distinctive aspect of each member of the Trinity was first referred to by the Greek term *hypostasis* (that which stands under or supports) and was also, after some confusion arose between the Greek and Latin terms, rendered by the Latin *persona*, a term derived from *personare*, "to sound through," which is probably derived from the Greek *prosōpon*, "face" or "mask." For our purposes, the point is that the value of distinctive individuality begins to emerge. For an accessible account of the etymological history, see William C. Placher, *A History of Christian Theology: An Introduction* (Philadelphia: Westminster Press, 1983), 75-85.

5. Thomas Aquinas, *Summa theologiae*, I.29.3.

6. For a fuller account of how analogy functions, see Philip A. Rolnick, *Analogical Possibilities: How Words Refer to God* (Atlanta: Scholars Press, 1993).

7. Thomas A. Langford, "The Concept of the Person: A Comparison of C. C. J. Webb and John Oman," in *Religion in Life* 33/3 (Summer 1964): 420. Langford is summarizing (and advocating) Webb in the statement cited.

8. Sequential ordering is a necessary concept for us, but it cannot be univocally applied to the interactions of eternity. Due allowances must be admitted when that which is finite attempts to discuss the Infinite and Eternal.

9. W. Norris Clarke, *Person and Being*, The Aquinas Lecture, 1993 (Milwaukee: Marquette University Press, 1993), 74. An important insight of both process thought and some neo-Thomists is that *receptivity* is a positive quality, not the indication of an ontological lack, as medieval thinkers insisted.

10. Macmurray, *Persons in Relation*, 60.

11. The understanding of person as constituted by its relations is exemplified by John Macmurray's work in *Persons in Relation*, 24 and passim. Although this work has much to commend it, it overemphasizes relationality at the expense of substantiality. The terms "self-possessing, self-communicative, and self-transcending" are from Clarke, *Person and Being*, 5. Clarke has amended his earlier characterization of the person as "dyadic" to include originating grace and so now writes of a "triadic" structure to the person. See Clarke, *Explorations in Metaphysics: Being, God, Person* (Notre Dame: University of Notre Dame Press, 1994), 119.

12. Clarke, *Person and Being*, 16.

13. This point has been made by Nicholas Berdyaev in *Slavery and Freedom*, trans. R. M. French (New York: Charles Scribner's Sons, 1944), 20-59.

14. Ibid., 25.

15. Ibid., 8.

16. Karol Wojtyla, *The Acting Person*, trans. Andrzej Potocki and in collaboration with Anna-Teresa Tymieniecka, ed., Analecta Husserliana Series, vol. 10 (Dordrecht, Holland, and Boston: D. Reidel, 1979).

17. Macmurray, *Persons in Relation*, 36.

18. Ibid., 17.

19. Louis Dupré, *Transcendent Selfhood* (New York: Seabury Press, 1976) as cited in Clarke, *Person and Being*, 121 n. 68.

20. Langford, "Concept of the Person," 418.

21. Clarke, *Person and Being*, 38.

22. David Burrell, *Aquinas: God and Action* (Notre Dame: University of Notre Dame Press, 1979), 101.

23. Macmurray, *Persons in Relation*, 108.

24. Michael Polanyi, *Personal Knowledge: Towards a Post-Critical Philosophy* (Chicago: University of Chicago Press, 1958, corrected edition, 1962), 63.
25. Ibid., 310.
26. Ibid., 309.
27. Wojtyla, *The Acting Person*, 138.
28. Eberhard Jüngel, *God as the Mystery of the World: On the Foundation of the Theology of the Crucified One in the Dispute Between Theism and Atheism*, trans. Darrell L. Guder (Grand Rapids: Wm. B. Eerdmans, 1983), 359. Some years before Jüngel, Berdyaev offered a similar definition of sin, in *Slavery and Freedom*, 42.
29. Wojtyla, *The Acting Person*, 194.
30. Ibid., 155.
31. *Summa theologiae*, I.3.5.2.
32. Polanyi, *Personal Knowledge*, 60-61.
33. Clarke, *Person and Being*, 79-80.
34. Martin Buber, *I and Thou*, trans. Walter Kaufmann (New York: Charles Scribner's Sons, 1970), 89.
35. See Macmurray, *Persons in Relation*, 188-89.
36. Ibid., 198.
37. Polanyi, *Personal Knowledge*, 203.
38. Macmurray, *Persons in Relation*, 119.
39. Wojtyla, *The Acting Person*, 293.
40. Gerard Manley Hopkins, "God's Grandeur," in *The Norton Anthology of English Literature*, rev. ed., vol. 2, ed. M. H. Abrams (New York: W. W. Norton and Co., 1968), 1433.

PART IV:
CULTURAL ESSAYS

GRACE WITHOUT REMAINDER:
Why Baptists Should Baptize Their Babies

WILLIE JAMES JENNINGS

Love is a corporate reality. We have overindividualized our notions of love, as though it is just a matter of one with one. But genuine love creates true community; it is enhanced by community; it includes the dimensions of community. The most adequate concrete expression of love is the existence of the Body of Christ. As Christians, we have received love, now we pray that we shall be shown how to walk in love.

—THOMAS LANGFORD[1]

C lassroom hospitality is the sign of a good theological teacher. It is the ability to turn theological positions that some students would consider foreign or hostile to their Christian understanding into invitations to deeper and broader ways of understanding their faith. This is no easy task, but Thomas Langford in his many years of teaching theology made it look easy. It is in the spirit of Dr. Langford's wonderful ability and in hope of carrying out another invitation that I wish to suggest something to my Baptist sisters and brothers. In this essay, I wish to argue that baptism is the primary way Christians are introduced to the grace of Jesus Christ. Baptism is the grammar of grace. It gives us the way in which we may begin to speak of grace in all its manifold actions in and among us. With this task in mind I wish to venture a proposal for Baptists—that infant baptism is exactly what Baptists (of all types) ought to do. How can I make this claim? I do not take lightly the significant communal divides between Baptists and on the one side those Protestant traditions which baptize infants and on the other side Catholic and Orthodox traditions which also baptize infants.[2] Nor do I believe that I can in the space of this brief essay present a decisive argument that will forever end Baptist objections to pedobaptism. My goal is to suggest that we Baptists ought to baptize infants if we genuinely believe that the grace of Jesus Christ is present in all Christian baptisms.

I am not going to offer an account of infant baptism that focuses on grace and ignores the real question of the nature of faith and confession in relation to baptism. Instead I wish to consider another route to this important question and to the grace of God witnessed in infant baptism. I will begin with some thoughts on baptism by baptist theologian James McClendon and then turn to the important critical treatment on infant baptism by the Swiss Reformed theologian Karl Barth. Finally I will turn to an interesting and little-known defense of infant baptism by the historical theologian and preeminent translator of Karl Barth's works, Geoffrey Bromiley. Taken together all three theologians render an account of baptism that is essentially the character and shape of grace, the grace given us by Jesus himself.

Baptism's Repair

James Wm. McClendon, Jr., in his *Systematic Theology: Doctrine*, presents a wonderfully provocative treatment of baptism.[3] McClendon understands baptism as what he calls a "remembering sign," which marks "the conversion of one who takes the way of Jesus."[4] Baptism, prophetic preaching, and the Lord's Supper stand as remembering signs between the primary signs of salvation, such as the resurrection of Christ, and the intimate signs of relationship with God, such as prayers being answered by God. McClendon understands baptism to have a future orientation toward the "coming rule of God."[5] We upon our baptism enter this expectation and are marked by our conversion. Our conversion is in fact the convergence of Jesus' baptism and our own baptism into Christ. Baptism is nothing less than a convergence of life narratives, Jesus' and our own, which establishes the moral power of baptism. For McClendon, baptism is a moral act in which God, the candidate, and the church (through the baptizing minister) all work together to bring the baptized into the "ongoing 'life-story' of the people of God."[6] McClendon views baptism as both a moral act of concrete discipleship and the act of God. He wishes to move beyond notions of baptism as mystery, sacrament, or symbol toward an understanding of baptism as a sign of communal partici-pation in the rule of God. God is an agent along with the candidate and the church in the act of baptism.

McClendon sees in the New Testament two narratives for how we come to baptism. One is that of Saul become Paul. Paul's story shows us the radical reversal in which a life is turned toward Jesus. The other narrative is that of Jesus himself in which a life becomes a fulfillment of the will of God. Both stories indicate baptism as a sign of salvation open to all who would come. Remarkably, McClendon the baptist theologian is making room for infant baptism in his construal of believer baptism. Infants may be included in the invitation. However, the mistake infant baptizers have made, McClendon contends, is losing the sense of the openness of the invitation of baptism and turning it (for those baptized as infants) into an unrepeatable act. Thus the New Testament thrust, its primal power as turned toward the world (i.e., the Gentiles, barbarians, women, and slaves)[7] was sacrificed for the sake of pediatric nurture. McClendon understands as do many others that the so-called Constantinian shift or compro-mise meant a disastrous turn for baptism tied to pediatrics: baptism became a cultural reflex without deep theological commitment. Even with infant baptism's two edificatory regimes, (1) Christian educa-tion—confirmation—ending with admission to communion, indicat-ing an earlier infant conversion or (2) infant baptism, infant confirmation, and immediate communion as members of the church, the damage was done—the sense of radical commitment to the way of Jesus Christ in baptism that grounds the invitation itself was lost.

McClendon sees this damage as being exacerbated by the tendency of some Baptist churches (and others who do not hold to infant baptism) to discount the infant baptisms of those who enter their communions. This discounting of the earlier baptism undermines the unity of all Christian baptism and feeds ecclesial divisiveness. Those baptized as infants must be welcomed and may be invited to rebaptism as an act of baptismal repair. Here McClendon is reaching for conti-nuity of salvific grace rooted in the life of those baptized as infants who now as adults have come to confess the rule of God in their lives. With this baptismal repair the earlier baptism is acknowledged (though as impaired) and bound to this later act of confession and commitment.

Why should this be done? Because for McClendon this repairing work is inherent in the logic of conversion-baptism. Baptism stands always with the commitment to walk with Jesus, even if that commitment comes from those baptized as infants. McClendon finds heartening possibilities from the recovery in liturgical studies of early Christian initiation practices. Those practices were shaped by a demonstrative process of initiation for those deemed ready that included immersion baptism, then exorcism, then anointing, and finally prayers. After this process, catechumens become communicants were admitted to the Eucharist. Like Baptists' conversion-baptism, this understanding of initiation confirmed (a) freedom against social control, (b) clarity of the difference between the church and its environments, and (c) identification with Jesus' first disciples. Infant baptism in McClendon's vision is an unfortunate development that may be corrected in time as the church rediscovers the roots of baptismal practice in ancient initiation rites. Those baptized as infants, McClendon believes, may be given this ancient (Baptist-like) vision of initiation by means of a baptismal repair through rebaptism.

McClendon is addressing the problem of those who, baptized as infants, are now articulating their faith and trying to make sense of their infant baptism. He addresses this problem while seeking to hold to his baptist vision of baptism. He does not wish to throw them into confusion or further any baptismal disunity, but he does wish to point to the importance of their present commitment to Jesus and his way of life through baptism. What McClendon has done is to begin to articulate the grace of Jesus Christ to those baptized as infants. He wishes to claim that earlier baptism as part of the redeeming work of God. Of course, he does not wish to promote infant baptism or claim its unrepeatability. He wishes to join that early baptism to the new baptism enacted as a believer. However, McClendon, by making this gracious gesture, has now opened himself to what all Baptists should see and indeed must see: the compelling inclusiveness of grace witnessed in baptism.

Baptism is always a matter of grace, grace that permeates lives joined to Jesus. McClendon's treatment of baptism shields him from two powerful realities that haunt its work. In all his biblical examples (e.g., Jesus, Paul, the disciples of Jesus, the disciples of John) he refers to people raised within the covenant of God with Israel, people born in and with the story of God bound in Israel. Equally important, McClendon's biblical exemplars share in yet another powerful reality: the nature of hope. Their baptism is a matter of hope, but hope is not simply a matter of the future but also of the past, of the beginning.

McClendon's account of baptismal repair explodes his account of baptism. If believer baptism may reach back and take hold of the life of an infant (baptized) in hope of now making clear the continuous grace of God in Jesus Christ, then believer baptism is fully open to the nature of hope that lives in baptism. Hope in Jesus Christ demands that our entire lives be offered up to him as the place of God's working, past, present, and future.

This offering up is not in itself a justification for infant baptism, but consider the relation of Christian baptism to the life of Israel embodied in Jesus' disciples. Those disciples shared in Israel's life and story in which a past filled with disobedience, pain, and suffering may in Jesus be woven into a present salvific word. This salvific word given in Jesus and heard by his disciples pointed toward the future restoration of all things in the rule of God. Their individual stories must be cast against the background of God's own story of forming a people in covenant faithfulness. These disciples are both simultaneously in and out from Israel, both old and new in Israel. They are those who have found in Israel its long-awaited hope and who have been chosen to follow Jesus as a sign of God's election of Israel. And this following of Jesus is a decisive new moment, a fresh beginning that separates and clarifies the calling and destiny of these individual disciples. Yet it is always, and intensely so, a matter of hope. McClendon, by saying that baptism may be repaired, has wandered into the field of hope that permeates baptism. Yet we must turn to the work of the theologian Karl Barth to gain a clearer grasp of the nature of this hope in its unbreakable connection to faith, even in the midst of Barth's unrelenting criticism of infant baptism.

Baptism's Folly

Karl Barth near the end of his epic work, *Church Dogmatics*, stunned the theological world by criticizing the practice of infant baptism.[8] It is indeed ironic though telling that in the preface to this important text, Barth praises the work of his eldest son Markus Barth, who was baptized as an infant, but who later as a defiant fifteen-year-old refused to be confirmed, and whose later work as a New Testament scholar *(Die Taufe ein Sakrament?)* had been instrumental in Barth's abandonment and critique of infant baptism as a sacrament.[9] It is also ironic that in this work, Barth, who has been commonly (though inarticulately) criticized for overemphasizing the decision of God for us at the cost of authentic human action and decision, is profoundly concerned with the intimate relation between God's action and human decision in Christian conversion. Barth, in his treatment of baptism, is not primarily concerned to defeat the doctrine of infant baptism. His primary goal is to examine the nature of the Christian life beginning with its grounding in baptism.

In his treatment of baptism, Barth comes to the conclusion that infant baptism is an ecclesial practice that can no longer be justified as part of the doctrine of baptism. How did Barth come to this conclusion? He begins his treatment with a fundamental distinction between baptism with the Holy Spirit and water baptism. Herein lies the roots of Barth's critique. Barth wishes to situate the Christian life firmly in the freedom of God. To clarify the freedom of God, Barth adds three levels of specificity. (1) God is freely faithful to humanity and makes possible by that faithfulness the freedom for humanity to be faithful to God. This is the freedom we find in the Christian life. (2) The heart of the Christian life is found in the history of Jesus Christ, where the faithfulness of God meets the faithful response of humanity. A Christian is one who has been joined to that history of Jesus Christ. (3) The Christian life is the gracious discovery of our lives in the history of Jesus Christ. In this discovery we find that an internal change of heart is not the subject of this conversion to the Christian life; rather Jesus himself is the subject. We have been joined to him in such a way as to give us our own history and our freedom to be for God.

The Holy Spirit joins us to Jesus. Barth establishes a crucial link between this baptism and the life of Jesus. The Holy Spirit brings to us the history of the resurrected Jesus as the history of our own salvation. This joining in which we truly find our lives in the history of Jesus is the baptism in the Holy Spirit. Jesus himself comes to us in this baptism of the Spirit, because Jesus is the author of faith (Heb 12:2). This coming to specific persons is a form of grace which demands gratitude in obedience to the Spirit. Along with gratitude and obedience, what also follows from this divine work is what Barth calls "a distinctive fellow-humanity,"[10] in which we desire to be with our sisters and brothers in Christ. A future orientation follows this desire in which we look for the future fulfillment of life in Christ as we seek to bear the fruit of the Spirit (Gal 5).

Barth understands this spirit baptism to be a form of grace as opposed to water baptism. Water baptism is not a form of grace. This baptism in the Spirit is prior to water baptism and the joining of a church. What then is the purpose of water baptism? Water baptism signifies both a change in us wrought by God and our decision to be faithful to God. Barth situates water baptism within an act of obedience that closely follows the obedience of Jesus and obedience to Jesus. We are commanded to be baptized in accordance with the life of Jesus. Barth contends that with this act of obedience we are at the beginning of the history of Jesus Christ. Indeed, we follow the obedience of Jesus in our baptism. Jesus was baptized to indicate his own submission to the lordship of God, his fellowship with sinful humanity, and his desire to live in service to God. For Barth, our goal in baptism is oneness with God in Jesus. Thus our baptism always points to the baptism in the Holy Spirit in which we are reconciled to God. Thus baptism is fundamentally a confession of our faith, the faith of the community and the candidate. Yet Barth wishes to make clear that the community and the candidate are not confessing their faith in the act of baptism. "They confess the divine act of grace and revelation which is the origin, theme, and content of their faith. Christian baptism is confession of this."[11]

Barth in pressing this distinction between what we do in baptism to what has been done for us by Jesus and in us by the Spirit's baptism wishes to undermine a sacramental understanding of water baptism. Simply and pejoratively put, a sacramental understanding of baptism for Barth would be baptism as an operation of grace (*ex opere operato*) in which something salvific is done to the individual in baptism. Barth questions the use of sacrament for baptism on exegetical grounds. If it is this sacramental view of baptism that grounds the doctrine of infant baptism, then this practice has no substantial theological or biblical justification. For Barth, if infant baptism cannot be seen as inherently central to a doctrine of Christian baptism then it is a mistaken direction followed by the church through the Reformation up to our present situation. Barth finds the arguments of Luther and

Calvin to generate more heat than light precisely because they offer weak justification for the practice of infant baptism.[12]

Equally important, Barth finds a sacramental view of baptism, such as that which guides the doctrine of infant baptism, to be fundamentally contrary to the nature of Christian conversion understood from the history of Jesus Christ. Christian conversion which is witnessed in baptism is the dual action of God working redemption in us through the Holy Spirit and our response to Jesus Christ in which we renounce all other claims on our existence, all former ways of life, in pledge to life with God in Jesus. Baptism is our yes to God's yes. We each must utter this yes in baptism. Baptism requires genuine human response. In light of this requirement, Barth concludes that infant baptism fails to rise to these basic realities. Clearly, Barth has in focus the problems also noted in McClendon's account—infant baptism's historic folly, baptism as a cultural reflex. For Barth, baptism as a convention of Christian communities fails to hold to the authenticity of baptism's work:

> The Christian life cannot be inherited as blood, gifts, characteristics and inclinations are inherited. No Christian environment, however genuine or sincere, can transfer this life to those who are in this environment. For these, too, the Christian life will and can begin only on the basis of their own liberation by God, their own decision. Its beginning—this is no part of their distinction but would run contrary to it—cannot be made for them by others through the fact that, without being asked about their own decision, they receive baptism. How can one expect any growth of the living community of the living Lord Jesus Christ in this way?[13]

It would seem that Barth wishes a decisive end to the practice of infant baptism. Barth's treatment powerfully presents a vision of baptism that demands human response seen visibly in confession of faith. However, we find an interesting final twist in Barth's treatment. Barth concludes that the work of baptism continues in the way the Christian life is lived out. Baptism becomes for Barth the context for moving through the Christian life. All its tasks and gifts, responsibilities and privileges, have their logic in baptism. Because baptism is a beginning, the first step of faithful obedience to God, it must take the character of hope. Baptism recognizes the need for growth in the Christian life, for continuity in commitment to Jesus Christ. Barth sees the danger of baptism's folly, the forgetfulness of one's baptism. But this can be overcome only in the recognition that baptism in hope is also baptism as an act of prayer. Here Barth points us finally in a direction similar to McClendon's. That is, to take baptism seriously requires we enter into the field of hope (and prayer).

Barth, however, wishes to take away from the church in its practice of baptizing its children the very thing he understands to be at the heart of baptism, the history of Jesus Christ. Barth grounds Christian baptism in the baptism of Jesus and the baptism by Jesus in the Holy Spirit. If baptism is grounded in Jesus in this way, at what point must water baptism be given to be consistent with this grounding? Barth contends that the candidates' decision is the point where they may be baptized. But here Barth has hidden from himself the implications of his deep commitments to the life of Jesus and the life of the Holy Spirit. Baptism, as Barth admits, is a beginning. It is a matter of hope and a prayer to God that life lived in the Spirit and with Jesus will be lived in faithful obedience to God. Does such hope begin with the decision of the candidate? Does this prayer turn on the confession of faith of an individual before the church? I suggest that Barth would need to turn away from the children in the midst of the church to answer these questions in the affirmative. More significant, Barth has rendered an account of the individual decision which is contrary to his understanding of the freedom God gives us in the Christian life. For Barth, our freedom is not a freedom to choose for or against God. It is the freedom that exists in the following of Jesus, in the conclusion that there was and is no other choice, no other possibility.

Barth is concerned to overcome baptism's folly. He wants the church to take seriously the commitment to the life of Jesus that must accompany baptism. Yet Barth closes himself off to the recognition that this folly can only be addressed in hope and prayer. Chronology cannot ensure a faithful Christian life anymore than a Christian heritage. Clearly, Barth is aware of this. His concern is to understand the practice of baptism from the biblical witness to Jesus Christ, and there he finds little to support pedobaptism. However, Barth misses another biblical absence: individual decision as the beginning of the life of faith. The story of Israel with its covenant with God, its history of hope and suffering, and its faithful waiting on God permeates the NT accounts of conversion. Barth is exactly right in seeing baptism as a matter of hope. However, he does not see that faith is also bound up in hope. What Barth teaches us even in his criticism of infant baptism is that hope is constituted by the life of Jesus Christ and activated in us by the Holy Spirit.

Barth's distinction between Spirit and water baptism is not sustainable if we take seriously the hope found in baptism. Our confession of faith is always a matter of hope. That is, it is made in hope of its realization throughout our lives. Baptism does not begin with the faith of the individual or the community, but with the faith of Jesus Christ who gave to us redemption in hope. But if faith confessed (by the individual) does not precede baptism, then do we not enter again into the problems recognized by Barth and noted by McClendon? I think not. What precedes baptism is the life of Jesus made real to us by the Holy Spirit. Barth shows us this. What is present in baptism is hope, the hope made real by Jesus. What follows baptism is a life always moving toward oneness with Jesus, to more and more clarity of confession of faith, to a joyful awaiting of its final consummation. Hope in baptism engages the possibilities of rejection, the turning away of an individual with one true and abiding word: from the beginning of your life God has sought you and loved you (and yes, saved you). In this construal building on Barth, I have not once used the term "infant baptism," but infant baptism is clearly within the vision of this understanding of baptism. Yet there is still the question of the content of hope and the nature of faith. To gain answers to these questions we must turn finally to the work of Bromiley.

Baptism's Hope

Ten years after the publication of Barth's treatment of baptism in *Church Dogmatics* his most important translator, Geoffrey Bromiley, wrote a little book defending the church practice of baptizing infants. In *Children of Promise*, Bromiley placed in print his greatest criticism of Barth's work without ever mentioning Barth's name.[14] More important, this quiet treatment of infant baptism offers a portrait of Christian faith that illumines the nature of baptism as fundamentally a disclosure of divine grace. Bromiley's goal was not to destroy the arguments against infant baptism. Rather he addresses the pastoral challenge of helping clarify the life of faith for those baptized as infants. In doing so, Bromiley has rendered an account of baptism wide and deep enough to hold together notions of both infant and adult ("believer") baptism.

Bromiley begins with an examination of the scriptures. Though not as detailed or exacting as Barth's treatment, Bromiley's work turns to the central question that Barth resists: what about the *children* of Israel? In Bromiley's account, Israel's life is more fundamental for understanding the relation of faith to baptism than in Barth's treatment of baptism. Moreover, Bromiley's reading of scripture presses forward a thesis that creates a number of problems for Barth and McClendon's positions. Bromiley, following the thinking of Luther and Calvin, contends that what we say about the children of the community of faith must begin with the reality of salvation. This simple thesis opens up levels of complexity and ambiguity that must be acknowledged for us to truly grasp the nature of faith in relation to the life of the Christian community.

Children are part of the community. Both Old and New Testaments point to this fact. However, Bromiley recognizes the scriptures open to us a complexity. In the OT, (male) children were made bearers of the covenant (as promise for their future) by circumcision. In the NT, the situation has changed radically. Circumcision is no longer required as the mark of covenant inclusion; rather, the Christian community, like the Apostle Paul himself, bears the mark of Christ (*to stigmata tou Iasou*, Gal 6:13-17). The children born to those who have been bought by Christ are marked in such a way as to be turned toward baptism. Bromiley understands this to be the point of continuity with the children of Israel in the OT. God deals with us (born in the community of faith, born to the community of faith) not in isolation but against the canvas of covenant care. The children of Christians, like the children of Israel, live in divine promise. Bromiley is clear that this sets up a direction in the scriptures which leads toward infant baptism. It certainly would be more difficult to see from scripture a trajectory that delayed baptism for church children until their decision to believe in the life of the community in which they are being raised.

Bromiley does understand that faith is fundamentally related to baptism. However, the meaning of baptism can be hidden from us if we place faith over it as a kind of hermeneutical grid to explain baptism. Rather, the doctrine of baptism gives us entrance to the nature of faith. Bromiley suggests that baptism is related primarily to what is done for us. Bromiley here echoes a traditional Reformed understanding of baptism that we also saw in Barth's approach. However, with Bromiley we find no sharp distinction between Spirit baptism and water baptism. It is the action of God that is signified in baptism. It is an action that precedes and constitutes baptism and yet works in and with our action of baptizing. Bromiley gains this insight from his reading of Jesus' life. Jesus' life is the life of God for us. Thus in Jesus' command that we be baptized we have the actual reality of salvation that is the ground for the action of baptism. The action of God is pointed to powerfully by baptism in the name of the triune God.

By explaining what it means to be baptized in the name of the Father, the Son, and the Holy Spirit, Bromiley renders an account of the Christian life that weaves together grace and faith bound to hope. Bromiley seems less concerned to define exactly what each triune name signifies in baptism; rather, the point seems to be to use the triune name to capture as much as possible the divine action signified in baptism. Baptism in the name of the Father "declares . . . God has a purpose of love for us."[15] The purpose of God unfolds in the giving of life and the renewal of life. In between this giving and this renewal is the history of our unfaithfulness witnessed in the life of Israel. Yet unfaithfulness, in Israel or with Christians, does not exhaust the divine purpose of love. Our unfaithfulness does not deconstruct the purpose of love for us witnessed in baptism. The faithfulness of God recasts for Bromiley the entire question of adult rejection or neglect of their infant baptism. The faithfulness of God establishes the challenge of our identity as the people of God. Our baptism places us in the midst of that challenge as we live between God's faithfulness and our propensity to be unfaithful. In this way, Bromiley captures the futility of using baptism as a means to divide true believers from nominal Christians or hypocrites. The "decision of faith" then becomes for Bromiley a declaration of identity rooted in our realizing the divine purpose of the Father's love in Jesus Christ, the Son of God.[16] For both an adult convert and one raised in the church, baptized as an infant, their decision of faith will mean the same thing in relation to their baptism—their entire lives are understood within the divine purpose of love.

Baptism in the name of the Son declares our reconciliation to God to be a reality through the life, death, and resurrection of Jesus Christ.

The death of sinful humanity and our rebirth in Christ is signified by this aspect of the baptismal name. Here Bromiley presses the connection of Jesus' life to our own. The Christian life must be understood in terms of an *imitatio Christi ex imago Christi*, the image of Christ that permeates our baptism. Our baptism is fundamentally immersion into Christ's death and resurrection, which illumines the life-pattern that must give shape to our living of the Christian life. That is, the life of Christ gives impetus to the living of our lives in holiness. Because we have been buried with Christ, in our baptism, we must live for him (Rom 6:4). Bromiley finds both the logic of adult conversion and infant baptism to be extractable from this New Testament motif. The point not to be missed though is that faith bound to baptism is a matter displayed in a life patterned after the death and resurrection of Jesus, and this is what constitutes the decision of faith. Thus the decision of faith is found not only in the confession of the moment but primarily in the confession of a life lived with Jesus.

Bromiley recognizes the Spirit as the one who brings into our lives (individually) the reality of Jesus' life in its profound healing of our existence. Here Bromiley sounds like Barth in his understanding of the work of the Spirit in baptism. However, for Bromiley the work of the Spirit establishes a critical ambiguity that is necessary for grasping the relation of the Spirit's work to baptism. Our baptism lives in the movement of the Spirit who works to convince us always of the love of God and seeks to establish in our speech and deeds full identification with Jesus. Bromiley is quite clear that personal commitment to Christ is a matter always of the Spirit's work.

This interplay of our agency and the movement of the Spirit does illumine for Bromiley a distinction between the Spirit's work and (water) baptism. Here the difference between Barth and Bromiley is subtle but important. Barth's distinction between the Spirit's work and water baptism suggests a chronological relation between them: water baptism must accompany the decision of faith and the confession of faith which is the work of the Spirit. This is not to say that every confession of faith is automatically authentic and thus the work of the Spirit, but authentic confession is to be distinguished from water baptism as the Spirit's work. In contrast, Bromiley's distinction points to the work of the Spirit in us as we live in Christian community. The Spirit *makes visible* what we cannot do in ourselves, that is, establish a life of loving commitment to Jesus. Yet this visibility awaits the final word of its authenticity which will be given by Jesus himself. We claim as a matter of hope the authenticity of this visible life of faith, and this we may identify as the work of the Spirit. This means the distinction does not build its boundary at the fount of baptism, but in the action of the Spirit and in the judgment of God.

Bromiley is prepared then to say that the Spirit has been and is at work in the lives of infants. The Bible gives us examples of those children of the community of faith in whom the Spirit was at work from the womb. The service to God visible later in life witnesses the Spirit's work. Yet in this regard Bromiley cannot avoid the central question of conversion. When is an infant converted? Bromiley's answer yields a beautiful picture of the Christian life:

> From the very beginning they are in the sphere of the word and Spirit, and the prayer of parents and congregation is made for them. They are not necessarily converted, and baptism itself will not convert them, but the gospel promises are before them and every reason exists to believe that the Holy Spirit has begun his work within them. They thus receive baptism as a sign and seal of the divine election, reconciliation, and regeneration. As they grow older, they may come quickly to individual repentance and faith. On the other hand they may move away for a period, or perhaps forever. But baptism is always there, bearing its witness to the will of the Father, the work of the Son, and the ministry of the Spirit. The church's proclamation tells them what they are to do. They are to die and rise again with Christ in personal repentance and faith, and are to begin the outworking of their renewal in conversion.[17]

This extended quotation underscores the hope that lies within every baptism. Bromiley's account of adult baptism shares with his understanding of infant baptism the hope that commitments made by the convert will issue in a life of commitment to Jesus Christ. The testimony of an adult convert is bound to the witness of an infant baptized. Thus the meaning of baptism is not exhausted with conversion; rather, baptism extends through the entire life of the Christian in community, from beginning to the end. Bromiley is convinced that all children born to those of the community of faith already belong to Jesus Christ and thus their baptism is a sign of their salvation. This means that in life (and death) these children will live before God.

Baptism's Invitation

If there is a thread that holds together McClendon's, Barth's, and Bromiley's treatments of baptism it is the saving life of Jesus Christ. Once that redemptive life is taken seriously then I believe that baptism must engulf all those touched by that life, specifically those who have come to faith in Jesus and who in their coming have brought their children. But while I may have addressed the arguments against infant baptism by McClendon and Barth, why would I suggest that Baptists ought to baptize infants? I do so believing that we Baptists must take more seriously our commitment to faith *in* Jesus Christ. Of course, this means I believe that being against infant baptism is not a defining point of being a good Baptist. I contend that radical faith in Jesus destroys the false boundaries between infant and adult (believer) baptism. Every baptism is a matter of hope so that the word of confession gives us no false security. The theological refrain of the pastor of the Baptist church I grew up in was Ephesians 2:8:

> For by grace you have been saved through faith, and this is not your own doing; it is the gift of God.

Like many Baptist children I listened and heard well these words, so that my faith was placed in me by the preaching of this word, the living of this word, and the playful growing in this word. I did not confess because I came to a decision for Christ, I confessed because the church (my mother, my father, my sisters and brothers, the mothers of the church, the deacons and trustees, the associate ministers, the chairperson of the usher board, they all) decided that this was what I must do, and in that decision God spoke to me.

We Baptists have the peculiar habit of not taking seriously the power of God at work in our children. We believe that we must withhold from them that which permeates our wonderfully incessant preaching and teaching, the grace of God. If, as Jesus taught (and preached), there was present the power to heal, then why can we not live in the hope that God is saving our children from the womb and baptize them as infants? To do so would yield our lives to the danger of grace, the grace of Jesus Christ. Grace is dangerous because once given it is inescapable. God's grace follows us in life and, if we have rejected Jesus, condemns us in death. More positively, the grace of

Jesus Christ means our daily walking with Christ in the shaping of a life patterned after Jesus. A community so shaped in this way will inevitably feel its baptism as both a cold shower awakening it to Christian commitment and a cool bath sheltering it from the heat of temptation. But baptism can never be a sign of sure faith, but only a sign of faith. Which brings me to a concluding story.

Several years ago I visited a Baptist church in another city with a colleague who teaches in a Baptist seminary. On this particular Sunday morning we would share the joy of seeing his eldest son baptized. Augmenting his joy would be his participation in the baptism of his son. As his then nine-year-old son descended the steps of the baptismal pool, the music that played between baptisms stopped and the lights dimmed. The son tentatively stepped in the slightly cold water and moved slowly toward his father. The only voice you could hear was the soft voice of this father speaking to his son. In his words, the father rehearsed the history of joy for him and his wife—from the birth of this son to the present moment. His final words before the invocation of the triune name in baptism were memorable: "We have waited all your life for this moment. I no longer call you my son but my brother in Christ."

I believe that we Baptists no longer have to wait.

Notes

1. *The Harvest of the Spirit: Reflections on Galatians 5:22* (Nashville: The Upper Room, 1981), 17.
2. See *Baptism, Eucharist and Ministry 1982–1990: Report on the Process and Responses.* Faith and Order Paper No. 149 (Geneva: W.C.C. Pub., 1990), 45ff.
3. James Wm. McClendon, Jr., *Systematic Theology: Doctrine* (Nashville: Abingdon Press, 1994), 386-97. Also see his *Systematic Theology: Ethics* (Nashville: Abingdon Press, 1986).
4. Ibid., 386.
5. Ibid.
6. Ibid., 390.
7. Ibid., 391.
8. Karl Barth, *Church Dogmatics,* IV/4: *The Christian Life (Fragment): Baptism as the Foundation of the Christian Life,* trans. G. W. Bromiley (Edinburgh: T. & T. Clark, 1969).
9. Ibid., IV/4, x-xi. Cf. Eberhard Busch, *Karl Barth: His Life from Letters and Autobiographical Texts* (Philadelphia: Fortress Press, 1976), 220. Also see John Bowden, *Karl Barth: Theologian* (London: SCM Press, 1983).
10. *Church Dogmatics,* IV/4, 36.
11. Ibid., 74.
12. Ibid., 167ff.
13. Ibid., 184.
14. Geoffrey W. Bromiley, *Children of Promise: The Case for Baptizing Infants* (Grand Rapids: Wm. B. Eerdmans, 1979).
15. Ibid., 38.
16. Ibid., 50.
17. Ibid., 80-81.

FAMILY GRACE:
The Christian Family and the Difference It Can Make for the American Family

STANLEY HAUERWAS

The Family: Reconsiderations

On the Feast of the Annunciation, March 25, 1998, Joel Adam Hauerwas was born. I am a grandfather. Nothing is more hopeful than the birth of a child. It defies the unknown, claiming that we can in fact trust in God's grace. So I write in the hope that the family names, and in gratitude to Adam and Laura Hauerwas for opening their lives, and thus mine and Paula's lives, to this new life.

Yet why should anyone other than our family care whether Joel has been born? It is good that he has been born, but such matters are "personal." Surely I should write about the family *qua* family, not the family Hauerwas. Yet, given some of what I have said in the past about the family—namely, that the first enemy of the family is Christianity, I think I need to make clear both that I care deeply that Joel has been born and why I see such a birth as a sign of God's grace.

I have been speaking and writing about the family for twenty-five years. Surely by now I have said what I have to say about the family. Why should I do it again if I have nothing new to say? If all I have to say is the same old thing (at least the same old thing for me), why use this opportunity in honoring Tom Langford to write again about the family?

217

Of course, such questions reflect what can only be understood as a kind of disease particularly prevalent among intellectuals. Once intellectuals have made up our minds about X or Y, we assume that we need to move on to matters that require further investigation—for example, now that I have had my say about the family, I should move on and think about other matters—maybe even about God. Of course such a characterization of the intellectual is caricature, but one worth naming because I think it locates one of the perverse forms the life of the mind can take; that is, the temptation of the intellectual to assume that we do not need to take responsibility for those aspects of life that make our life possible. As a result, the work of the intellectual can be quite imaginative but lack grounding in matters that matter. I hope Joel's birth is sufficient to remind me that if what I have to say about the family is true, then it cannot be said too often.

Yet the other reason I was hesitant to speak again about the family is I am not altogether happy with what I have to say. I believe, as many think, that the family in America is in profound trouble. I think I know why the family is in profound trouble, but I have no solution to offer. Indeed I fear that my understanding of the place of the family, theologically understood, can make things worse. I do not want to make things worse. I want Joel Adam Hauerwas born as he has been born. I want him to have the confidence to have children. But I want those wants to be shaped by the hope that is of God because other hopes can be demonic. How to say so in a child-fearing culture like ours is not easy.

The family is in trouble in societies like America because such societies, as I will try to show, have tried to create social arrangements that deny our lives are constituted by gift. We believe we can live in a manner that does not require acknowledgment that we are creatures of a gracious God. We believe if we are recipients of gifts, we are so because we first have achieved a standing that is our accomplishment. We simply do not have the resources to acknowledge that our very existence is gift.

This is why we fear our children. To acknowledge our children as gift would require the recognition that we also are gift. In order to protect ourselves from such knowledge, we assume we can only responsibly have children if we can make them safe. Yet gifts, particularly the gift of a child, cannot help rendering the world unsafe. Christians should understand such to be the case, believing that through a child has come our redemption and the world's. The grace that the Jesus child bestowed makes the family possible, makes our lives as gift possible. That is why, moreover, the Christian understanding and practice of the family is such a challenge to America. Thus, the gift of the child Jesus makes the world unsafe because it does not leave the world as it is. And it makes the American family unsafe because it forms the Christian family as an alternative. In this way, the Christian family becomes a witness to God's grace.

The American Family

Let me try to explain these last remarks by providing an overview of why, in spite of the celebration of the family by most Americans, the family that we celebrate is in such profound trouble. Indeed what I hope to show is that the very celebration of the family, the fact that Americans so desperately cling to the family as our anchor in the storms of life, is but an indication of the trouble in which the family in America finds itself. The more we are forced to make the family the be-all and end-all of our existence, the more the family becomes a problem not only for itself, but in particular for Christians.

Let me begin by sharing with you some reflections about the family by one of the great philosophers of the Christian era. This philosopher observes that, as the Stoics said, every man is first and principally recommended to his own care.[1] For it is surely the case that each person in every respect is fitter and abler to take care of himself or herself than of any other person. That we are best able to take care of ourselves is obvious because "every man feels his own pleasures and his own pains more sensibly than those of other people."[2]

After the care of ourselves, however, the members of our own family are those who are the natural objects of our affections. We are naturally bound to those with whom we live, influenced as we are by their happiness or misery. We are habituated to sympathize with them since we know better how "everything is likely to affect them, and [our] sympathy with them is more precise and determinative, than it can be with the greater part of people."[3]

Such sympathy is by nature more strongly directed toward our children than toward our own parents. For the existence of the child, for some time after it comes into the world, depends altogether on the care of the parent. But the care of the parent does not naturally depend on the care of the child. So from the eye of nature, it would seem, a child is a more important object than an old man; and excites a much more lively, as well as a much more universal sympathy. It ought to do so. Everything may be expected, or at least hoped, from the child. In ordinary cases, very little can be expected or hoped from the old man. The weakness of childhood interests the affections of the most brutal and hard-hearted. It is only to the virtuous and humane, that the infirmities of old age are not the objects of contempt and aversion. In ordinary cases, an old man dies without being much regretted by anybody. Scarce a child can die without rendering asunder the heart of somebody.[4]

A sobering observation, perhaps, but one in which we cannot help seeing ourselves.

It is surely the case, as this philosopher observes, that the earliest friendships—that is, the friendships that are naturally contracted when the heart is most susceptible to such sympathy—are those between brothers and sisters. Accordingly they have a particular intensity. Sympathy among siblings is necessary for tranquillity and happiness. Nature, by obliging them to accommodate to one another, renders their sympathy more habitual and thereby more lively and distinct. Such sympathy continues after they are separated into different families; but because they seldom live in the same family (though they are more important to one another than to the greater part of people), they are much less than brothers and sisters. For affection is but habitual sympathy, and when we are no longer in the situation that requires such habits, our relations cannot help growing less intense. That is why the children of cousins are of less importance as the "affection gradually diminishes as the relation grows more and more remote."[5]

Thus in pastoral countries—that is, countries where the authority of law is not sufficient to give perfect security to every member of the state—the tie between families is much deeper. In pastoral countries the different branches of the family choose to live in the neighborhood of one another. They are, from the highest to the lowest, of more or less importance to one another. In such societies, those who have positions of responsibility "consider the poorest man of his clan, as his cousin and relation."[6]

Such is not the case

in commercial countries, where the authority of law is always perfectly sufficient to protect the meanest man in the state, the descendants of the same family, having no such motive for keeping together, naturally separate and disperse, as interest or inclination may direct. They soon cease to be of importance to one another; and, in a few generations, not only lose all care about one another, but all remembrance of their common origin, and of the connection which took place among their ancestors. Regard for remote relations becomes, in every country, less and less, according as this state of civilization has been longer and more completely established. It has been longer and more completely established in England than in Scotland; and remote relations are, accordingly, more considered in the latter country than in the former, though, in this respect, the difference between the two countries is growing less and less every day.[7]

So wrote Adam Smith in *The Theory of Moral Sentiments,* first published in 1759. The rest, so to speak, is history. For I take it that Smith's observations about how the family is reshaped by the growth of a society governed by law, what Max Weber called a legal-rational social order, have come to pass. Scotland did and has become England and now the whole world will soon be California. Of course, Smith thought this to be a good thing. Indeed, the whole point of *Theory of Moral Sentiments* is to show how the weakening of the familial ties can increase the necessity of sympathy between strangers and result in cooperative forms of behavior not realized in the past.

Smith's aim was to articulate the philosophical presuppositions and institutional arrangements necessary for the creation of societies in which the poorest man of the clan would not need the regard or charity of the chieftain to survive. Such a system would no longer require individual acts of charity (though of course neither would it exclude such acts but now they are voluntary) since the system itself would supply the wants of each individual through free exchange. The family would still exist, but it too would increasingly be understood as but another instance of exchange relation. I think it not difficult to see that much of the current social and psychological literature, which is often written in the interest of saving the family or at least making the family work, reproduces Smith's understanding of "sympathy." From my perspective this is but trying to cure the illness by infecting more people with the disease.

The same is true, moreover, for those who would have the state intervene to save the family. That is surely to have the fox guard the hen house. That the state has increasingly taken over the functions of the family is the result of the changes Smith at once named and championed. For example, I think few developments have been more deleterious for the family in America than what we now call "public education" and its supporting services. The development of such bureaucracies legitimated by their commitment to helping children cannot but result, despite the best of intentions, in making parents feel incompetent to raise children. Indeed, as the Carnegie Council report on the family, *All Our Children: The American Family Under Pressure*, suggested in 1977, the primary role of the parent should be that of a manager coordinating the care their children receive through the appropriate experts. As the report puts the matter, "No longer able to do it all themselves, parents today are in some ways like the executives in a large firm—responsible for the smooth coordination of the many people and processes that must work together to produce the final product."[8]

One of the curiosities of our time is how many conservatives in America—that is, people who support capitalist arrangements—believe the family can be protected from capitalist formation. Calls for the importance of intermediate institutions fail to appreciate that to call the family an intermediate institution is to have already accepted the presuppositions of a legal-rationalistic social order based on making all relationships exchange relations. Appeals to support the family too often accept the capitalist presumption that the family exists primarily as the place where we receive and learn affection.

Yet as Robert Nisbet pointed out in 1953 in his wonderful book, *The Quest for Community*, familial kinship can never be sustained on interpersonal and psychological grounds.[9] The strength of the family has been its social, economic, and political significance. As Nisbet observes, and it is worth quoting him at length,

> In every enlarging area of population in modern times, the economic, legal, educational, religious, and recreational functions of the family have declined or diminished. Politically, membership in the family is superfluous; economically, it is regarded by many as an outright hindrance to success. The family, as someone has put it, is now the accident of the worker rather than his essence. His competitive position may be more favorable without it. Our systems of law and education and all

222

the manifold recreational activities of individuals engaged in their pursuit of happiness have come to rest upon, and to be directed to, the individual, not the family. On all sides we continue to celebrate from pulpit and rostrum the indispensability of the family to economy and the state, but in plain fact, the family is indispensable to neither of these at the present time. The major processes of economy and political administration have become increasingly independent of the symbolism and integrative activities of kinship.[10]

That the family is now economically and politically secondary has the ironic effect of making an idealized account of the family too important in our lives. In a world of strangers, we cling to the family as the one place that supplies us with relationships we have not chosen. Such relationships seem to promise to give our lives, if not purpose, at least an anchor. The problem, however, is that the family is unable to bear the burden of such intense psychological and moral expectations, which results in spawning whole industries of people who now take as their task to save the family or save us from the family—both projects undertaken in terms shaped by Adam Smith. Yet it is not clear what they have to offer as an alternative. Too often I fear the alternative turns out to be nothing more than a "career."[11]

The Christian Family

This alternative—that is, the assumption that the family is everything, or the family is but a beginning that we must leave behind in the interest of being free—is the reason I have tried to remind Christians that for us the family is constituted by a quite different politics from the politics of the world that was aborning when Smith wrote *The Theory of Moral Sentiments*. In particular I have objected to the view of some Christians that the main virtue of Christianity is the presumption that Christianity is very good for the family—particularly when the family is the one determined by capitalist practices. That seems to me to be nothing short of idolatrous. After all, Christianity has been and will continue to be, if we are faithful, a challenge to familial loyalties.

For example, Will Willimon notes that during the time he has been Dean of the Chapel at Duke, he has received four angry phone calls from parents. They have all been the same call. The parent says, "We sent Suzy to Duke with her head on straight. She was to major in economics and go on to law school. But she has become so involved in the Wesley Fellowship that she has now decided she is going to become a missionary to Honduras. How could you let this happen? You have ruined her life." That Methodism, pale a form of Christianity though it be, can still produce this kind of result indicates that the gospel is not altogether friendly to the family.

Of course the Christian challenge to the family goes deeper than the difference in expectations that may occur between parents and children. I take it that nothing embodies the Christian challenge to the family more determinatively than the presumption that Christians do not have to have children to be Christians. The most decisive difference between Christianity and Judaism is to be found here. God has willed the church to be reproduced not through biology but through witness and conversion. We must remember the most significant thing that single people give up is not sex. What the single give up are heirs, grandchildren named Joel Adam Hauerwas, and they do so because they now understand that they have been made part of a community that is more determinative than the biological family.

Singleness is the practice necessary for the church to be, to participate in, the hope God secured through Christ's cross, resurrection, and ascension. Singleness embodies the Christian hope that God's kingdom has come, is present, and is still to come. Accordingly, we cannot help witnessing this Good News to others, others who may be our children, but more likely to children who have come from families who have never heard the name of Christ. When the church loses the significance of singleness, I suspect it does so because Christians no longer have confidence that the gospel can be received by those who have not been "raised in it." Put differently, Christian justifications of the family may often be the result of Christians no longer believing that the gospel is true or joyful.

That singleness is the first way of life for Christians does not imply that marriage and the having of children is in any way a less worthy way to be Christian. Rather, that Christians do not have to marry means that for Christians marriage is given a new dignity. We are called to be married for the upbuilding of that community called church. Accordingly, the love required of Christians even in marriage imitates that love discovered through our brothers and sisters in Christ. Therefore, marriage is not, for Christians, where we learn what love is about; rather marriage is made possible for Christians because we have first been loved by God.

I realize such a view seems quite bizarre in a culture dominated by romantic accounts of marriage. We assume a couple falls in love and comes to the church to have their love publicly acknowledged. Of course, that results in the presumption that if the love that was initially present in the relationship is no longer present, the marriage no longer exists. Romantic accounts of marriage simply cannot comprehend the church's view that marriage names the time created through faithful promise that makes possible the discovery of the gift of love. Marriage is God's gift to the church through which the hope born by the gift of the Kingdom patiently learns to wait in the time made possible by the presence of children.

If this is not the fundamental theological presumption that sustains Christian marriage, then I do not see how we can make sense of the church's acceptance of arranged marriages. I am aware that we (that is, people with "modern" sentiments) tend to look on the institution of arranged marriage as a cultural mistake we have well left behind; but such a view seems to me to be myopic. As I often observed when I taught at the University of Notre Dame, the very existence of Notre Dame and Saint Mary's was dependent on the continuing belief in arranged marriages. To those institutions Catholic families rightly sent their sons and daughters in the hope that they would meet and marry someone of approximately the same social class and religious background. That is arranged marriage under the illusion of choice.

Moreover, that is why I always taught "Hauerwas's Law" to my classes in marriage and the family at Notre Dame: "You always marry the wrong person." Like any good law, it is, of course, reversible. You also always marry the right person. My law was intended not to instill in students a cynical view of marriage, but rather to help them see that the church rightly understands that we no more know the person we marry than we know ourselves. However, that we lack such knowledge in no way renders marriage problematic, at least not marriage between Christians; for to be married as Christians is possible because we understand that we are members of a more determinative community than marriage. In other words, baptism makes marriage possible.

Thus we expect Christians to have their promises to one another witnessed by the church as a reminder that we rightfully will hold you to promises made when you did not and could not fully comprehend what you were promising. How could anyone *know* what it means to promise lifelong monogamous fidelity? From the church's perspective the question is not whether you know what you are promising; but rather, whether you are the kind of person who can be held to a promise you made when you did not know what you were promising. We believe, of course, that baptism creates the condition that makes possible the presumption that we might just be such people.

It is only against this background that how Christians think about sex is intelligible. Christians do not have a sexual ethic based on some general account of human sexuality. Rather, we have marriage as a practice that governs how we think about sex. For Christians there is nothing called premarital sex because we believe that all sex is marital. The problem with sex outside a publicly acknowledged marriage is not that it is sex, but that it is without the purposes that come only from marriage. To name such purpose unitive and procreative is obviously shorthand for a very complex relation, but such a shorthand has its purpose in a time when people think they get to make up what sex is for.

My difficulty with the Roman Catholic argument against contraception is that it may involve the abstraction of sex from marriage. The argument that every act of sexual intercourse must be open to conception I fear tries to read too much off the act itself, thus divorcing the act from marriage. It is one thing to maintain that marriage as an institution is necessarily open to procreation; it is quite another to maintain that every act of sexual intercourse must be open to conception. The problem is how to make clear that marriage is a practice whose telos is children in a world in which marriage has been spiritualized in the name of love. If nothing else, the prohibition of contraception reminds Christians that sex has a purpose inseparable from our bodies.

The Christian refusal to separate marriage and the having of children can be usefully contrasted with Adam Smith's account of the place of children. Smith simply assumed that having children was a natural result of a particularly intense form of sympathy. Yet what he does not provide is why anyone would find having children a good thing to want to do. Indeed I think there is no greater sign of the incoherence surrounding the having of children in our culture than the pagan assumption that biology makes children ours. Such an assumption seems to draw on Smith's view that it is necessary for the child to be "like us" in order to create bonds of sympathy. That children are born of our bodies, that children can be the bodily form of the unity of a marriage, is no doubt a great gift. But it is not, from a Christian perspective, a necessary condition to account for our responsibility for children.

Christians, single and married, are parents. "Parent" names an office of the Christian community that everyone in the community is expected to fulfill faithfully. Those called to marriage are presumed to accept the call and responsibility to have and care for particular children in the name of the community. But the goods and the burdens of that office cannot be restricted just to those who "have" children. That is why the church rightly expects parents to bring up children in the faith. No responsibility is more important.

Accordingly, the church has rightly resisted state authorities when they attempt to educate children in a manner contrary to parental desires. The church does so because the church expects parents to represent Christ for our children. Parental rights over their children are derived rights drawing as they do their intelligibility from the church's command that parents are to bring their children up in the faith. Christian parents do not own their children; but are rather called to serve children by recognizing that the children of our bodies are gifts of God, not our possessions. That is the "right" the church protects in the name of parental care of children. Of course, the problem in America is that Christians have come to believe the public authorities are but an extension of the care we are to give our children.[12]

I am aware that the account I have just given of the Christian family may strike many as extreme. Surely the business of marriage and having children is a more straightforward affair. Indeed, there seems to be something distinctly "unnatural" about my account of Christian marriage. My account may even seem to risk creating a gulf between God's good creation of marriage and family as we generally know it, and how marriage and the family are institutionalized in the church. Or to put the objection in more Catholic terms, I may seem to risk divorcing nature from grace.[13]

I cannot deny that Christian singleness represents a challenge to what we may well consider "normal." But then the normal is scarcely a good indication of what is natural. Singleness does not deny the natural, but rather is a reminder that nature naturally has an eschatological destiny. In that respect singleness is not different from marriage. I can think of nothing more natural than lifelong monogamous fidelity.[14] I can think of nothing more natural than the desire for children, even in a world as dark as this one. What Christians have discovered about singleness or marriage is not unique to us. It is simply our privilege and responsibility to be for others what God has made it possible for us to be. Indeed, I think that Christians can do few things more important in a world like ours than to be a people capable of welcoming children. Such a welcome is made possible because we are a people who have learned to live by gift.

Where Do We Go from Here?

Which brings me back to how I began this essay. You may remember I expressed the worry that my critique of those who make Christianity a "good thing" for the family may play into the hands of the forces that are about the destruction of the family. Put more accurately, I am not at all sure how we as Christians can sustain the practices of singleness, marriage, and the having of children in a world that makes those practices a matter of individual satisfaction. The account I have just given of the Christian family (which I think is true) is also, I fear, too ethereal. Nisbet is right. The family, and in particular the Christian family, cannot survive unless the family in fact is necessary for our survival.

It is quite interesting in this respect to think about the poor. The poor go on having children in our society in a manner that those with money seem to think irresponsible. But I wonder if the poor are not prophetic just to the extent they understand that the having of children is not a matter of our being able to make sure the world into which children are born will be safe. What we are about as Christians is the having of children. That must come first, and then we must subject other aspects of our lives to that reality. I am suggesting not that children become an end in themselves, but rather that children are the way we remember that what matters is God, not making the world safe or becoming rich.

At stake in all this is the survival of the church. I am often accused of tempting Christians to withdraw from the world. I have no wish to do this, nor any idea how it might be done. Yet I am convinced that if the church is to be able to discipline marriage in the name of that politics called church, we are going to find ourselves as Christians in tension with the world—at least the world as envisaged by Adam Smith, in which we find ourselves today. My claim that the first task of the church is to be the church, in other words, may be exactly what is required if Christians are to be a people capable of bringing children into the world. Moreover, for the church to be a community capable of sustaining the having and care of children, we must also be a people who are not bent on the control of our economic destinies. No attitude is more destructive of children or the family than the presumption that having children is an economic zero-sum game. In this way we remind ourselves that nothing is easier or harder to remember than that children are a gift from God: a family grace. So I thank God for Joel Adam Hauerwas.

Notes

1. Adam Smith, *The Theory of Moral Sentiments,* ed. D. D. Raphael and A. L. Macfie (Oxford: Clarendon Press, 1979). For a sympathetic treatment of Adam Smith that challenges many of the false stereotypes that surround him and his work, see Jerry Z. Muller, *Adam Smith in His Time and Ours* (Princeton, N.J.: Princeton University Press, 1993).
2. Smith, *Theory of Moral Sentiments,* 219. It is fascinating to compare this observation with Aquinas's discussion of the order which ought to determine our care for one another. Of course for Aquinas the discussion of the order of charity is framed by his presumption that we are first to love God before all else. Thus we are first to love ourselves because

   > God is loved as the principle of good, on which the love of charity is founded; while man, out of charity, loves himself by reason of his being a partaker of the aforesaid good, and loves his neighbor by reason of his fellowship in that good. Now fellowship is a reason for love according to a certain union in relation to God. Wherefore just as unity surpasses union, the fact that man himself has a share of the Divine good is a more potent reason for loving than that another should be a partner with him in that share. Therefore man, out of charity, ought to love himself more than his neighbor: in sign whereof, a man ought not to give way to any evil of sin, which counteracts his share of happiness, not even that he may free his neighbor of sin. (*Summa theologia,* II-II, 26, 4, 1291)

   Aquinas suggests that we ought to love our kindred first since we are told to do so by the commandment of the Decalogue. He even suggests we ought to love our parents first and then our children because the father is the source of our origin and "in which respect he is a more exalted good and more like God" (II-II, 26, 9, 1295). Although I would not want to defend every aspect of Aquinas's understanding of the order of charity, what makes him so interesting is how the order is determined first by our love of God.
3. Ibid.
4. Ibid.
5. Ibid., 220.
6. Ibid., 223.
7. Ibid.
8. I discuss this report extensively in *A Community of Character: Toward a Constructive Christian Social Ethic* (Notre Dame, Ind.: University of Notre Dame Press, 1981), 155-66 (here, p. 17).
9. Robert A. Nisbet, *The Quest for Community: A Study in the Ethics of Order and Freedom* (New

York: Oxford University Press, 1953); later published as *Community and Power* (New York: Oxford University Press, 1962), then reissued as *The Quest for Community* (1976).

10. Nisbet, *Quest for Community*, 60. This quotation also appears in my *Community of Character*, q.v. "The Family: Theological Reflections," 167-74. The place of my reflections on the family in my overall work has, I fear, been poorly understood. Accordingly I cannot refrain from directing readers to Grady Scott Davis's wonderful footnote in his *Warcraft and the Fragility of Virtue: An Essay in Aristotelian Ethics* (Moscow: University of Idaho Press, 1992), 25. Davis rightly sees that my reflections on these matters constitute my most sustained critique of liberalism. As Davis puts it, "It is in coming to grips with the constitutive institutions of the community—marriage, family, religion, political participation, and health care, for example—that the limits of the contractarian tradition become clearest and Hauerwas' writings on these topics more telling in their critical implications than even the best of Rawls' more 'philosophical' critiques."

11. The idea that "career" too often becomes the alternative to the family indicates the class nature of much of these discussions. The role money has in the destruction of the family I think has not been appropriately appreciated.

12. In *After Christendom* (Nashville: Abingdon Press, 1991), I use Bertrand Russell's account of marriage to show how the contractual version of marriage and sexual relations, contrary to Russell's belief, must lead to the growth of the state.

13. For my extensive reflections on the relation of nature and grace, see *Sanctify Them in the Truth: Holiness Exemplified* (Nashville: Abingdon Press, 1998).

14. This subject is well argued by Catherine M. Wallace, *For Fidelity: How Intimacy and Commitment Enrich Our Lives* (New York: Alfred Knopf, 1998).

GRACE,
CHRISTIAN CONTROVERSY,
AND TOLERABLE FALSEHOODS

MARY McCLINTOCK FULKERSON

Grace and controversy. Both are familiar elements of the Christian community; both are crucial to its well-being. My first point is obvious. As a recent handbook of Christian theology says, grace is the central reality of the Christian faith.[1] Controversy, the second, is a less obviously desirable part of Christian life. Less desirable, that is, unless we take some cues from its historical resilience, in this case in important debates about grace. To think constructively, even "graciously" about controversy in this essay, I want to move from historic debates on the topic of grace focused on the recurring opposition between divine and human agency to reading a current controversy in terms of such an opposition—that between feminist and orthodox theologians. By reading such a contentious debate within the history of difference over agency and assuming that each "side" is important, I will suggest a more helpful way to think about controversy than the terms of opposition would suggest and, consequently, its contribution to Christian life.

First, a reminder of historic controversy. Grace is a definitional claim about God's character, as the handbook says; it is also "a needed remedy for something in the human situation, a sign of the divine favor, the agent of a restored relation." Yet despite the fact that grace has to do with both God and humanity, Christians have continually disagreed over which should get the most attention. Martin Luther's concern about the radical sinfulness of humanity, for example, led him to reject works righteousness, which he associated with sacramental practices of his day, and to ascribe all to God. Many in the church, however, heard justification by faith as a form of antinomianism. The concern for real change in human lives led some to fear that this notion of salvation by grace through faith alone would undermine human responsibility.[2] Another debate over agency in the operation of grace occurred with differing practices of baptism. In such traditions as the Reformed, the primary concern was to protect the priority of God's agency, an emphasis that underwrote the practice of infant baptism. On the other side were the Anabaptist traditions, where concern with human agency and responsibility— the serious transformation of the sinner—led to the practice of believers' baptism, a public display of accountability, to ensure the reality of saving grace had "taken."

Still another debate occurred with the emergence of nineteenth-century Protestant liberal theology, a debate explicitly about epistemology, but also about grace and agency. After Kant, theology entered a period of self-consciousness about the limitations of the knowing subject. Friedrich Schleiermacher's constructive response, developed to describe and render intelligible the shape of redeemed human experience for a modern audience, took the form of an exploration of the nature of the experiencing subject of faith.[3] This turn to the subject provoked a counterposition in early-twentieth-century dialectical theology. Decrying the status Schleiermacher allowed the human subject, Karl Barth and his successors judged this turn to be the triumph of an implicitly autonomous human subject over the Divine Subject. To neoorthodox theologians, such as Barth and his successors, an epistemology (like Schleiermacher's) that took its cue from the limits of the experiencing subject constituted a challenge to God's primacy in the work of salvation. Although the disagreement over the focus on the human subject adds a new issue, epistemology, the debate resonates with earlier ones. The neoorthodox complaint on one side is analogous to the fear that focus on human being undermines the priority of God in salvation. The Schleiermacherian concern, on the other, is that theology describe actual human experience for the sake of affirming the reality of changed lives. A continuation of neoorthodox God-talk unconnected to the shape of historical human experience, this theology worries, courts irrelevance, and produces a new way to endanger the reality of transformed lives.

These examples illustrate that grace and controversy are linked in our tradition, but can we say any more than that Christians can always disagree on a subject? The debates themselves offer hints. Although they come out of different historical contexts, the debates share similar concerns. Focus on God's agency in each is theological advocacy of human dependence upon God. This acknowledgment of our need for divine favor is central to the reality of grace. We confess that *God* is "the agent of a restored relation" as Marty put it. Yet the idea that human life might remain unchanged is equally unacceptable. The other trajectory of concern— whether it be focused on the requirement that works of love are necessary, that a responsible decision be made for Christ, or that taking account of the shape and limits of human experience is essential to commending Christian faith—is that the "restored relation" shows its effects in human agency.[4]

A similarity of concerns, however, does not mean the two interests can be folded together. The debates are different, and the interests *are* expressions of *opposition*. What does it mean that both affirmations have to be made, but are difficult to maintain at the same time? If we take our cue from what these oppositions express—interests—and acknowledge that theological interests are attached to practitioners of faith, we may find it is least useful to adjudicate certain kinds of oppositions as mutually exclusive claims. To develop an alternative to framing these questions in conventional terms of who is right and who is wrong—a more "gracious" frame for opposition between the concern with divine and human activity—let us look at one more debate, a highly contentious contemporary controversy over God's name.

Using the debate between feminist and orthodox theologies, not typically thought of in relation to grace, I will reframe opposing views as interest-driven practices. With this definition, questions of adjudication become more complicated, and we must speak of tolerable falsehoods attached to truths. I will contend that this frame, or something like it, allows an account of theological opposition apposite to grace as the truth to which all of these debates testify.

Feminists vs. the Orthodox

A contemporary debate as oppositional as any is that between orthodox theologians and feminist theologians. The debate is caused by the rise of feminist theology, now identified in its second-wave version with the work of Mary Daly, Valerie Saiving, Rosemary Radford Ruether, Elisabeth Schüssler Fiorenza, and Letty Russell, among others. Feminist theology is known for the preeminent status it gives the phenomenon of "women's experience." This status is granted in order to correct for the dominance of male-produced accounts of Christian faith, accounts which feminists judge to render women invisible at best and denigrated at worst. In service to that corrective end, feminists offer critiques of the gendered language of the Christian tradition, particularly its God-language. In response, a number of theologians argue that biblical God-language as adumbrated by classic trinitarian doctrine is itself the form in which God's gracious revelation appears. They interpret the language change called for by feminists as a violation of Christian faith itself, tantamount to the creation of another religion. To simplify a complicated conversation I will present the debate by drawing from two essays, one a position characteristic of orthodox theologians that argues against the feminist call to alter the male-dominant imagery of the trinitarian formula, and the second a feminist essay which takes the other "side." Following this summary, I will try out a frame for these positions which might allow a more "gracious" approach to difference.

The essay "Conversation on Grace and Healing: Perspectives from the Movement to End Violence Against Women," by Mary D. Pellauer with Susan Brooks Thistlethwaite, provides a good example of a feminist position on grace. As the title suggests, feminist theology takes up the doctrinal loci of the tradition as they relate to concrete struggles for liberation, in this case, situations of sexual abuse and violence against women. It is theology done in the context of the rape crisis and domestic abuse center.[5] Recorded as a conversation between feminist theologians Thistlethwaite and Pellauer, the essay draws upon their experiences and those of women they have known in their work with victims of abuse and violence to define grace. Transcribing a conversation in Pellauer's home, including the interruptions of everyday domestic life, the essay's very form reflects the feminist epistemological claim that theology should arise from

234

women's experience. Richly intensified by the contributions of two thinkers, it has a fragmented and unfinished character like any conversation—a feature celebrated by the authors.[6]

Drawing from her Lutheran training and her own experience as a victim of abuse, Pellauer defines the healing of victims of sexual abuse as a process of experiencing grace.[7] Healing is the overarching rubric for the process of restoration from violence, the end of the process. This healing is interpreted in the discourse of justice and liberation, rather than therapy, and framed as a continuing process of grace. Although the invocation of grace entails some comment on the priority of divine agency, as we will see, the primary focus is on the shape of human experience in the explication of the process of gracious healing.

To respect its character as grace, Pellauer insists, we must allow for the slowness of this healing. A victim needs to move through the many dimensions of the process without being pressured to "get over it." The rush to resolution that typifies a traditional road map for grace, she insists, often violates the process of healing. A premature call for forgiveness for the abuser may also violate the process and is linked to another potential problem from the tradition. Some instances in the tradition that associate victims of suffering with culpability for sin have been known to connect women's sexuality with that state of guilt. Thus a victim of rape or sexual abuse has been suspected of complicity in the sin. Such complications as these provide good reason, Pellauer says, to attend to the well-being and innocence of the abused woman and to forgo any requirement that she be responsible for the condition of the perpetrator.

Developing the hermeneutic of grace further, Pellauer says that a theological interpretation of the healing process finds that its very independence from our control is a sign of its graciousness. Necessary moments include coming to the point where a victim is ready to remember the past, periods of anger, and mourning. These, too, are a sign of prevenient grace, she observes. Healing comes, although not always, and it cannot be forced. We must recognize that healing may be discontinuous, even as we must continually offer healing possibilities. It may be on "the back burner" for periods of time. As such it can be helpfully thought about with the images of slow creation that characterize many women's activities. The "gifted" and uncontrollable nature of the healing process is not simply the theologian's observation. Part of the spiritual discipline of participating in healing, Pellauer remarks, is being able to say, "It's not up to me." This posture points to the double agency of grace at work. Somehow "I am healing" and "I am being healed" are not mutually contradictory statements. Another feminist testifies, "I did everything I could to survive, but I know it was the grace of God."[8]

The issue of language about God arises, as do all theological topics in liberation theology, out of the particular setting of the oppression. Ministering in the context of rape crisis centers, Pellauer says, requires a "phenomenology of women's religious or spiritual experience in the context of these violations."[9] Part of respecting the gracious independence of the process—its "objectivity"—prohibits a rush to correlate the experience with traditional Christian terms and categories. The minister-interpreter must let the victim speak in her own language. Pellauer relates a "big mistake" she made with a clergy-woman victim of sexual abuse. "I asked her something with 'God' in it, like, 'How does your faith, or your belief in God, connect up to what you've been saying?' And she said, 'There's a hole in God's plan. He'll never forgive a little girl who fucked her daddy.' " This was a self-incriminating cry, Pellauer exclaims, "from a woman who had been assaulted by her father between the ages of three and twelve." Describing her shock and dismay at this response, Pellauer tells of a different approach tried later. When she put her question in terms of the spiritual resources that might have helped the woman survive, rather than invoking a traditional God, Pellauer got a different set of healing images.

> She talked about going down into the abyss, further and further down until she touched bottom, and the bottom held her up. That there was something coming up from underneath her that held her up and without that she would not have been alive. It was totally different from the earlier punitive response. I think maybe it was just the use of the word "God" that pulled this whole punitive strand out and . . .

The associations happen automatically, Thistlethwaite comments, like punching a computer program.[10]

Although both feminist theologians agree that victims' own language about the Transcendent constrain the conversation, they refuse to simply "baptize" "everything that happens." The dilemma for the feminist theologian here is figuring out the proper approach—a way between a theological objectivity that imposes theology and ignores the victim's religious world, and the other extreme—what Thistlethwaite calls "psychobabble—if it happens to you, it's religion." The theological task, then, is the task of ministry, of discerning grace in its most hidden and ordinary expressions, looking for "the extraordinary in the ordinary . . . when the very mundane thing begins to shimmer around the edges and to speak values beyond itself, or to point at something else," as Pellauer puts it.[11]

In sum I would say that on the one hand this feminist notion of grace has form. It is the events of healing and survival, events that are typically marked by stages of restoration. Its chief character is gift, the occurrence that (sometimes) comes to restore life and well-being when they have been brutally violated. On the other hand, this feminist notion of grace is not tied (at least in this essay) to a normative language or tradition. In attempting to correct for the effect of theological patriarchy—the valuing of theological discourse over the messiness and multiple resonances of human experience—it takes most seriously the presenting spiritual resources and associations, Christian or not, of the sufferer.

We find a very different theological approach in *Speaking the Christian God: The Holy Trinity and the Challenge of Feminism*. A collection of academic essays by various writers , the book is unified thematically by the conviction that "the trinitarian language for God—Father, Son, and Holy Spirit—is biblically given, and cannot be changed."[12] From this shared base the authors develop critiques of feminist theological proposals for changing the traditional formula. One author identifies the stakes of such fiddling with the tradition: feminist theology is an example of both heresy (apostasy) and an extreme version of Cartesianism, the use of the autonomous "I" as the primary criterion.[13] For purposes of this comparison I will draw from the essay by the editor, a good representative of the oppositional position to our feminist proposal.

Alvin F. Kimel, Jr., takes up the question "How to name God?" in order to address the issue feminist criticism has forced on the church. The answer appears in his introductory paragraph: the "triune God has named himself, and he likes his name"—it is essential to the gospel.[14] Contrasting in form from the fragmented conversational feminist piece, Kimel's extended elaboration of this claim proceeds as a scholarly argument offering evidence to the reader along the way that will commend agreement with the claim that God's trinitarian name is essential to the gospel and endangered by feminist alterations. The three sections in the essay do not connect as a tightly reasoned case. Rather, they elaborate in different ways what the essential trinitarian name conveys. The sections do dispute contrary positions very briefly, however, and in the process appeal to certain data such as scripture or doctrinal tradition. From these and throughout the exposition we find the specifics of an evidential apparatus, namely, the *warrants* for that data (what authorizes the data as reliable), and the *backing* for the warrants (why we should accept the warrants).[15] By identifying these elements at the end, we get the commitments and driving interest of Kimel's opposition to feminism into focus.

Kimel uses three themes to flesh out the meaning of the name of God. First is the "interlocking whole" (baptism, creed, liturgy) that constitutes Christian life. The corporate life of Christians, especially as signaled by baptism, provides the context for the name. The logic for presenting this life is its grammatical ordering by the Trinity. This grammar is warranted by the work of theologians who forged trinitarian doctrine and by scripture itself.[16] A second important theme is the exposition of the centrality of historical particularity to the Christian understanding of God. This historicity is communicated by the genres of biblical narrative. Not only is their scriptural locus a warrant for the narratives about God, narrative is commended by appeal to the notable postliberal theologian George Lindbeck in order to underscore the normative force of "story." It is identity-constitutive.[17]

There is an objective event preceding these discourses, both narrative and the biblical and doctrinal tradition—the objectivity of God's presence in the Incarnation.[18] Moving to a narrative-type theology, Kimel speaks of the history of God and its display in the story of Jesus of Nazareth, the Christ. This is key to our knowing who God is, because history and specificity protect us from speculative travels into "the infinite, unknowable, homogeneous abyss of motionless deity." Such an argument comes from the conviction that the real gracious character of God must be given priority in our theology, and that "any old account" will not do.

Kimel backs up the appeal to historical specificity in a variety of ways. Although presented as an appeal to the biblical story, which in itself might suffice, the argument from determinacy includes at least two, possibly three subthemes. The argument for the distinctiveness of the biblically narrated God is elaborated by means of a stark contrast with nondeterminate or historical notions of deity; thus a proper theology is threatened by any Greek, philosophical, or "antecedent construals of deity," any that abstract deity. With this theme, Kimel appeals to a philosophical distinction between the general and the particular.[19]

A second, related subtheme is Kimel's argument based on linguistic grammar, the distinction between a proper name and a common noun. With the proper triune name we get the specificity of the biblical God, not a generic deity (a common noun). The Father, Son, and Holy Spirit is "our deity's *proper name.*" In a third underdeveloped subtheme to warrant the God of historical particularity, Kimel refers to the function of history to display identity.[20]

The connecting rubric for these ideas is the tight correlation of the history of this God in this life of Jesus Christ with the trinitarian name. In other words, the grammar of the Trinity, economic and immanent, becomes the crucial hermeneutic for Kimel's argument that what is distinctive and must be protected in the Christian understanding of God is its historical particularity and specificity. Trinitarian doctrine in its full complexity contains the rules for reading the story correctly. Even God depends upon the trinitarian grammar, Kimel tells us. "When the deity seeks to know who he is, he looks at Jesus the Israelite; when he seeks to understand who he has been and will be, he tells himself the biblical story of the Father, Son, and Holy Spirit."[21] The inner relations in the Godhead are thus matched to the determinacy of the God who has a history with us and are necessary to getting him right.

Consideration of how this essay's exposition is defended leads to the question of evidence, that is, its data, warrants, and backing. The most important of the warrants and backing for the claim appears in Kimel's opening resolution—that we use the trinitarian language because God provided it and approves it. The remainder of the essay is threaded through with the various elements of what is thought to constitute God's self-communication. Primarily the data come from scripture, particularly certain sayings of Jesus, and from doctrinal tradition. Although the two subthemes mentioned served to explicate the trinitarian account of God attested to by dominical scripture and classical doctrine, they are less important in status than the data of scripture and tradition. None, however, exceeds the sufficiency of the divine warrant Kimel has initially claimed—that the trinitarian name is God's own choice.

Given these notions of evidence, I would summarize the orthodox essay as follows. The thesis of the essay that feminist alterations of God's name are an "alienation from the gospel" is primarily articulated as a defense of a trinitarian naming of God. According to this orthodox position, God's nature or character is displayed in a particular history of three economic persons; their interrelations are mapped by this doctrine, and access to this God depends upon our faithful attention to these expressions of the objective truth contained therein about this God. If we are to think of the centrality of grace as gospel and agree that God's giving of Godself is the very essence of grace, then Kimel is arguing that God's giving of this name *is* the mediated form in which grace is available to us. "Through it we are given access into the triune life of the Godhead."[22]

On this view the problem with feminist alterations of the name of God, to which he actually gives little space, is simply that their names do not map the same story, history, and inner relations of this God. They constitute the creation of "a new religion, a new God."[23] As we saw, the evidence for the arguments is drawn from two general sources: (1) the argument from historical specificity—the refusal of generic deity by appeal to a specific traditionally denominated story of God, the Father, Son, Holy Spirit; (2) the evidence of an objective God incarnate in history, the mediation of this history in scripture, and its correct elaboration in doctrine. The backing for much of the latter, which would seem to stand on its own, is the claim that this name is divinely revealed in scripture, most directly by Jesus—in short, God is the backing for the second source. The least significant warrants for these claims are the arguments from linguistics, the notion that personal names and generic nouns are qualitatively different entities. A bit of the evidential apparatus, in other words, seems to serve the purpose of accentuating and illustrating a point—helping us understand the import of specificity vs. abstractness by seeing it in the function of language. The argument itself, however, is sufficiently warranted by the divine sanction of the language. The primary evidence—dominical scripture and doctrine and its backing as God-given—is found to be so clear on the issue of the Holy Name, that the feminist alternatives and their very different sources take up very little of the essay's attention. The feminist position is, after all, neither biblical nor an expression of doctrinally correct grammar. For Kimel, correlating the feminist position with the orthodox position would be like going up to a complete stranger and claiming her or him as a relative.

Reframing Contention: Interest-driven Practices

As with every theological disagreement, it is difficult to say that orthodox and feminist theologians differ over one thing; they disagree as much about the nature of authority and the use of sources, as about gender and grace.[24] Were we to pursue these differences within a frame that assumes claims are either adequate matches to reality or they are not, the options are bleak. On the one side there is the claim that a version of Christian faith is simply not Christian. It does not provide access to the Christian God. On the feminist side we have the opposing view that grace is accessible whether one is Christian or not. Although they do not comment on the orthodox view, it is likely that Pellauer-Thistlethwaite feminism would find it patriarchal. These theological views are, at best, strongly antithetical, and may be mutually exclusive. (It is difficult to imagine that one could find a little truth in both to add together.) Yet if taking sides is the only option, how does one account for the other (wrong) side? Given that these positions come from strongly convicted communities of thought, how does one account for the other (wrong) side? Is the wrong position due to stupidity on the part of its authors and their supporters? sloppiness? moral corruption? their failure to be given God's grace? Here I must simply assert rather than argue that the material conditions for such epistemological certainty do not currently exist, even if they were thought to at one time.

To find another way to think about the opposition, I turn to a conversation about the long-standing opposition in social theory between the notions of structure and of agency. Judging the very framing of this problem to be the problem, philosopher Anthony Appiah lays out a proposal that is suggestive for an alternative theological framing of opposition. As traditionally posed in social theory, the argument is between proponents of individual responsibility, creativity, expressiveness, and even genius, and the view that social systems or the structuring of the social world produces reality. Whether it be the romantic notions of the origins of literature in the expressive individual, on the one side, or the ostensible structural determinism of a Foucaultian notion of discourse, on the other, or some older liberal individualism vs. Marxist view, Appiah insists that the dilemma is fundamentally misleading. Its very construction is problematic, he says, whether we think that one is right and one wrong, or take the view that a little bit of each will solve the impasse. If a little of each resolves it, we see agents as not completely determined by structures such as capitalism, but as occasionally contributing something, a "gradual series of concessions." This view ends "by conceding too much" and basically undermines the meaning of the terms. In place of any version of the opposition, he argues that these concepts are not even about the same thing at all. The opposition "structures vs. individuals" does not designate competition for the "same causal space." Rather it is a competition for "narrative space, as different levels of theory, with different constitutive assumptions."[25]

If narratives are judged by how interesting they are and what ends they serve, as I think they are, then Appiah's view shows that the "theories" represented by these oppositions are each constituted by practices, practices that are defined by interests. Appiah's analysis exposes the differences between these "opposed" positions. Once we consider their differences in social theory, we will be able to see how they provide another way of understanding the feminist and orthodox positions.

Theories that focus on structure come from practices aimed at *emancipatory social changes:* "Structure is central because of a series of preferences and beliefs; . . . above all because of a preference for social life without exploitation, originally conceived of as the expropriation of surplus labor." Theories that focus on individuals, or better, discourse about agents, are rooted in interests derived from our practices of *living with others* —"commonsense psychology," as Appiah puts it.[26] Thus different interests construct different areas of inquiry, with attendant forms of justification, and teleological ends.[27]

Of equal importance in this reframing is the recognition that these forms of articulation, particularly as they develop the patterns that get termed "theories," always—of necessity—*idealize.* Idealization is required in order to define a region of inquiry, for to map reality is necessarily to occlude some of the terrain, the data, the bits of stuff that do not fit the relevant pattern. All theories, Appiah reminds his readers, commit some form of obfuscation, whether it be a theory about the human psyche, deep space, or the Christian past. In any discernment of patterns some things are not accounted for, described, or made part of the picture that is made visible. To say this is not to say that the theories or patterns are useless or false. Rather, Appiah says we may speak of "approximate truth" or "good enough" truth in the employment of different kinds of theories toward the ends for which they are constructed. Examples abound. The science developed to serve the interest that requires assessing energy regulation at the cellular level would not serve a chemistry adequate for developing industrial dyes, where a relevant theory works with relatively more cumbersome units.[28] The history that constructs "significant event" as military or political action occludes "significant events" of "kitchen history."

What is noteworthy in recognizing different interest-constitutive theories is that areas of inquiry are partly determined by the *falsehoods* indulged and whether they can be tolerated. In a theory of rationality developed to serve the interest in human responsibility, for example, it must be tolerable that no one acts in consistently rational ways. In industrial chemistry, the invisibility of certain cellular levels must be tolerable for the industrial level "grid" to work.

Appiah's proposal is suggestive for theologians because of an already widely shared view that theologies are practices driven by interests.[29] To develop it a bit we would say that each such practice is commendable insofar as we recognize first the importance of its interests. We would assume that its articulation as theory cannot avoid the obscuring of some realities; *it entails falsehood that we can tolerate.* Again we assume that any claim with commendable interests and ends must ignore some aspects of reality to get at others and must identify reality in ways that falsify some of its dimensions.

To return to Appiah's claim that the problem is set up wrong as opposition, we can see now that it is not a real choice to say that one must choose between the theory of structures or individual agency. One is never engaged in only one practice, and the practices attached to these theories prove to be no exception. Even those committed to socialist and emancipatory interests that come with the structural theories are most likely also engaged in practices driven by the psychological need to speak of individual agency—"I love," or "I commit," "I buy," and so forth. Defined as interest-driven practice, this "bourgeois discourse" of individualism opens access to a region of reality different from the discourse of capitalist structures. It is judged as a product of corruption, yet it cannot be dispensed with or simply replaced. It produces access to some realities. One must connect the two in much more complex ways than opposition or addition afford.

What would it look like, then, to reframe the debate between orthodox and feminist positions by taking Appiah's suggestion that the problem is set up wrong? I think we would find something better than the unhappy choices of true or false, or adding together everybody's "piece of the puzzle." Thus I propose that these theologies are different practices, led by different interests. They both occlude different dimensions of the realities into which they inquire.

The practice invoked in the Kimel essay is directed by an interest in proper reference to God. The setting invoked for the practice is a liturgically ordered life. The means for that practice are supplied by ancient theologians (Basil, Athanasius), scriptural passages referring to God as Father, especially those attributed to Jesus, and participation in the liturgical life of the church. The priority of God's agency is captured in the conviction that there are traditions that God has "spoken," and that a central communication is the giving of his Name. Characteristic of this interpretative community is reliance upon these loci, which function as warrants for claims and directives for behavior. There is no semiotic "fuzz" or confusion in this interpretative community. Meaning is one-directional; there are texts which refer (send) and readers-hearers who correctly receive (understand). What must be said about God and what the rules are for speaking properly of the gracious transcendent Agent of salvation are the concerns of the orthodox theologian.

The interest of feminist theologians directs a practice of ministry and area of inquiry that are very different. The acknowledged setting of a rape and abuse crisis center tells us that the interest is corrective of what is perceived as the confluence of patriarchal religious images, but more immediately as the violence perpetrated against women, and the ways that religious discourse is entangled with the sustaining of such oppression as well as its relief. The social space of those practitioners of ministry or healing with victims of sexual abuse and domestic violence is a complex space where economic dependence, fear, self-hatred, and local pieties, both ecclesial and regional languages and habits, constitute the "real world." Thus the means for the practice of critique and liberation are drawn from overlapping languages produced by the multitude of institutions (church, cultural, legal, economic, etc.) contributing to the oppression of women. The open-ended and pragmatic way liberatory responses are crafted—dependence upon a phenomenology of women's experience, for example—displays the crosshatch character of commitments and languages, as well as ends of this practice.

On the one hand, then, the orthodox theologian is affirming the prevenience of God's agency in the event of grace. The protective normative moves concerning the trinitarian name of God are fundamentally about the transcendence and a priori character of God in our salvation. The identification of the particular biblical and doctrinal patristic texts as warrants-evidence simply protect the givenness of that divine agency. (The biblical texts are revelation, not human constructions.) If we were to describe this posture in relation to the continuing dilemmas about agency that come with the debates about grace, it seems most closely associated with acknowledging God's prior agency in the work of grace; it underlines human dependence upon God and excoriates the practices that emphasize human agency and construction.

The feminist essay, on the other hand, is about the interest the church has always had in "real transformation." Whether it be in the tradition of the Catholic church's stress on human acts that display salvation or in the tradition of Schleiermacher's concern to render the experience of redemption intelligible, the phenomenology of women's experience is driven by an interest in attending to the actuality of graced lives. What it looks like when women victims heal and how to minister to them in the process constitute the feminist "text." We can identify the theological character of the feminist interest, at least as exemplified in the Pellauer essay, within the tradition of the church that has concern with the actual transformation of communities, in this case, the concern that real change happens in the lives of abused women, and the role that language for God has in that transformation.[30]

Given that these are different interest-driven practices, what do they falsify? What can we assume is distorted by the feminist essay? What are its "tolerable falsehoods"? The theory or pattern operating in the Pellauer essay includes the prioritizing of women's experience, the interest in the critique of the patriarchal character of both theological and biblical traditions, as well as current social realities for the ends of liberation from gender oppression. Some aspects of reality which do not fit this pattern will be overlooked. For example, any claim that Christianity is patriarchy, hinted at here, overlooks that about Christian history which is *not* harmful to women. Such a judgment surely does not result from the consultation of all instances of Christian faith so as to warrant the judgment empirically and statistically. The insistence on the oppressive function of God-language could not hold in all cases. Nor would all women agree. Not all women associate the language of "fatherhood" with domineering men, the denigrating of women, or sexual abuse. Would the historical invisibility of women of all races, classes, and sexual preferences be significant enough to merit such interest, and how would one know? These counter situations suggest occlusions that can be identified in feminist approaches.

Another falsehood tolerated in this essay has to do with the aspects of traditional theological reflection that would require some distinction between traditions. The detachment in Pellauer and Thistle-thwaite's discussion of grace from any particular language could be taken to suggest that grace is some reality prior to discourse, or that a number of religious (or nonreligious) traditions name it, that the reality of Jesus Christ has no central bearing on its definition. Since the orthodox position associates language so closely with the reality itself as to make of it virtually a relation of identity—language constitutes reality—we find a serious difference here. However, Appiah's frame would suggest that Pellauer's detachment of discourse from a process called grace in fact indicates an overlooking of some issues in the interest of allowing other realities to come into focus. What is overlooked is the question of how a narrative and community reproducing such a narrative might be fundamental elements in shaping graced lives. The account ignores the real possibility that healing cannot happen without a stock of traditions and stories from which to draw. For this eclecticism to be tolerable means that in the work with abused women (or others) something believed to be true and good appears when such realities as continuity of tradition are overlooked. When victims' languages may be deficient, where shelters may be lacking constant communities and traditions, an interpreter must feel that it is more important to claim grace—the moments when a move into recovery, hope for a future, or restoration happen—than to gatekeep a particular normative language. In sum, the falsehoods tolerated by the feminist piece are related to an unwillingness to pull out a normative religious tradition for naming grace, and a willingness to remain content with affirmations of well-being, provision of safe space, and freedom from pressured accountability. However, a false-hood is being tolerated: that one might know what grace is without a story.

Turning to the orthodox position, a first example of the falsehoods deemed tolerable is found in the evidential apparatus. When the tradition is invoked in citable segments—like theological sound bites—and used to authorize current practice, the assumptions about the world that characterized the earliest decades and centuries of the Christian faith are treated as irrelevant to an author's deliverances on a doctrinal truth. An ancient thinker's views on God, his cosmology, on the way in which language, meaning, and reference work are thereby treated differently than his or her view of the workings of human anatomy, disease, the galaxy, and other worldly regions, all of which a scholar would want to contextualize in their historicity. Thus the views on God's name and resulting heresy found in biblical passages, Basil, Athanasius, and other early fathers are treated as context-transcending data that should compel practice today.

A second example is toleration of a contradiction. As noted earlier, the two sources of warrants and backing in the defense of the trinitar-ian name are really separate and could easily be disconnected. Kimel's appeal to historical particularity is disconnected from his claim that the classic authorities are revealed. If the scripture is divinely revealed, then its content is to some extent immaterial; scripture could repre-sent a generic or female God and one would still need to follow its command. The argument from specificity and history, on this basis, seems superfluous. To put it a bit differently, is the real bottom line that God has revealed "his" name in Jesus as witnessed to us by Scripture? or is it that *this particular kind of God* is authenticated by virtue of the attractiveness of "his" nature, and so forth, and thereby authenticates the witness? The contradiction arises in that the appeals to linguistics, historical particularity vs. abstraction, and such all function as evidence that invokes non-Christian knowledges. They go beyond God's revelation. As such, they are concessions to human understanding and imply (contradictorily) that we need more than God's revelation to understand God. Kimel's two sources of evidence for his claim that the trinitarian name is the correct one are not only disconnected, but are not coherent together.

Third, the argument assumes that the language of the tradition, when properly grammatical and biblical, works together as a cohesive whole in a community and is not made complex by the meaning-laden world of hearers. Hearers do not bring any signifiers to the process of meaning-making that give texts the associations that come with place and difference. Hearers and (we assume) readers are like blank slates on this view, and the force of meaning, when it works properly, is one-way. Thus, the semantic world of gendered terms is assumed to be a fixed one, such that neither historical distance nor experiential and ability-differences need to be addressed.

What is tolerated, in short, is the "falsehood" that hearers and readers in fact could and can all *understand* the formula in the same way, and thus, correctly. This requires the overlooking of complicating questions like, what if we lived before the fourth-century trinitarian formulation was consolidated and spoke differently of God, say with modalist images? Was the wrong god given to us? Or, what if we were or are uneducated and do not understand or have access to the complexities behind the formula? Or, what if we are like the woman whose experience of sexual abuse makes the associations of correct God-language with "Father" continually problematic, despite her best intentions to be faithful?

What, then, is the benefit of this frame for opposition? I think three things are accomplished by accepting Appiah's frame for oppositional positions. First, the notions that some debates are not about the same things and that all positions constructed out of the interest-driven patterning of reality must tolerate falsehoods are suggestive of a complex view of reality. They invite more alternatives than relativism or the forms of objectivism, where correctness means offering representations entirely adequate to reality. We are invited to tie theological positions to the practices in which they are embedded and the interests they serve. When looked at in their thickness, different practices and their ends can appear more sympathetic, more appropriate, than when considered simply as propositional truth claims. Pellauer's story forces us to hear the interconnections denied by the orthodox proposal. The experiential associations that constitute signifiers such as "Father" cannot be denied in situations which acknowledge the intersections of other discourses. The feminist view is more likely to elicit sympathy when viewed as a strategy in a practice of ministry where the harmful and abusive associations that may come with certain images of God must be taken seriously. The end of the practice is defined as the terms of transformation for particular women—transformation which will not be advanced by the insistence that orthodox doctrine must be followed.

For its part, orthodoxy might appear more feasible when seen as a part of a practice whose end is the continuation of a tradition of dependence upon a God whose reality and givenness precedes the human being. Insofar as it invokes a yearning for a world where all talk could be talk that was God's gift, that is itself mediating of the divine, it is a yearning that other "camps" might have some sympathy for, if not share. The trinitarian grammar can be taken as a meta-ordering of the elements of transformed creation, an ordering that may not be enforceable in every context, but reminds us that determinate stories and their patterns are crucial for identity, God's or anyone's. How else might we know the shape of grace? The benefit, then, in this frame is that attention to the interests and success at furthering their ends provide more interesting ways to compare different theological positions.

As interest-driven practices, however, both theological positions distort reality. An important second benefit to this frame is that it *relocates the terms of acceptability* for opposing positions. If this is not simply pluralism of an undiscriminating sort, it is because we can make judgments about which falsifications are tolerable and which are not. Here we move to the question of whether the falsehoods feminist theology tolerates or those orthodoxy allows *should* be tolerated. We may decide that the continued interest in the mixed discourses of contextual life which drives feminist theology generates damned lies if we think from a certain theological view. Or that the continued interest in signifying processes in abstraction from the hybridity of contemporary discourse is intolerable from another view. Whatever the case, theological reflection can only benefit by discernment of what is being occluded by any position rather than pretending a false adequacy.

A third benefit of this reframing is a theological reason to agree that falsification comes with all theological positions. Falsification seems undeniable if we take seriously the setting in which theological practice happens for most theologians connected to the academy.[31] The "true enough" character of a particular theory, we remember, is not undermined by the fact that it ignores, or does not describe the full dimensionality of reality. It "works," in other words, but it does not work for all regions of reality. A theological discourse that insisted that only one form of Godly talk was true would be badly misdescribing the social space of most Christian institutions with which I am familiar. The evidence is not simply that there are other religious discourses competing with our theological discourse; it is the *participation* of theologians in *other* discursive practices. It fundamentally matters that discourse occurs in practices; creeds and confessions are attached to human actors who reside in institutions. They may invoke a Godly utopia, but they do not consistently enact it. More specifically, the discourse of most theological institutions is still the discourse of individual achievement and merit. We are not, in other words, living in a fully transformed world, where our capacities to name our dependence upon God are steadily in play. As long as we occupy other social spaces, that orthodox discourse does not "work" everywhere.

This is not to suggest that there are no faithful who live life as constant prayer. It is to suggest that by and large the locus for the production of much theology is the academy in the United States, which is constructed out of the discourses of the social formation of the liberal democratic state and global capitalism. Thus try as we may to create alternative liturgical and "redeemed" social space in our institutions, attached as we are to churches, our use of the language of *my* raise, *my* social security, *my* tenure, *my* book, displays our constitution by the secular processes of the United States and is a manifestation of the "leaks" of the "nonredeemed" world into our liturgically shaped world.

This discourse still signals the world of "my accomplishments," as opposed to the world where the paradox of grace is displayed in every human act. In such a world it would be a mistake to think that one side is right and should "win": either orthodoxy and other theologies most concerned to sponsor God's prior agency, *or* feminism and those interested in the messy multidiscursive character of human experience. The first point here is that orthodoxy as an aspiration for a world where our discourse can match God's own cannot expect theologies more focused on mixed discourses and their associations to go away, just as socialists with preference for the language of structure cannot expect the language of individual agency (bourgeois individualism) to disappear quite yet, however unredeemed it is.

In a world of such institutions as I describe, theology cannot yet fully display the reality for which orthodoxy yearns. However, in such a world, theology also needs a signal conviction that feminist theology fails to provide. That conviction is the paradox of grace. Grace as a paradox stands for the Christian hope that theological discourse must witness to, but cannot yet fully display.[32] As Paul puts it, "By the grace of God I am what I am: and his grace which was bestowed upon me was not in vain; but I labored more abundantly than they all: yet not I, but the grace of God which was with me" (1 Cor 15:10 KJV). The paradox of grace is that the most completely human action is the action that one recognizes to be sustained, made possible by God, and exemplified in the Incarnation. "In ascribing all to God it does not abrogate human personality nor disclaim personal responsibility. Never is human action more truly and fully personal, never does the agent feel more perfectly free, than in those moments of which he can say as a Christian that whatever good was in them was not his but God's."[33]

That paradox signals the resolution of the contraries between God's and our agency. This resolution is not yet fully evident, however, in our worlds of materially located discourse. We cannot speak of our economic and institutional lives in these paradoxical terms. This does not refute the truth of grace; however, it means that it is premature to demand a singular theological logic or to deny that our theological discourse is built upon tolerable falsehoods. What may be intolerable, in light of this paradox of grace, would be to ignore either the conditions of real transformation in human life or the need to depend upon the God who is already there before us.[34] Finding that grace is a paradox, in other words, suggests that a uniformity of claims may be the last good that we should seek.

Notes

1. Martin E. Marty, "Grace," in *A New Handbook of Christian Theology*, Donald W. Musser and Joseph L. Price, eds. (Nashville: Abingdon Press, 1992): 209-11.
2. It is not accurate to say that the interest in human responsibility was taken to exclude God's grace. Marty is surely right that for Christians grace is an expression of "the character of God" as love undeserved, unconditional, "a needed remedy for something in the human

situation, a sign of the divine favor, the agent of a restored relation." Eventually, however, the issue arises over what humans contribute. Is it given or deserved? (Other issues which seem related to agency include, Is grace irresistible? How is it related to the will?) (Marty, "Grace," pp. 210-11).

3. Descriptions of the subject's determination by the historical realities of sin and grace took the place of metaphysical claims about God and traditional accounts of revelation as the primary subject matter of doctrine in Schleiermacher's chief work, *The Christian Faith*. Not only did Schleiermacher understand divine agency to be a condition of the redemptive experience of the Christian community, but his description of the Christian affections and reinterpretation of doctrine have grace as the central experienced reality of Christian faith. The "evidence" of God's agency was in a sense the experience of forgiveness as the reduction of the misery of sin through the christomorphic shaping of the community, as Niebuhr called it.

4. Marty, "Grace," 211.

5. Mary D. Pellauer with Susan Brooks Thistlethwaite, "Conversation on Grace and Healing: Perspectives from the Movement to End Violence Against Women," in *Lift Every Voice: Constructing Christian Theologies from the Underside*, ed. Susan B. Thistlethwaite and Mary Potter Engel (New York: HarperSanFrancisco, 1990), 169-86. A liberation "rule of thumb" is that theology must have a "consistency between the theory and the practice" (ibid., 171).

6. Ibid., 170.

7. Shaped by Lutheran theology of law and gospel, sin and grace, and by working-class poor white abusive families, the theologians' interpretation is an important element in the account of grace, but it is not theorized here relative to the reflective task of theology.

8. Ibid., 174, 183.

9. Ibid., 180.

10. Ibid., 181.

11. Ibid., 182, 181, 185.

12. Promotional sheet on *Speaking the Christian God* from Eerdmans New Book Information.

13. Leslie Zeigler, "Christianity or Feminism?" in *Speaking the Christian God: The Holy Trinity and the Challenge of Feminism*, ed. Alvin F. Kimel, Jr. (Grand Rapids: Wm. B. Eerdmans, 1992), 318-19.

14. Alvin F. Kimel, Jr., "The God Who Likes His Name: Holy Trinity, Feminism, and the Language of Faith," in *Speaking the Christian God*, 188.

15. I am thinking of Stephen Toulmin's anatomy of argument in *The Uses of Argument* (Cambridge: Cambridge University Press, 1958).

16. Kimel cites (pp. 189, 190) Basil the Great, Athanasian strictures against heresy, for example, for the properly named practice. Repeatedly, the appeal to the practice is warranted by the textual authorities, which are authorized by God. Baptism governs the proper God-language and God authorizes it, evidenced by a scripture citation (Matt. 28:19)—spoken of as the "canonical mandate." The biblical backing for these warrants, Kimel insists, means that the grammar is stipulative for proper speech, not simply a suggestion or option, nor a historically relative practice.

17. Kimel, "Language of Faith," 191.

18. It is possible to argue that this appeal is the backing for scripture's status as a warrant for the proper name; i.e., the objectivity of the Incarnation authorizes scripture, which has status because it reports it. However, the more forceful argument in the essay is that the biblical mediation is a warrant because it is revealed by God—thus God's self-revelation is the ultimate backing.

19. Kimel, "Language of Faith," 202.

20. Ibid., 201-2.

21. Ibid., 202-3.

22. He doesn't put it just this way. J. A. Dinoia does, in "Knowing and Naming the Triune God." But see Kimel, "Language of Faith," 208.

23. Kimel, "Language of Faith," 208.

24. I see it in the tradition of the neoorthodox vs. the liberal Protestant view on the use of "human experience" in the task of theological reflection. Feminists assume that religious

discourse is constructed, it is produced by human beings. At least here they do not ascribe special status to any religious tradition or system.

25. Anthony Appiah, "Tolerable Falsehoods: Agency and the Interests of Theory," in *Consequences of Theory*, Selected Papers from the English Institute, 1987–88, New Series, no. 14, ed. Jonathan Arac and Barbara Johnson (Baltimore: Johns Hopkins University Press, 1991), 69, 74.

26. Ibid., 82, 80-81.

27. Just as interest in women generated the field of women's studies, for example, it generated an attendant redefining of historical periodization. The passion for recovering women's agency itself scrambled and redefined what counted as evidence and agency and still does in historical studies shaped by feminism.

28. Appiah, "Tolerable Falsehoods," 77.

29. A number of authors—James Wm. McClendon, Craig Dykstra, among others—think of theology as practice, using Alasdair MacIntyre's definition of "practice" as a model.

30. If there is an ancestor for this feminist focus in some of the historic debates it might be Schleiermacher in his concern that grace-redemption be rendered intelligible in terms of the structures of human experience.

31. See Appiah, "Tolerable Falsehoods," 84-85. I realize academies differ. I generalize and assume that divinity schools and seminaries, as well as most churches, operate mostly within today's social formation.

32. My inspiration here is grace as interpreted by theologian D. M. Baillie, whose work in the first half of the twentieth century took up central doctrines of the Christian faith, the Incarnation and Atonement. Baillie interpreted these doctrines through an understanding of grace as the central paradox of Christian life. D. M. Baillie, *God Was in Christ: An Essay on Incarnation and Atonement* (New York: Charles Scribner's Sons, 1948), 108.

33. Baillie, *God Was in Christ*, 114. As for Jesus Christ as the God-Man: the important analogy here is that he was the Man who would "claim nothing for Himself as a Man, but ascribed all glory to God." "I, . . . yet not I but the Father" (p. 126).

34. Is this trinitarian? Isn't the Trinity the distinctively Christian view of God? Baillie thinks so and remarks that the trinitarian conception is just what has been expressed devotionally in these descriptions of grace (ibid., 122). Extrapolating from Baillie, nowhere is it ever said that the paradox of grace is that I am most fully human when I call God "Father-Son-Holy Spirit."

CONTRIBUTORS

C. Clifton Black

Black is the Otto A. Piper Professor of Biblical Theology at Princeton Theological Seminary, Princeton, New Jersey. Among his books are *Jesus Christ: Holy Week and Crucifixion,* with Thomas A. Langford (Graded Press, 1985), *Mark: Images of an Apostolic Interpreter* (University of South Carolina Press, 1994), and the commentary on First, Second, and Third John in *The New Interpreter's Bible, Volume XII* (Abingdon Press, 1998).

Mary McClintock Fulkerson

Fulkerson is Associate Professor of Theology in the Divinity School at Duke University, Durham, North Carolina, with a joint appointment in Women's Studies. She has written *Changing the Subject: Women's Discourses and Feminist Theology* (Fortress Press, 1994) and is currently working on a book on the intersection of cultural theory and theology.

Beverly Roberts Gaventa

Gaventa is Helen H. P. Manson Professor of New Testament Literature and Exegesis at Princeton Theological Seminary, Princeton, New Jersey. She is the author of *From Darkness to Light* (Fortress Press, 1986), *Mary: Glimpses of the Mother of Jesus* (University of South Carolina,

1995), and *I and II Thessalonians,* Interpretation (John Knox, 1998).

Stanley Hauerwas

Hauerwas is the Gilbert T. Rowe Professor of Theological Ethics in the Divinity School at Duke University, Durham, North Carolina. His books include *Resident Aliens,* with William Willimon (Abingdon Press, 1989), *Christians Among the Virtues* (University of Notre Dame, 1997), and *Sanctify Them in the Truth* (Abingdon Press, 1999).

Richard P. Heitzenrater

Heitzenrater is William Kellon Quick Professor of Church History and Wesley Studies at the Divinity School at Duke University, Durham, North Carolina. He is the General Editor, *Bicentennial Edition of the Works of John Wesley,* 35 volumes (Abingdon, 1976 –). His books include *The Elusive Mr. Wesley,* 2 vols. (Abingdon Press, 1984 –85) and *Wesley and the People Called Methodists* (Abingdon Press, 1995).

Willie James Jennings

Jennings is Associate Dean of Academic Programs and Assistant Research Professor of Systematic Theology and Black Church Studies at the Divinity School, Duke University, Durham, North Carolina. He is currently at work on two projects dealing with theology, racial identity, and anthropology.

Robert K. Johnston

Johnston is Professor of Theology and Culture at Fuller Theological Seminary, Pasadena, California. His books include *The Christian at Play* (Wm. B. Eerdmans, 1983), as coeditor, *The Variety of American Evangelicalism* (University of Tennessee, 1991), and as coeditor, New International Biblical Commentary, 18 vols. (Hendrickson, 1995–). He is working on a book on theology and film.

L. Gregory Jones

Jones is Dean and Professor of Theology in the Divinity School, Duke University, Durham, North Carolina. He is coeditor of the journal *Modern Theology* and the author of *Transformed Judgment* (Notre Dame, 1990), *Reading in Communion: Scripture and Ethics in Christian Life,* with Stephen Fowl (Eerdmans, 1991), and *Embodying Forgiveness: A Theological Analysis* (Eerdmans, 1995).

Philip D. Kenneson

Kenneson is Associate Professor of Theology and Philosophy at Milligan College, Milligan, Tennessee. He is the author of *Selling Out the Church: The Dangers of Church Marketing,* with James Street (Abingdon Press, 1997), *Beyond Sectarianism: Re-Imagining Church and World* (Trinity, 1999), and *Life on the Vine: Cultivating the Fruit of the Spirit in Christian Community* (InterVarsity, 1999).

James C. Logan

Logan is E. Stanley Jones Professor of Wesleyan Studies and Evangelism at Wesley Theological Seminary, Washington, D.C. He is the author of *Theology as a Source in Shaping the Church's Educational Work* (United Methodist Church, 1974), *Theology and Evangelism in the Wesleyan Heritage* (Kingswood Books, 1994), and *Christ for the World* (Kingswood Books, 1996).

Roland E. Murphy

Murphy is George Washington Ivey Emeritus Professor of Biblical Studies at the Divinity School, Duke University, Durham, North Carolina. The author of many books, especially on Old Testament wisdom literature, his work includes *The Song of Songs* (Hermeneia, Fortress Press, 1990), *The Tree of Life* (Anchor, Doubleday, 1990), and *Proverbs* (WBC, Word, 1999).

Philip A. Rolnick

Rolnick is Professor of Religion, Greensboro College, Greensboro, North Carolina, and director of the college's Ethics Across the Curriculum program. He is the author of *Analogical Possibilities: How Words Refer to God* (Scholars, 1993) and the editor of *Explorations in Ethics: Readings Across the Curriculum* (Greensboro College, 1998).

Jean Miller Schmidt

Schmidt is Professor of Modern Church History at Iliff School of Theology, Denver, Colorado. She is the author of *Souls or the Social Order* (Carlson, 1991) and *Grace Sufficient: A History of Women in American Methodism* (Abingdon Press, 1999). She is working with colleagues on a two-volume history (sources and narrative) of *The Methodist Experience in America.*

D. Moody Smith

Smith is George Washington Ivey Professor of New Testament in the Divinity School, Duke University, Durham, North Carolina, where he and Langford have been colleagues for three decades. His books include *Anatomy of the New Testament,* with Robert Spivey (Macmillan, 1969, continuously in print), *The Theology of the Gospel of John* (Cambridge University, 1995), and *John* ANTC (Abingdon Press, 1999).

David C. Steinmetz

Steinmetz is Amos Ragan Kearns Professor of the History of Christianity at the Divinity School and Director of the Graduate Program in Religion, Duke University, Durham, North Carolina. His books include *Luther and Staupitz* (Duke University, 1980), *Luther in Context* (Indiana University, 1986), and *Calvin in Context* (Oxford University, 1995).

Jonathan R. Wilson

Wilson is Associate Professor of Religious Studies and Chair of the Religious Studies Department at Westmont College. His books include *Theology as Cultural Critique* (Mercer University, 1996), *Gospel Virtues* (InterVarsity, 1998), and *Living Faithfully in a Fragmented World* (Trinity, 1998).

PUBLICATIONS OF THOMAS A. LANGFORD

Books

Philosophy of Religion. Coedited with George L. Abernethy. New York: Macmillan, 1962, 542 pages. 2nd ed. New York: Macmillan, 1968, 586 pages.

History of Philosophy. Coedited with George L. Abernethy. Los Angeles: Dickenson Publishing Co., 1965, 620 pages.

Intellect and Hope, Essays in the Thought of Michael Polanyi. Coauthor and editor with William H. Poteat, Durham, N.C.: Duke University Press, 1968, 464 pages.

In Search of Foundations: English Theology 1900–1920. Nashville/New York: Abingdon Press, 1969, 349 pages.

Introduction to Western Philosophy: Pre-Socratics to Mill. Coauthor with George L. Abernethy. Los Angeles: Dickenson Publishing Co., 1970, 339 pages (also Recording for the Blind, recorded on magnetic tape and paperback edition 1976).

Christian Wholeness. Nashville: The Upper Room, 1979, 129 pages. Translation into Czechoslovakian: *Krestanska Celost.* Prague, Czechoslovakia, 1984, 132 pages. *Christian Wholeness* also translated into Korean, 1986.

The Harvest of the Spirit. Nashville: The Upper Room, 1981, 96 pages.

Practical Divinity: Theology in the Wesleyan Tradition. Nashville: Abingdon Press, 1983, 303 pages.

Prayer and the Common Life. Nashville: The Upper Room, 1984, 109 pages.

Wesleyan Theology: A Sourcebook. Durham, N.C.: Labyrinth Press, 1984, 309 pages.

With C. Clifton Black, II, *Jesus Christ: Holy Week and Crucifixion.* Nashville: Graded Press, United Methodist Publishing House, 1985, 64 pages.

The Centenary of Duke Memorial Church. With Ann Marie Langford. Durham, N.C.: Seamans Press, 1986, 61 pages.

Doctrine and Theology in The United Methodist Church. Editor. Nashville: Kingswood Books, 1991.

Preface, Afterword, Revisions, and Articles

"Introduction: A Wesleyan-Methodist Theological Tradition," "Conciliar Theology: A Report," "Doctrinal Affirmation and Theological Exploration," "The United Methodist Quadrilateral: A Theological Task." *God Made Known.* Nashville: Abingdon Press, 1992, 114 pages.

Practical Divinity: Theology in the Wesleyan Tradition. 2nd ed. Vol. 1. Nashville: Abingdon Press, 1998, 288 pages.

Practical Divinity: Readings in Wesleyan Theology. Vol. 2. Nashville: Abingdon Press, 1999, 324 pages.

Exploring Methodism: Methodist Theology. London: Epworth, 1998, 112 pages.

Booklet

Grace Upon Grace: The Mission Statement of The United Methodist Church. Nashville: Graded Press, 1990, 1-41.

Scholarly Articles

"Preaching the Doctrine of Atonement." *Encounter* (Spring 1955): 16-18.

"The Recruiting of Ministers." *North Carolina Christian Advocate* (October 27, 1960): 8-9.

"The Beginning of Prayer." *Motive* 21/6 (March 1961): 37-38.

"Theology and Prayer." *The Christian Scholar* 44/3 (Fall 1961): 253-58.

"Christianity Under Persecution." *Adult Teacher* 15/5 (May 1962): 2-4.

"Discipline and Devotion." *Response,* Duke Divinity School, 6/1 (October 29): 4 -5.

"The Gospel of Mark." *Wesley Quarterly* 22/1 (January-February-March, 1963): 13-20.

"The Gospel of Mark," *Wesley Quarterly* 22/2 (April-June, 1963): 13-20.

"Secular Realm/Secularism: An Important Difference." *Christian Advocate* 7/8 (April 11, 1963): 7-8.

"The Life and Teaching of Jesus." *Adult Teacher* 16/10 (October 1963): 25-32.

"Jesus' Growing Years and Early Ministry." *Adult Teacher* 16/11 (November 1963): 25-32.

"Jesus' Growing Years and Early Ministry." *Adult Teacher* 16/12 (December 1963): 14-23.

"Focus on Faculty," Autobiographical Sketch. *The Duke Divinity School Bulletin* 28/3 (November 1963): 227-29.

"The Wisdom and Witness of the Cross." *The Duke Divinity School Review* 29/1 (Winter 1964): 42-45.

"Giovanni Miegge on Jesus as a Martyr." *Interpretation* 18/2 (April 1964): 183-90.

"The Concept of Person: A Comparison of C. C. J. Webb and John Oman." *Religion in Life* 33/3 (Summer 1964): 407-20.

"The Cost of Discipleship," Dietrich Bonhoeffer. *Adult Teacher* 18/9 (May 1965): 11-13, 65.

"Religion and the Department of Religion at Duke." *The Duke Divinity School Review* 30/3 (Autumn 1965): 181-90.

"The Natural Theology of John MacMurray." *The Canadian Journal of Theology* 12/1 (Spring 1966): 9-20.

"Michael Polanyi and the Task of Theology." *The Journal of Religion* 46/1 (January 1966): 45-55.

"The Theological Methodology of John Oman and H. H. Farmer." *Religious Studies* 1/2 (Summer 1966): 229-40.

"Campus Turmoil: A Religious Dimension." *The Christian Century* 84/6 (February 8, 1967): 172-74.

"Campus Turmoil: A Religious Dimension," reprinted in *Training Young People.* (The Sunday School Board of the Southern Baptist Convention, Nashville, Tennessee), January, February, March 1968, vol. II, no. 2, pp. 14-16.

"Seeking Strength Through Prayer." *The Upper Room Disciplines* (Nashville, Upper Room, 1970), 154 -60.

"Christian Ministerial Education." *The Duke Divinity School Review* 36/3 (Fall 1971): 155-62.

"T. F. Torrance's Theological Science: A Reaction." *Scottish Journal of Theology* 25/2 (May 1972): 155-70.

"Style of Ordained Ministers." *Christian Advocate* 14/16 (August 30, 1973): 7-8.

"Baccalaureate Address." *Salem College* 15/9 (Fall 1973): 15-16, 20.

"Authority and Faith: A Theological Reflection." *Religion in Life* 42/2 (Autumn 1973): 346-87.

"Theology and Social Change." *New York Times* (October 7, 1973), section 2, p. 7.

"The Place of Meeting." *The Christian Century* 90/35 (October 3, 1973): 965-66.

"The Resurrection." *Adult Leader* 6/3 (March 1974): 8-10.

"The Holy Spirit and Sanctification: Refinding the Lost Image of Creation." *The Holy Spirit,* ed. Dow Kirkpatrick (Nashville: Tidings, 1974), 187-208.

"The Minister as Scholar." *The Duke Divinity School Review* 39/3 (Fall 1974): 135-41.

"The Family of God." *The Upper Room Disciplines* (Nashville: Upper Room, 1975), 192-98.

"The Conveyance of Personal Knowledge." *Excellence in University Teaching.* Thomas H. Buxton and K. W. Prichard, eds. (Columbia: University of South Carolina Press, 1975), 147-56.

"Authority, Community, and Church." *Creation, Christ, and Culture.* Studies in Honor of T. F. Torrance, ed. Richard W. A. McKinney (Edinburgh, Scotland: T. & T. Clark, 1976), 167-80.

"A Theological Assessment of Theological Education." *Hannavee* 3/1:2-3.

"Goodness Gracious." *The Upper Room Disciplines 1979* (Nashville: Upper Room, 1979), 313-19.

"John Wesley's Doctrine of Justification by Faith." *Proceedings of the Canadian Methodist Historical Society* (Toronto, 1979), 19 pages.

"John Wesley's Doctrine of Sanctification." *Proceedings of the Canadian Methodist Historical Society* (Toronto, 1979), 15 pages.

"Wesley's Doctrine of Church, Ministry, and Sacraments." *Proceedings of the Canadian Methodist Historical Society* (Toronto, 1979), 21 pages.

"Excerpts from *Christian Wholeness in Alive Now!* " (July/August, 1979): 4, 8-9, 25, 28, 53, 65.

"The World Methodist Council and Ecumenism." *World Parish* 19/3 (November 1979): 7.

"Pluralism and Unity in The United Methodist Church." *Occasional Papers.* United Methodist Board of Higher Education and Ministry (November 11, 1979): 1-7.

"Theological Education and Liberation Theology: An Invitation to Respond." With Thomas Ambrogie, Robert McAfee Brown, et al. *Theological Education* 16/1 (Autumn 1979): 7-12. Responses, pp. 12-68.

"The Range of Mission." *The Military Chaplaincy.* The Board of Higher Education and Ministry, The United Methodist Church (1979): 32-44.

"Theological Tasks Today." *The North Parker: Seminary Review*. Address for installation of Dr. Robert K. Johnston (November 1982): 8-10.

"Gnade Als Theologische Norm in der Theologie Wesleys," *Mitteilungen* (November 1983): 4-23.

"Schubert M. Ogden's *The Point of Christology: A Critical Response.*" *Perkins Journal* 36/4 (Fall 1983): 33-39.

"Reflections on the Ministry Study Report." *Occasional Papers*. United Methodist Board of Higher Education and Ministry (February 20, 1984): 1-7.

"Lake Junaluska." *Encyclopedia of Religion in the South*. Ed. Samuel S. Hill (Macon, Ga.: Mercer University Press, 1984); "Lake Junaluska," p. 399, and "Theology (Southern)," pp. 774-79, ibid.

"Constructive Theology in the Wesleyan Tradition." *Wesleyan Theology Today*. Nashville: Kingswood Books, 1984, pp. 56-64.

"Is There Such a Thing as Wesleyan Theology?" *Epworth Review* 15/2 (May 1988): 67-71.

"Conciliar Theology: A Report." *Quarterly Review* 9/2 (Summer 1989): 3-15.

"The Teaching Office in The United Methodist Church." *Quarterly Review* 10/3 (Fall 1990): 4-17. Also appears in *Teaching and Religious Imagination*. Charles Foster, ed. Nashville: Abingdon Press, 1991.

"Theological Reflections." *Lectionary Homiletics* 2/11 (October 1991): 4-5, 13-14, 21-22, 28-29.

"Teaching in the Methodist Tradition: A Wesleyan Perspective." *By What Authority*. Elizabeth B. Price and Charles R. Foster, eds. Nashville: Abingdon Press, 1992, pp. 57-72.

"Charles Wesley as Theologian." *Charles Wesley: Poet and Theologian*. S. T. Kimbrough, Jr., ed. Nashville: Abingdon Press, 1992, pp. 97-105.

"John Wesley and Theological Method." *Rethinking Wesley's Theology for Contemporary Methodism*. Ed. Randy L. Maddox. Nashville: Kingswood Books, 1998, pp. 35-48.

"Church and Authority." *Kirche und Welt Am Beginn Des Dritten Jahrtausends*. Ed. Helmut Nausner. Vienna, Evangelische-Methodische Kirche in Osterreich, 1998, pp. 87-93.